PRAISE FOR Worry-

D0091343

Arnie and Michael have developed a tool that can assist us all in our dialogue with one another. The "Recap and Reflect" feature helps me to hear from God through others—and that may be the most important thing of all.

Brian Doyle
President, Iron Sharpens Iron National Men's Equipping Conferences

Great advice for *every* worrier in your life—from an anxious child to a stressed-out spouse.

Dr. Trina Young Greer
Founder and Executive Director of Genesis Counseling Center

This honest and well-written book empowers sufferers of all ages to face the doubts they encounter and equips them to deal with worry wherever and whenever it strikes.

Adam Lewis, D.Min.
Lead Pastor, Connecting Pointe Church of the Nazarene

More than another "self-help" book, *Worry-Free Living* is a developmental spiritual fitness plan for individuals or small groups who are seeking to live more effectively for Christ.

Dr. Rick Ryding
Pastor and Professor Emeritus (Mount Vernon, Ohio)

God is not just interested in our souls; He wraps his salvation around the *whole* person. This is why the mind, body, spirit approach to handling worry here is essential for wholeness and healing.

Rev. Connie Larson DeVaughn
Co-Pastor, Altadena Baptist Church

Worry-Free Living is outstanding, excellent in truth, very well written, and highly practical.

Dr. Steve and Megan Scheibner
Founders of CharacterHealth, Creators of "In My Seat: A Pilot's Story"

WORRY FREE LIVING

Dr. Arnie Cole & Michael Ross

Authentic

Published by Authentic Publishers
188 Front Street, Suite 116-44
Franklin, TN 37064
Authentic Publishers is a division of Authentic Media, Inc.

Library of Congress Cataloging-in-Publication Data
Cole, Arnie and Ross, Michael
Worry-Free Living : Finding relief from anxiety and stress for you and your family / Arnie Cole & Michael Ross
p. cm.
ISBN 978-1-78078-226-3
       978-1-78078-344-4 (eBook)
Printed in the United States of America

 21 20 19 18 17 16 15 14   10 9 8 7 6 5 4 3 2 1

To our growing *goTandem* community:

"Peace I leave with you; my peace I give you. I do not give to you as the world gives. Do not let your hearts be troubled and do not be afraid."

JOHN 14:27, NIV—JESUS CHRIST

Contents

ACKNOWLEDGMENTS

We are deeply grateful to several psychology, medical, and ministry professionals who helped us shape these pages. Here are six we'd like to highlight:

Pamela Ovwigho, Ph.D.—executive director of the Center for Bible Engagement. She directed all of the research that became the foundation of this book and contributed to chapters 3, 4, and 9.

Theresa Cox, PAC—writer, missionary, and a pediatric physician's assistant in Colorado with more than three decades of experience in medicine. She holds an M.A. in counseling and has written several articles for the American Academy of Pediatrics. She contributed to chapters 6 and 10.

Trina Young Greer, Psy.D.—licensed clinical psychologist, is the founder and executive director of Genesis Counseling Center (www. genesiscounselingcenter.com) and co-founder of Genesis Assist (www.genesisassist.com).

Nanette Gingery, M.A.—therapist and addiction specialist, is the president of Summit Care and Wellness Treatment and Counseling (www.summitcareandwellness.com).

Eric T. Scalise, Ph.D., LPC, LMFT—is the vice president for professional development, executive director, international board of Christian care, and senior editor of American Association of Christian Counselors (www.aacc.net). In addition, he is the vice president for academic affairs at Light University online, as well as an author, a national and international conference speaker, and a consultant with organizations, clinicians, ministry leaders, and churches on a variety of issues.

Michelle DeRusha—author and blogger ("Graceful" at www. michellederusha.com), is the former associate editor for *Art & Antiques* magazine. She is the mother of two rambunctious, bug-loving boys— Noah and Rowan—and wife to Brad. Michelle contributed to our Bible study at the end of the book, "30 Days to a Peaceful Home."

INTRODUCTION

How to Use This Book

Since 2003, the Center for Bible Engagement at Back to the Bible has studied the spiritual lives of believers around the world—so far, more than 100,000 in twenty-two countries. Our research has primarily focused on how people grow spiritually, how they engage (or don't engage) the Bible, and what temptations they encounter each day.

Worry is one of the most common struggles among Christ-followers. The findings discussed in *Worry-Free Living* come from our ongoing program and from two additional studies specifically focused on worry. In the first, 2,110 teen and adult Christians completed survey questions on what they worry about, how they think about worry, and what helps them deal with worry. Our participants are a diverse group ranging in age from thirteen to over seventy and representing every state in the nation. In the second study, five hundred eight- to twelve-year-olds also shared about their worries and how they deal with them.

Through these studies, we've learned that . . .

- Feeling worried and stressed is fairly common regardless of gender and age.
- Worries about family are the most common among teens and adults. Other common worries focus on finances, the future, and faith.
- Tweens (ages eight or nine through twelve) worry most frequently about school.
- How comfortable we are with life's uncertainties affects how much we worry. How we think about worry (e.g.,

"it's helpful for solving problems" or "it shows a lack of faith") can also impact what we call the fear-worry-stress cycle (see chapter 1).

- Believers often use spiritual methods to cope with worry and stress. Seeking God's love and care, asking Him to help us let go of the situation, and spending time reading His Word are some of the most frequent means of handling these struggles.

I'm Dr. Arnie Cole, and as a behaviorist I've charted successful programs for fellow "wounded strugglers," including those who feel trapped by fear and worry and stress. I and my partners—Michael Ross, a bestselling journalist and family expert, and Dr. Pam Ovwigho, a psychologist and leading researcher—have witnessed and been part of lasting change in thousands of lives during our many decades of combined ministry experience. In this book, which contains an engaging mix of real-life stories, reliable research, and biblical guidance, we'll demonstrate dependable and practical ways you can resist worry's grip, unplug its power, and steer clear of its unhealthy consequences.

Here's what we've packed into this unique resource—it's three books in one:

a hands-on reference guide
a faith-building devotional
a personal and small-group workbook

Explore these pages on your own, journaling and completing the steps you'll discover in each section, referring back to them as you would with any practical reference guide. Read it with a partner or with your entire Sunday school class or small group. Each chapter concludes with questions designed to spark lively discussions, making *Worry-Free Living* ideal for couples and group study. There's even a thirty-day devotional at the end.

Various chapters uncover the most common worries and stress-points for men, for women, for children (including tween and teens), and for twenty-somethings—for those we love or who are in our care. This resource is designed to help readers:

- become self-aware, by evaluating the stress in our lives and households and plotting realistic steps toward change
- reach out to those we love—from spouses and in-laws to teens and kids
- understand the difference between the *mind* (what we think) and the *brain* (the physical processes of chemical reactions) . . . and how they contribute to worry
- learn to de-stress our thinking and calm down our bodies
- give up unhealthy religiosity, e.g., a false belief that "worrying shows we lack faith"
- reject the myth that we're in control and learn to take Jesus at his promise: "Come to me, all you who are weary and burdened, and I will give you rest."[1]

Features You'll Find in These Pages

*"**Our Research Says**"—key findings from our survey analysis (at end of chapter).* Our conclusions and advice aren't based on mere opinion. This book's foundation is built on years of research by the Center for Bible Engagement. Now and again you'll discover the latest findings from Dr. Pamela Ovwigho, the lead researcher on our staff in Lincoln, Nebraska. To date, she and a team of smart folks at our headquarters have studied the spiritual lives of more than 100,000 Christians from around the world—men, women, and children ranging in age from eight to eighty. Further, we've included insights and treatment options from a variety of medical professionals.

*"**Recap and Reflect**"—thought-provoking questions from our conversations (at end of chapter).* This book is filled with biblical principles and

pragmatic action points you can apply to your life. Beginning with chapter 2, these sections will get you thinking, listening, sharing, and ultimately acting on what you'll read. In addition to being well-researched, our advice is drawn from the understanding of God, our Master Creator, the ultimate Counselor and Healer.

"The Worry-Wise Plan"—easy-to-follow solutions for relief from fear, worry, and stress. You'll find these interactive strategies in chapter 8. Our plan is presented from three interrelated perspectives: how worry affects our *mind, body,* and *spirit.* It isn't enough to just say "stop fretting" or "trust God more." Most of us wish we didn't spend so much time worrying, but often we simply aren't managing to truly change it. Thus, we must consider physiological and emotional factors unique to each one of us. For some, overcoming worry means unraveling wrong thinking and learning new ways of coping. (Many of us have been taught—or have caught—a worry habit.) For others, struggles with chronic worry are caused by hormonal imbalances. And, for everyone, our ability to handle negative circumstances is affected by our genes, our health, and the substances we put into our bodies. Connecting these factors with eternal wisdom leads us to the ways of overcoming worry.

"Worry-Wise . . . and Live Well"—realistic steps you can customize for yourself and those in your care. This practical material, at the end of each chapter in Part Three, shows parents, caregivers, and ministers (for example) how the Worry-Wise Plan can be applied to various age groups. The goal is to break the cycle of unnecessary suffering and find peace in Christ.

"Bible Study: 30 Days to a Peaceful Home"—verses you can study and questions that will help you ponder what you've read. Everything we've created for this feature is designed to move you and your family or group deeper into Scripture, challenging you to replace worry with God's Word—engaging it, reflecting on it, and learning how to live it out. Bible engagement leads believers into a thriving relationship with Jesus Christ. And, as we get more of

him in our lives—more of his heart, more of his story, more of what he wants for each of us—the more we discover and grow. As the truth is worked into our hearts, we learn how to . . .

> . . . *develop the right mindset so we can better live out the words of Jesus.*
> . . . *take our eyes off ourselves and begin to love our neighbors.*
> . . . *pray with power and passion.*
> . . . *nurture our families.*
> . . . *live healthy and well within the community of believers.*
> . . . *serve the needy.*
> . . . *praise and worship our Creator.*
> . . . *become more like Jesus.*

www.goTandemBooks.com—*a website that can help you and your family and friends and church grow.* Periodically we'll invite you to pop over there for video clips, spiritual growth assessments, and other faith-building resources. Go ahead: try it and get a taste of what you can experience in the days ahead.

* * * * *

Using the personal pronoun "I" can get a little confusing, so to keep things simple we'll keep letting you know who's talking. For example, right now it's me (Arnie); soon the "I" is Michael; a bit later it's Pam. And, in general, the collective pronoun "we" refers to you and us . . . strugglers who want to live a little more like Jesus every day.

We believe this book also will help parents identify what's bugging their families, learn how to clarify individual and shared worries, and sort them into those they can and cannot do something about. And *Worry-Free Living* has something for every worrywart, from the chronically stressed to the occasional ruminator.

So let's not waste another minute. Turn the page and begin finding how you can chart a path toward growth . . . and ultimately put an end to cyclical fear and worry and stress.

MORE ABOUT THE AUTHORS

Dr. Arnie Cole is a behaviorist, researcher, and gifted speaker. During his career, he has developed programs that have helped men, women, and children successfully overcome their struggles and begin growing spiritually. He is passionate about sharing the power of Bible engagement.

Michael Ross is an award-winning author and veteran communicator who has written thousands of articles and has interviewed hundreds of athletes, musicians, actors, as well as amazing people from all walks of life. He is passionate about helping families thrive in Christ.

Contact Arnie and Michael

goTandemBooks.com

backtothebible.org

Back to the Bible: (402) 464-7200
Attn.: Director of CEO Communications

GOTANDEM.COM

Spiritual growth just the way you need it.

PART ONE

WHEN WORRY HITS HOME

By the End of Part One You'll Be Able to:

- See how the fear-worry-stress cycle is affecting millions of lives
- Grasp the health dangers of worry and anxiety
- Understand the worries of men, women, and children
- Identify how worry is impacting you and your family

Random Facts That Can Make Common Fears Less Scary

- If you live in the US, you have much higher odds of becoming a millionaire than of dying from the avian flu virus (or "bird flu," a strain of H5N1).[1]
- Vampire bats, which very rarely bite humans and are generally harmless, also are the only bats that adopt their neighbor's young if the bats' mother dies.[2,3]
- More people are killed in the US each year by vending machines than by sharks.[4]
- In a typical year, fewer than seven people in the US die of a poisonous spider bite.[5]
- Every year deer kill more people in the US than bears, dogs, wolves, alligators, sharks, spiders, bees, wasps, scorpions, and snakes. *Combined.*

A TOXIC WEB OF "WHAT IF?"

A PEOPLE IN NEED OF RELIEF

If you're in a bad situation, don't worry, it'll change.
If you're in a good situation, don't worry, it'll change. [1]
JOHN A. SIMONE SR.

It's a boisterous, kid-centric weekend in the Meyer household, and thirty-nine-year-old Marci won't have it any other way. While other moms would give anything for a bit of quiet—*an hour at the spa would be heaven, right?*—she savors the noise.

The squeals and giggles of her three children are music to her ears, a reminder of what's most important: her family's well-being. *Life itself.*

The young Florida mom shudders as she looks back over the past six months: the fear, the worry, the stress . . . all the what-ifs that have incessantly plagued her and her husband's thoughts. It's the possibility of losing what's so precious to them.

From across the family room, Marci watches eight-year-old Andrew, her middle child, sprawled on the floor, lost in a world of play. She can't take her eyes off of him.

Andrew meticulously snaps Legos into place as he carefully inspects his creation. "Here's the command center," he tells a playmate. "And these lasers blast enemy destroyers."

"That's so cool," his buddy says as he skillfully lands a ship behind Lego walls. "The good guys can hide their cruisers around the arena."

A mishmash of white, red, and yellow bricks rise into an eclectic fortress—complete with medieval towers, battlements, and working catapults. On the other side of the wall are futuristic spaceships and what looks like a giant stadium. Is it an interplanetary outpost? An academy for brave cadets with a *Hunger Games* twist?

"Time for the Beyblade battle!" shouts another friend.

Andrew's eyes light up. "Let it rip!" he shouts, in the words of his favorite game.

The kids scramble to claim the coolest spin-top toys: brightly colored discs with names like "Guardian Leviathan," "Pirate Orochi," "Ninja Salamander." Seconds later they pull plastic ripcords and launch their Beyblades into the makeshift arena.

Soon they're immersed in an imaginary world of adventurous and courageous warriors, fighting for justice against evil, dystopian kingdoms in far-off galaxies.

Marci smiles at all the commotion.

Just how it should be, she thinks. *Kids lost in play.* Not *how it's been lately. Day after day after day full of stress and anxiety, with challenges no child should face.*

She quietly watches Andrew interacting, savoring his expressions, making mental audio files of his laughter and snapshots of the joy that always seems to radiate from his precious face.

With the exception of his shiny bald head, nobody would think the boy had a care in the world. No one would suspect he's ill.

Terribly ill.

A real-life war is being waged within the Meyer home. Andrew is battling a mostly invisible monster—a growth of abnormal cells in his body that threatens his young life.

I wonder if he gets it, Marci thinks. *I wonder how much he understands what's going on. Maybe it's okay if he doesn't. Maybe it's okay if I do all his worrying for him.*

A few months earlier, Andrew was diagnosed with Hodgkin's lymphoma—a cancer that affects the lymphatic network, part of the circulatory system. Its nodes or glands are positioned all around the body, and one of its main responsibilities is fighting infections. The trouble all started in August 2012.

* * * * *

Marci and her husband, Jeff, had noticed that Andrew, suddenly, was talking differently—much as if he'd developed a slight speech impediment or maybe had just returned from a trip to the orthodontist. The concerned mom examined his tongue. "Nothing strange here," she said. Then she squinted and ran a fingernail over a tooth. "That is—nothing a toothbrush and a good cleaning can't fix!"

Andrew laughed.

The boy had no past health issues and rarely got sick. And, at the moment, he wasn't complaining of, for instance, a painful tongue or a sore throat. But a few weeks later—on September 19, to be exact—his condition began to worsen.

"It hurts a little," he told his parents, "like when I eat or swallow."

Marci put her hand on his forehead. "You don't feel hot, but if your throat hurts it's possible you caught a bug, maybe strep. We'll go see the family doctor."

Later that day Andrew sat on an exam table with his mouth opened wide. Their concerned physician was nodding her head and scribbling notes on a pad. "Makes complete sense that he's having a hard time talking," she said, finally turning toward Marci. "He has a 'golf ball' in the back of his throat. Take a look."

Marci bent to inspect, followed the light, and gasped. "That's *huge*. Exactly what is it?"

"An enlarged tonsil," she said. "To be on the safe side I'm sending Andrew to a specialist; a very good ear, nose, and throat doctor who I'm quite certain will get to the bottom of this."

Two days later, another examination, followed by more jotting and nodding.

However, the otolaryngologist's tone and expression seemed especially serious. He pulled off his glasses and rubbed his eyes. "Do you mind if we go into the other room and talk?"

Marci looked uneasily at Jeff and swallowed. *I don't like the way he said "talk,"* she thought. "Wonder what this is about," she whispered, as they got up and started for the door. "Could something else be lodged in Andrew's throat?" Then she turned to their son and smiled. "You'll be fine with the nurse, okay? We'll be right back."

* * * * *

Lymphoma? CANCER?
Neither Marci nor Jeff could get past those two frightening words. So much of what the doctor said afterward had gone in one ear and out the other. But then hearing terms like "treatment options" and "success rate" effectively snapped them back to the moment.

"Our first step is removing the tumor," explained the specialist. "And we recommend doing it right away. The color and characteristics of the mass are consistent with Hodgkin's lymphoma. Let's get him into surgery on Monday."

"Absolutely," Marci said.

"Whatever we need to do," Jeff agreed.

* * * * *

A week later, both parents sat at another table, this time with an oncologist.

Marci's head was still spinning. *None of this is turning out how I expected. I'd hoped for simple: Remove the problem, and that's it.*

Despite a flawless surgery, and though the child was recovering well, the cancer cells had metastasized—were spreading throughout his body. Chemotherapy was now entering the picture.

"We're confident Andrew will beat this," one doctor had said. "There's a high success rate for this type of lymphoma. We've been researching it for twenty years. He will be fine."

It was a ray of hope.

Marci remained calm, vowing to do everything necessary to get through. *It's hard right now, but we will get through this. Six months of chemo, and then it will be over.*

Andrew is going to be okay.

*   *   *   *

As the Beyblades skimmed across the arena and the boys high-fived wildly, a pang of fear stabbed at Marci's stomach. Her optimism was being challenged by worry.

Even after all the treatments there's still the possibility of a relapse.

And then there are the chemo's side effects.

What if something worse happens to him?

How would our kids grow up, knowing they lost their brother?

What is God telling us?

What if we lose him?

The Fear-Worry-Stress Cycle

WHAT IF?

Whether these two simple words roll off our lips or ripple through our minds, they set into motion our most common form of suffering: a cyclical experience of fear, worry, and stress.

And no one is immune.

For most of us, worry is second nature—often more like a reflex than a choice. On any given day we fret about countless smaller things: whether an accessory matches our outfit, what people will think of us when we open our mouths to speak, about waistlines and wrinkles and workloads. And then plenty of bigger things can hold our thoughts hostage: growing debts and thinly stretched paychecks, protecting our families, strained relationships and social snubs, health scares, parenting challenges, overcoming mistakes, working through painful memories . . . coming to grips with an unthinkable dilemma.

Just as for the Meyers, it isn't hard to see how we can get caught in a toxic what-if web.

"My wife, kids, and I are Christians," Jeff says, "so we have hope in Jesus Christ. Yet the pain is no less real. My faith and my loved ones are everything to me."

This weary dad talks candidly about a bleak moment right in the middle of their family trial; a point when the heavy weight of stress was almost too much to bear.

"Andrew began to fight us with the treatments—he didn't want to take his medicine. 'It tastes bad, and I don't like it,' he told me. 'But you have to,' I snapped. 'If you don't take it, you could die.' Suddenly it felt as if the words just hung in the air. I couldn't believe they came out; they shouldn't come from any parent's mouth. That shouldn't be anyone's reality."

Can you relate?

Does anything about Jeff and Marci's struggle read like your story?

An Agonizing Equation: Fear + Worry = Stress

Medical doctors and psychologists agree that worry is a key component of anxiety and chronic stress and that it's often at the heart of so many problems we face: overeating, alcoholism, cigarette smoking, drug abuse, and a long list of other compulsive behaviors. Over the span of our lifetimes, worrying accounts for untold quantities of invaluable time we'll never get back. We even worry about being worried: *Is all this stress killing me?*

Most neuroscientists and psychologists think our brain is actually hardwired to manage stress. They point to early humans who engaged their fight-or-flight instinct daily as a way to survive.

Our ancestors used worrisome thoughts as motivators to solve problems, find protection, and prepare for the worst.

Yet in modern times the stuff of sleepless nights and sweaty palms has grown into a loop of unnecessary suffering and is fast becoming a public health crisis. "America is at a critical crossroads when it comes to stress and our health," reports the American Psychological Association (APA). "Most of us are suffering from moderate to high stress these days, with 44% reporting that their stress levels have increased over the past five years."[2]

The so-called Millennials (broadly, those born between 1979 and 1995) claim higher stress levels than their parents' and grandparents' generations. Of those in this age group—right now there are between seventy-five million and eighty million in the US—more than half say worry and stress keeps them up at night.[3] Even our nation's youth are fearful. According to the Report of the Surgeon General, anxiety is the most common emotional disorder during childhood and adolescence. About 13 of every 100 children and adolescents ages nine to seventeen experience some kind of anxiety disorder; girls are affected more than boys in about a 2:1 ratio. And, troublingly, even though one-fifth of all children say they "worry a great deal or a lot," only 3% of parents rate their children's stress as extreme.[4]

We've observed children as young as three caught up in worry. What's wrong with this picture? Everything! Worried parents raise worried children; this can rob them of emotional well-being. And we're not just talking about nonreligious households. Our research shows that Christians are every bit as worried as the rest of the world.

What triggers worry for most of us? Ten factors:

- personal finances
- work-related stresses
- family
- parenting
- relationships
- health concerns

- personal safety
- body image and appearance
- temptations (including addictions)
- social acceptance

Nonetheless, there's no reason that circumstances or situations must dictate our peace and our joy any more than our emotions must determine our actions. Worry and anxiety are negatively affecting most and profoundly harming many; it's time for us to learn how to spend each moment more wisely and to establish more quality connections. We need to stop the cycle of worry—and, by God's strength, we can. We *can* begin experiencing the life He wants for us!

All of us who follow Jesus are learning to surrender to the one true Source of peace. He came "that [we] may have life, and have it to the full"[5]—to bring us into intimacy with God, which is foundational to overcoming worry. "Seek first his kingdom and his righteousness," He tells us, "and all these things will be given to you as well. Therefore do not worry about tomorrow, for tomorrow will worry about itself. Each day has enough trouble of its own."[6]

As the Meyers will admit, it's much easier to say we believe these truths than it is to live them out day by day—especially amidst a crisis. Yet their family is managing to do it, and the faithful steps they're taking have been nothing short of transformational.

Let's head back to their story to discover what's making a difference.

What Jeff and Marci Are Learning (and We Can Too)

One evening, while six-year-old Alison was with her grandparents and Andrew was at the hospital undergoing treatments, their oldest son Nathan (ten) had Jeff all to himself for some much needed father-son time.

The two loaded up on snacks and watched TV. They talked, and wrestled, and Jeff cracked a few jokes—anything to deflate the stress they'd been feeling. Yet he knew his boy's thoughts were miles away—no doubt in the hospital room, right by Andrew's side.

Nathan, fidgeting with the remote, turned toward his dad. "I need to know something," he said, then paused and glanced away.

"Yes, son?"

Then he looked Jeff in the eye. "Is Andrew going to die?"

Jeff sighed before responding. "It's so hard. The hardest thing we've ever had to go through. We don't want that to happen. We'll keep praying, and hoping, and doing all we can to fight the illness. But I have to be honest with you, Nathan—"

Now he also paused, fighting emotion, mustering the strength to let out the words. "It's possible—it could happen. It's hard to imagine life without him, but it *could* happen. If he died, you'd have Ally and mom and me, and we'd keep on loving each other. And we'd be okay."

Jeff smiled and put his hand on the boy's shoulder. "And, guess what? So would Andrew. He'd be in heaven with Jesus. He's a Christian—just like you and our whole family. Jesus loves us and takes care of us and will be with us forever. Hold on to that. Never stop believing it."

* * * * *

A few nights later, Jeff sat on the edge of the bed with his wife, telling her all about his talk with Nathan.

Then he shared another conversation; one he'd had with God.

"Marci," he said, tenderly. "I sense the Lord asking me a question. I feel He's asking this of us: 'If I take Andrew away, will you still worship Me?'"

She nodded in agreement.

He continued. "I know our faith is being tested—and it's so difficult, so painful. I don't want to lose Andrew—or any of you. I've felt so worried and stressed these past few months. I don't understand why any of this is happening."

He wiped tears from his eye. Marci squeezed his hand.

"Here's what I said to God," Jeff explained. "I told him, 'Yes, Lord, I will worship you. I will trust you. No matter what you decide to do. All of this is in your hands.'"

Marci opened her Bible to Ephesians. "Here's what's getting me through this," she said. "'Now to him who is able to do far more abundantly beyond all that we ask or think, according to the power that works within us, to Him be the glory in the church and in Christ Jesus to all generations forever and ever. Amen.'"[7]

She then spoke about the many questions swirling through her head—most prominent was *What are we going to do if we lose Andrew?*—and her own honest conversations with God: "If you take away the most important thing to me—my kids—yes, I will be devastated, but I will not turn my back on you. I know that you love me, and I know you're in control of everything. No matter what you choose, I know there's a reason for it."

She repeated the simple truth Jeff had shared with Nathan: "Jesus takes care of us."

"I know with all my heart that God is going to do something bigger and greater than we can imagine," she said. "Whether He takes Andrew or heals him . . . He has a purpose for all of this. All we need to do is surrender—and trust. We don't have to waste time in fear, and we don't have to worry about the outcome. Jesus takes care of us!"

Note: As we went to press, Andrew was given a clean bill of health. He is cancer free. He and his friends broke out the Beyblades and Legos and had a fun-filled celebration!

Worry, Anxiety, and Stress: Similar but Different

"Are you worried about something?"

"I'm anxious to get going."

"This job is stressing me out!"

We often use worry, anxiety, and stress interchangeably, in everyday conversation. While all three terms describe states we want to avoid, and though they often occur together, they are in fact distinct. Understanding the differences can help us get a better handle on our own situation.

Worry

Here are two psychological definitions of "worry":

- A chain of thoughts and images, negatively affect-laden and relatively uncontrollable.
- An attempt to engage in *mental* problem-solving on an issue whose outcome is uncertain but contains the possibility of one or more negative outcomes (emphasis mine).[8]

Emerging research underscores worrying as one of several types of repetitive *thought*; others include reminiscing, anticipating, and reflecting. Dr. Suzanne Segerstrom, a professor of clinical psychology, has researched repetitive thought among older adults and found that the thoughts vary in terms of whether their content is positive or negative (valence) and whether the tone is of uncertain searching or more certain problem-solving (purpose). Worry typically involves negative thoughts regarding uncertain situations.

Anxiety

"Anxiety," typically described more as an *emotional* state consisting of restlessness, panic, or a sense of impending doom, is often accompanied by physical symptoms like muscle tension, sweating, heart palpitations, and shortness of breath. Anxiety may also include thoughts such as fear of embarrassment or of dying from a heart attack. Anxiety frequently (but not always) arises out of stressful circumstances.

Sometimes people experience anxiety to the extent that they're suffering from an anxiety disorder. Of these there's a wide variety, comprising one of our nation's most common mental health problems. Types include generalized anxiety disorder, obsessive-compulsive disorder, panic disorder, post-traumatic stress disorder, and social phobia (or social anxiety disorder).

Stress

"Stress" represents this trio's most nebulous term. Dr. Hans Selye, an endocrinologist, coined it in 1936 to describe "the non-specific response of the body to any demand for change."[9] It can refer to external circumstances and also a person's response to those circumstances. Stress can be productive or harmful. For example, the Stressful Life Events Checklist developed by the psychiatrists Thomas Holmes and Richard Rahe (displayed below),[10] includes both "positive" and "negative" stress-producing events.

SOCIAL READJUSTMENT RATING SCALE

Death of spouse * Divorce * Marital separation
* Jail term * Death of close family member
* Personal injury or illness * Marriage * Fired at work
* Marital reconciliation * Retirement * Change in health
of family member * Pregnancy * Sexual difficulties
* Gain of new family member * Business readjustment
* Change in financial state * Death of close friend
* Change to a different line of work * Change in number
of arguments with spouse * A large mortgage or loan
* Foreclosure of mortgage or loan * Change in
responsibilities at work * Son or daughter leaving home
* Trouble with in-laws * Outstanding personal achievement
* Spouse begins or stops work * Begin or end school/college
* Change in living conditions * Revision of personal
habits * Trouble with boss * Change in work hours or
conditions * Change in residence * Change in school/college
* Change in recreation * Change in church activities

* Change in social activities * A moderate loan or mortgage
* Change in sleeping habits * Change in number of family
get-togethers * Change in eating habits * Vacation
* Christmas * Minor violation of the law

Understanding "The Cycle"

You'll read about the fear-worry-stress cycle throughout *Worry-Free Living*. This isn't an official medical term; we coined it for the sake of clear communication in this book. However, therapists and doctors do often study and refer to specific cycles of worry and anxiety.

For the sake of our discussions in each chapter, we want to ensure that you understand two key factors about the book's primary subject:

A. Worry, anxiety, and negative stress frequently have one thing in common: *fear*.
B. Despite distinctions, they often overlap and sometimes feed on each other.

Here's how we define "the fear-worry-stress cycle":

The process whereby a person feels fearful of a particular object or event, worries about encountering that object or situation in the future, experiences a stress reaction, and may then begin to fear and worry about being stressed or worried.

Worry begins with a pang of fear. Thereafter our minds can become stuck on repetitive, negative thoughts about uncertain situations. Eventually this can lead to anxiety and/or harmful stress, and then we may start to fear and worry about the adverse effects of stress on our health.

If you feel trapped somewhere in this cycle, your issue could be physiological, in which case it might be poor nutritional choices or chemical imbalances (such as the overproduction of adrenaline in the brain) causing you to feel anxious. Maybe you're battling a disorder (see chapter 5 for details about common conditions). Or maybe your problem is more spiritual in nature; God feels distant to you, and you're struggling to trust Him and surrender to His will.

Whether you're grappling with one of these causes or another one, tackling worry, anxiety, and stress in a single book—as you may suspect—is a daunting task. There's a lot to consider, and some aspects can get complicated. To avoid bogging down our conversations with psychobabble, and as a way of helping you get to the root of what's affecting you and those in your care, we will endeavor to walk you through the issues as straightforwardly and engagingly as possible, with strategies, stories, and scripturally based guidance.

IN THE GRIP OF FEAR

WHAT IF THE UNTHINKABLE ACTUALLY HAPPENED?

You will never fully understand how God could give you peace in some of the situations you face, but you do not have to understand it in order to experience it. . . . Scripture says to be anxious for nothing. God's Word clearly indicates that there is nothing you can face that is too difficult, too troubling, or too fearful for God.[1]

HENRY T. BLACKABY

Safe. At peace with God.

That's how seventeen-year-old Haley Havlik feels as she soaks in the rugged scenery of Wallowa Whitman National Forest in northeastern Oregon—her favorite place to hike.

"It's incredible," she says. "How could anyone claim that God doesn't exist?"

Two strong arms gently slip around her waist, and the words that always make her knees weak are whispered into her ears: "It's not as incredible as *you.*"

Haley turns and looks up at the handsome grinning face. Deep inside, she can't stop thanking God for her boyfriend, eighteen-year-old Brian Sakultarawattn (pronounced skoon-tra-WATT)—a guy who walks his talk. A guy who's made up his mind about living for Jesus.

"Yep...God definitely broke the mold when he made you," Brian says. She punches him on the arm.

"I'm serious—you like my kind of music, you aren't afraid to eat my cooking, you keep up with me on the trails. What more could I ask for in a girl?!"

Secure in his arms, Haley can't imagine anything destroying their love for each other—or their faith in God.

* * * * *

A year later, on a warm summer day, they're at Jesus Northwest, a music festival in Vancouver, Washington. As dc Talk leaves the stage, Haley and Brian take a break from the crowds and go for a walk.

"Remember the first time we came here?" he asks, taking her hand.

"Yep—summer of '92. Three years ago! We were just starting to get interested in each other."

"A lot has happened between us." Suddenly he stops walking, looks around, and drops to one knee. She begins to laugh.

"I love you, Haley Havlik," says Brian. "Will you marry me?"

"Stop it, okay?" she says. "And get up before someone sees you."

He holds up an engagement ring. She's stunned to realize he's not kidding.

"Will you be my wife?"

Tears are already streaming down her cheeks. "*Yes!*" she says. "Yes. I will marry you."

"I always want to take care of you."

"That's my job too, you know."

"We'll build a cabin."

"That's where we'll start a family."

Neither can fathom the challenges ahead. There will be a fiery test of their faith, of their commitment to each other and to God.

* * * * *

It's 1:15 p.m. on December 26, 1995. Haley's at home organizing her junk drawer, thinking about more exciting activities—like hanging out with Brian when he's done at work.

The phone rings, and her thoughts dissipate.

"Hello?"

"Haley, this is Angellee."

On the other end of the line, Haley's sister sounds strained. "There's been an accident. Brian's been burned. We need you here right away."

Within minutes Haley's in a frenzied emergency room at St. John's Medical Center in Longview, Washington.

"The ambulance is standing by," a doctor tells Brian's parents. "We'll rush him to a burn unit in Portland. That's his only chance."

A sickening pain stabs at Haley's stomach. "What happened?" she pleads. "Where's Brian?"

Angellee has her in a firm hug. "It's serious, Haley. There was a fire, an explosion. Brian was burned—very badly. He's in critical condition. Dan suffered burns on his hands but saved his life."

* * * * *

A mistake.

An explosion.

Instantaneous disaster, and life is altered forever.

Alone in the woods, Brian is devoured by a massive ball of flame. He drops to the ground and begins to roll, but the fire won't go out, doesn't even diminish. He screams. No one's there.

Exhausted, he stills, and closes his eyes. Suddenly, silently, he's waiting to die.

My life is over, he says inwardly. *I trust God.*

Then Brian hears a voice. When he opens his eyes, everything's fuzzy. The flames are gone, but he can't move his arms or legs. Above him hover the worried faces of his friend Dan, and Angellee, Dan's wife.

Before long the worried faces belong to a frenzied medical crew in white masks. Needles and IVs are jabbed into his ravaged body. Across the sterile room a monitor blips irregularly. Life teeters on the edge. *Is this a dream? Will I wake up and go on living—normally? What about Haley? Will we get married and build our log cabin? Will I still be able to work? I trust God.*

"Hang in there," he hears from somewhere above. "We're taking care of you. You're going to make it."

Just before everything goes black, Brian takes a labored breath, and a dozen words roll off his tongue: "I trust God. If I die, tell Haley that I love her."

* * * * *

Less than an hour earlier, Brian had been cleaning the shop at Teen Trees International, a tree farm near his home in St. Helens, Oregon. He'd worked there for two years, learning forestry management skills.

Brian and his supervisor, Dan Kloppman, Haley's brother-in-law, had dumped a few loads of discarded paper into a parking-lot burn barrel and lit a match. Then they'd broken for lunch around 12:30 p.m., letting the fire smolder.

When he'd returned a short time later, Brian had again built up the fire. The flames had begun to shoot above the barrel's rim, so he'd hurriedly proceeded to search the shop for a bucket of rainwater to dowse the fire. In the rush, he'd inadvertently grabbed a can of gasoline.

KABOOM.

Immediately, a swirling fireball torched his hair and clothes. Immersed in flame, all he could see was gravel. He dove to the ground anyway, rolling frantically, yet the flames seemed unaffected. He scrambled to his feet, raced to a steep dirt embankment, and rolled some more. Nothing diminished the fire. Brian screamed but heard no response.

"I just relaxed my body and waited for God to take me home," he says. "I don't remember feeling a thing. The pain didn't come until later—not until my body began to heal."

Dan, who in fact had heard his screams, raced to the scene, managed to put out the flames with his hands, and quickly loaded the teen into a van for the twenty-mile drive to the hospital. "I knew it was Brian's only hope," he says. "He was too badly burned to wait for an ambulance. I feared he might go into shock."

"You're not going to die," Angellee told Brian, holding his head. "I knew he was barely holding on," she recalls. "I knew I had to do everything I could to encourage him."

About an hour-and-a-half after the accident, and fifty miles away, at Emanuel Hospital in Portland, Dr. Joe Pulito of the Oregon Burn Center took Brian's family into a private room.

"There's a 90 percent chance Brian will die," he said. "Maybe not in the next twenty-four hours, but infection will set in during the next few weeks, and he'll eventually die."

"So there's a 10 percent chance that my son will live?" asked Jani, his mom.

Dr. Pulito rubbed his eyes and took a deep breath. "Perhaps even less." (Later he admitted that the survival odds had been only 1/10th of one percent, or one in a thousand.)

"Doctor, we won't hold you responsible for the results," she said. "Just do your best. God will decide the outcome."

The physician nodded his head.

Brian's parents and siblings and Haley kept a constant prayer vigil. "That night, we slept in waiting-room chairs," Haley says. "And the next day we were joined by dozens of people from the community." At one point more than sixty scrunched into the waiting room.

They prayed for the burn unit crew, who had the phenomenal challenge of racing against time to reconstruct Brian's exterior shell—the body's gatekeeper against lethal infections. Unlike a skin-reddening first-degree burn, such as from spending too much time at the beach, third-degree burns leave the body defenseless against invading germs by destroying the dermis—the capillary-rich layer beneath the outermost (epidermal) surface. Nevertheless, despite alarmingly slim odds, Brian had youth on his side, and his heart was strong. He even had a few patches of unburned skin on his lower stomach and back that could be used for grafts.

With skin from cadavers and grafts from what little flesh he had left, surgeons stapled together an intricate "quilt." This covering was merely temporary; it bought the doctors enough time to have Brian's own skin grown in a lab from a small graft, a process that usually takes about four weeks. When this skin later arrived—cut into Mini-Post-It-note-sized squares—doctors repeated grueling procedures of scraping off the old skin and stitching on the new.

To keep Brian alive, surgeons had to sacrifice his infected limbs. He endured *nineteen* surgeries—nearly one a week during his stay at the Oregon Burn Unit.

After one operation, Dr. Andrew Cramer, who assisted Dr. Pulito, told Brian's family, "I really did feel the presence of God during surgery. Keep praying."

Three weeks in, the teen regained consciousness.

"I was wrapped in bandages," Brian said, "and didn't realize that my limbs were gone. I thought I could still feel them."

Haley broke into tears when her fiancé awoke, and everyone in the waiting room that day began praising God.

But the young man's condition was still critical. "It gave us hope when Brian regained consciousness," Haley recalls, "yet we knew there was a long road ahead. It wasn't until two months after the accident that doctors told us he would survive."

Several days passed before Brian began to ask about his hands. (He'd known only he was blind, which at the time was thought to be temporary.)

Jani took a deep breath. "You were burned really badly . . . and, in order to save your life, doctors had to amputate your forearms."

He then asked about his legs.

"I told him that part of his left leg was gone and that infection might cost him his right foot," she remembers.

Brian was angry. "Why didn't the doctors just go ahead and cut off my head while they were at it?!"

Then she asked her son a hard question. "Do you think we made the right decision . . . keeping you alive?"

He paused, then replied, "Yes. I'm glad I'm alive. God spared me and will use me."

When Jani called the family from the waiting room to gather around his bed, Haley, who'd barely left her fiancé's side, leaned close.

"I love you very much," she said.

Brian turned in the direction of her voice. "Why?" he asked, knowing his life would never be the same.

Jani spoke up. "Brian, if something like this had happened to Haley, would you still love her?"

Brian paused again, then answered. "Yes."

He thought for a minute. "I guess it's gonna take longer to finish the cabin now."

* * * * *

Nearly a year and a half after the fire, Haley (then nineteen) and Brian (then twenty) still didn't question their commitment to each other. In fact, they married.

"We had a small wedding with family and close friends," Haley says. "Brian's parents added a special room on their house—that's where Brian and I live.

"It just doesn't matter to me how he looks on the outside," she adds. "It's what's on the inside that makes the outside handsome. And Brian's still the same on the inside. I still see that boyish smile. I still share the dream of someday raising a family. But right now my focus is on helping him to recover."

What does Brian think?

"After the accident a newspaper reporter asked, 'Wouldn't it have been better to die than to live like this?' My answer: 'Life is precious and we can't take it for granted.'

"I thank God every day for another chance to live. I especially thank him for Haley. We will have kids. Doctors say I can father a child.

"My advice to anyone reading this: Live each day for Jesus. Don't wait until tomorrow to get right with Him. No one knows what tomorrow will be like.

"And no matter how hard life gets—the worries and fears and struggles you encounter—don't give up. Just because of what happened to me, I'm not ready to check out of this world. God has plans for me—and you."[2]

From the Author's Notes: Time to Put Worry in Its Place

On the afternoon when I (Michael) interviewed Brian and his family, I was worried.

I was worried about my appearance. *I hate flying. My clothes are wrinkled from three hours of being crammed into a chimpanzee-sized space.*

I was worried about being on time for the interview. *I can't read this map. Where's Highway 30? And was I supposed to cross the Columbia River. Oh, perfect—now I'm in Washington, with no exits until Seattle* (exaggerating only slight).

I was worried about making a good impression. *Will I ask the right questions? Have I done sufficient research? Did I use enough mouthwash?*

The truth is, worry's nothing new for me. I'm pretty proficient with it. A day, an hour ... probably not even a minute goes by in which at some level I'm *not* battling against getting caught up in fearful rumination: deadlines, finances, first impressions, health concerns, meetings, parenting (usually associated with guilt over not spending enough time with my son), pleasing God, pleasing my wife, pleasing my boss, pleasing my pastor—my list goes on and on.

But, when I met Brian . . .

His mom wheeled him into their living room, right next to my chair, and Haley held a straw to his mouth so he could sip Coke as we talked. Mesmerized by his story, I asked numerous questions; they seemed to roll off my tongue. He answered each one, very honestly.

Brian was relaxed, at peace. He smiled a lot and laughed a few times. He shared about how much he loved God and his family. And about how excited he was for the future.

No bitterness.

No fear.

No worry.

I looked down at my rumpled clothes and felt as if the words *MISGUIDED...VAIN...UNTRUSTING GRUMBLER* were flashing across my forehead. My problems seemed so petty compared with Brian's challenges.

It reminded me of something God's Word says about self-obsession and selfish behavior:

> Don't be naïve. There are difficult times ahead. As the end approaches, people are going to be self-absorbed, money-hungry, self-promoting, stuck-up, profane, contemptuous of parents, crude, coarse, dog-eat-dog, unbending, slanderers, impulsively wild, savage, cynical, treacherous, ruthless, bloated windbags, addicted to lust, and allergic to God. They'll make a show of religion, but behind the scenes they're animals. Stay clear of these people.[3]

Had I been acting like a bloated windbag?

Was my tendency to worry making me allergic to God?

Forgive me if I seem to be slinging any here. That's not at all my intention. For so many (myself included), just surviving in this fast-paced, adrenaline-driven world is ... well, stressful. And the worry instinct in us sure doesn't usually feel like a mere "choice," as if we might flick a switch to shut it off—sometimes it seems far more like an electrified ball and chain. Though we feel we'd give anything to break free from it, there are cultural, spiritual, psychological, and physiological factors in play that often manage to reel us in.

For example: In addition to being a worrier, I battle social phobia (also known as social anxiety disorder).

There's a real tug-of-war going on inside my heart: part of me hates the spotlight, part of me loves it. While I'm not a bad speaker, I panic just before I set foot in front of a crowd or begin speaking into a radio mike. (I don't mean a few pangs of nerves, I mean actual panic.) And that's a true stumbling block in my line of work—public speaking comes with the territory. Even as I write these words I'm also preparing for (and ruminating on) a sermon for this Sunday's service; my pastor asked me to share spiritual lessons from one of my past books. I did the same thing last week at a men's retreat in New York, and soon I'll be taping a Focus on the Family radio show—sharing with millions about our research at Back to the Bible.

Even as God keeps opening doors, my inner fears tempt me to avoid them. And, as the tug-of-war persists, I find that I'm caught up in an exhausting cycle of worry. Further, I know for a fact that as difficult as my struggles seem to me, so many others face circumstances and challenges indescribably more daunting—maybe you or a member of your family is one of them.

Where Do We Go from Here?

As to our worry, our stress, our anxiety, our fear, Jesus has said:

> Are you tired? Worn out? Burned out on religion? Come to me. Get away with me and you'll recover your life. I'll show you how to take a real rest. Walk with me and work with me—watch how I do it. Learn the unforced rhythms of grace. I won't lay anything heavy or ill-fitting on you an. Keep company with me and you'll learn to live freely and lightly.[4]

My purpose is to give them [my followers] a rich and satisfying life.[5]

Peace I leave with you; my peace I give to you. Not as the world gives do I give to you. Let not your hearts be troubled, neither let them be afraid.[6]

I have told you these things, so that in me you may have peace. In this world you will have trouble. But take heart! I have overcome the world.[7]

Brian is living proof that we can trust Jesus and take Him at His word. Meeting this young man helped to put so many of my hang-ups in the right perspective, including some *don'ts* that I really want to stop *doing*:

Don't give up.

Don't stop living.

Don't cling to fear, to worry, to anxiety.

Instead, I want to put these things in their place—beginning with the countless small worries (like wrinkled clothes) and then moving on to the big issues (like social panic disorder).

Are you ready to walk this path with me?

* * * * *

As we step forward and move ahead together, you'll meet people like you and me, hearing in their words what helps as well as what often has held them back. You'll learn also from Arnie's expertise in psychology and behavioral science. We hope and pray that primarily and foremost, in *Worry-Free Living*, you'll encounter God.

This book is all about what God's Word says regarding worry, fear, and anxiety.

And that's exactly where we'll begin.

With our blessing, you can photocopy the following section. Tape these truths and verses to your fridge, medicine cabinet, dashboard, or your forehead. The point is, learn them—commit them to memory in the days and weeks ahead. Make what you read here part of your mindset, your mode of living.

We can **TRUST** God in the midst of a crisis. We can lean on and find comfort in the truth that we're not the ones in control.

- "Be still, and know that I am God; I will be exalted among the nations, I will be exalted in the earth." The LORD Almighty is with us; the God of Jacob is our fortress (Psalm 46:10–11).

We can **TRUST** that He will not abandon us. In any distress we can call out to Him, and He will empower us through his Spirit. He will help us to handle whatever it is we must face.

- The LORD himself goes before you and will be with you; he will never leave you nor forsake you. Do not be afraid; do not be discouraged (Deuteronomy 31:8).
- For the sake of his great name the LORD will not reject his people, because the LORD was pleased to make you his own (1 Samuel 12:22).
- The Spirit God gave us does not make us timid, but gives us power, love, and self-discipline (2 Timothy 1:7).
- We say, with confidence, "The LORD is my helper; I will not be afraid. What can mere mortals do to me?" (Hebrews 13:6).

We can **TRUST** His Word when life feels out of control.

- The LORD is good, a refuge in times of trouble. He cares for those who trust in him (Nahum 1:7).

- Christ . . . suffered once for sins, the righteous for the unrighteous, to bring you to God (1 Peter 3:18).
- God so loved the world that he gave his one and only Son, that whoever believes in him shall not perish but have eternal life (John 3:16).
- Jesus said, "Peace be with you! As the Father has sent me, I am sending you." And with that he breathed on them and said, "Receive the Holy Spirit" (John 20:21-22).
- This is love for God: to keep his commands. And his commands are not burdensome, for everyone born of God overcomes the world (1 John 5:3-4).

Our Research Says . . .

- If you struggle with worry and anxiety, you're in renowned company. Abraham Lincoln, Barbara Bush, John Steinbeck, Charles Schultz, Sir Isaac Newton, and Oprah Winfrey, for example, have had to deal with one or more conditions known as an anxiety disorder.[8]
- According to the World Health Organization, the US has the highest prevalence of anxiety disorders (18.2%) among fourteen countries surveyed; France's rate is second highest (12%). The lowest rates were in China and Nigeria (around 3%).[9]
- The most common fears are of spiders, snakes, heights, crowded areas/open spaces, dogs, thunder and lightning, blood, injections, social situations, flying, germs or dirt, terrorist attacks, dentists, and water/drowning.

Recap and Reflect
Talking Points for Couples or Group Study
• • • • • • • • • • • • • • • • • • • •

Imagine facing the kinds of challenges Brian and his family endure. A violent explosion cost him his sight, both arms, and one leg. Here on earth he'll never again look into the eyes of his loved ones, let alone bathe and dress himself or go for a walk.

> **True or false?** *When my life sails along smoothly, I feel better about myself. When problems hit, my confidence takes a nosedive.* (Explain your answer.)

• Pause for a moment and take inventory of your own struggles.

> *To what extent is my life affected by or weighed down with unnecessary stresses and worries? Is it time to change my "worry perspective"? (Is it time to stop sweating small stuff?) If so, how—in what ways?*

• Close your eyes and try to envision Brian's world.

> *How would I react if a horrible accident scarred my body? Would I still value my life? Would I want to die? (What would be MY response if something I deeply fear—if something "unthinkable"—actually happened?)*

Despite the fact that Brian's world is greatly altered, his foundation—his faith in God—remains unshaken. His identity in and commitment to Jesus Christ defines who he truly is. "I don't ask God why this happened to me," he says. "I ask, 'What's next? How do you want to use me?'" And remember what Haley said? "It's what's on the inside that makes the outside handsome. And Brian's still the same on the inside."

Is Jesus Christ the foundation of my life? Do I trust Him,
with everything, or is there something I'm holding back?

Even though most of our worries and fears never come to fruition, sometimes they actually do. And, though it happens to a very small percentage of people, occasionally the very worst thing we can imagine does happen. As Brian and Haley have shown, whether or not we're in that small minority, God holds us in His arms, is always ready to give us hope, and never stops encouraging us or showing us how to keep placing one foot in front of the other as we hold to our trust in Him. People can survive the unthinkable and nevertheless thrive in their faith.

Here's What's Next

Now that we've done some needful soul-searching—and briefly considered the effects of the fear-worry-stress cycle in our lives—let's dive into some survey results and learn about what's bugging people like us.

A PEEK AT WHAT'S BUGGING US

STRESS-POINTS OF HUSBANDS, WIVES, KIDS, AND ADULT CHILDREN

*The first thing, when one is being worried as to whether one will
have to have an operation or whether one is a literary failure,
is to assume absolutely mercilessly that the worst is true, and to ask,
What then? If it turns out in the end that the worst is not true,
so much the better: but for the meantime the question must be
resolutely put out of mind. Otherwise your thoughts merely go round and
round a wearisome circle, not hopeful, not despondent, then hopeful
again—that way madness lies. Having settled then that the worst is true,
one can proceed to consider the situation.*[1]

C. S. LEWIS

Anxious thoughts swirl through our brains when we're tired, when
we're sick, when we're crawling through snarled traffic, when we're late
for a big meeting. Fear kicks in as our safety is threatened and our circumstances slide out of control. Our brain, on full alert, launches into
a fight-or-flight state; adrenaline surges and races everywhere inside us.
(No need for a highly caffeinated supersized double shot of anything.)

The fear-worry-stress cycle is on the rise, in us and in our families.
And, Christ-followers are every bit as worried as the rest of the world.

- Ben feels trapped by a dead-end job and frets about his future.
- Leslie is panicked about some bad choices her college-age
  son is making.

- Sarah wonders who will take care of her now that she's eighty—and alone.
- And four-year-old Evan feels so anxious that his teachers don't know how to help. The moment his mother leaves after bringing him to preschool, immobilizing fear washes over him and holds on tight.

What's going on? A small child's world should be filled with wonder, not inundated with worry. And, how can it be that of 2,600 respondents, more than half described themselves as "often worried and fearful"? (As to whether they worry most days of the week, 66% of Christian women and 56% of Christian men said yes.)

It's partly because of what we've come to expect and accept. Most of us believe it's normal to be busy—frantically racing through day after day, multitasking from deadline to deadline. Combine that with how we've become depersonalized and isolated on our computers and devices, at our jobs, in our communities—even in our homes and our churches. These cultural conditions make commonplace the maladies of stress and anxiety. Something else is at play too: Many of us thrive on the excitement of an adrenaline rush, especially those who crave exhilaration and chase after energy that they perceive will spur them to achieve great things.

Yet adrenaline is addictive, and the crashes after the rushes, which our bodies bring about in order to recover, tend to result in persistent fatigue and even depression. (Much more on this in chapter 5.) With worry and stress also in the mix, myriad health problems can arise: dizziness, racing heartbeat, rapid breathing and/or shortness of breath, headache, inability to concentrate, irritability, muscle tension, nausea, nervous energy, and more. Over time, a state of adrenalized anxiety can lead to serious physiological consequences:

- Depressed immune system (making it harder to fight off diseases like cancer)
- Digestive disorders

- Muscle tension
- Increased chances of triggering clinical depression
- Changes in blood chemistry (heightening risk of [for instance] adult-onset diabetes)
- Impairment of the body's ability to form new cells
- Short-term memory loss
- Premature coronary artery disease
- Elevated blood pressure
- Heart failure

At the same time, doctors point out that stress isn't the sole culprit. Actually, it's just a trigger—it's how we handle stress that matters most. There are effective steps and lifestyle changes every member of the family can take! Christians really do hold the keys to real transformation and meaningful growth. Our lives can be different— less stressful, freer, happier, and far more fulfilling. Our Worry-Wise Plan (we'll get to this in chapter 8) will walk you through a mind-body-spirit approach to finding relief. After identifying the relevant physiological and emotional factors, you can plot a God-centered solution to handling worry.

* * * * *

Before we find solutions, though, we've got to understand the problem: what's negatively affecting us, and why. As Arnie and Pam analyzed the spiritual lives of 2,600 Christians, I pursued and conducted the interviews for this book. Together we met men, women, and children whose worry tendencies stem from a wide range of difficult struggles, sometimes including panic disorder, obsessive-compulsive disorder (OCD), and post-traumatic stress disorder (PTSD).

We'll touch on these and other issues and conditions in Part Two. In this chapter, we'll dive into the data, explore what worries us, and examine beliefs about worry. Then we'll talk about ways of coping with worry: How do we stop the worry cycle once it's started? Is it possible to sidestep worry altogether? We'll conclude with a focus on the spiritual side of worry.

How Stressed Are We?

Since 2007, the American Psychological Association has conducted an annual "Stress in America" survey, which examines how stressed we are, what causes our stress, and how we cope with it. According to the findings of the 2010 APA survey, about half of all adults have experienced a moderate amount of stress in the previous month, and about one in four were extremely stressed.[1] Those who participated in our study reported similar stress levels. However, there are notable differences by age and gender:

Figure 1. Average Stress Level Among U.S. Christians.

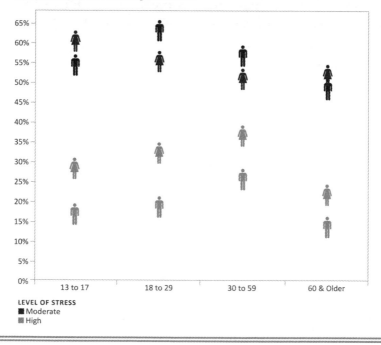

LEVEL OF STRESS
■ Moderate
■ High

Worry's Most Frequent Facets

Ask a couple thousand people what they worry about most and you'll quickly recognize that, whether presently at a high or a low point of stress (stress-point), nearly everyone can name something they worry about, even if only occasionally. Details of specific worries certainly vary depending on circumstances, yet there are themes to what sends most of us into worry mode.

We find many ways to ask *What if?* and then proceed to imagine what could go wrong. Let's explore what these most often center on, at different life stages.

What if . . . something happens to my family?

Our most frequent worries center on those closest to our hearts, the people we love. Family concerns are by far the most common. This is true overall as well as across genders and across all age groups except tweens. Women do worry about family more than men do, and family worries increase as we age, peaking in the aged thirty-to-fifty-nine range.

For tweens, family worries focus primarily on their parents—from parents' health to parents' financial concerns. Kids worry that they'll split up, especially when hearing them argue. They also fear their parents won't be proud of them, or that circumstances such as parental separation or incarceration would result in their parents not living with them anymore.

Later life stages bring family worries that expand to include emotional health and spiritual concerns as well as physical safety. Believers often question whether certain loved ones will choose to follow Christ. In addition, as we age our worries focus more on children and grandchildren, even though concerns about our parents remain. Sometimes we fret about our relational roles—*am I a good husband/wife? Am I nurturing my kids as I should?*

The following answers illustrate many of our worries about family:

"I worry about . . ."
   . . . *my family. My [infant] son was diagnosed with a food allergy, and we've been in the ER twice with him in his first fifteen months, due to severe reaction . . . Most of my worry is [from being] constantly on alert to make sure he doesn't eat something he shouldn't.*
   . . . *my children and their friendships, if they're associating with Christian friends.*
   . . . *my wife, [that she] may cheat on me. I am a stepfather and dealing with the deadbeat that doesn't pay for much of anything, yet he's looked at as a hero by his kids.*
   . . . *[whether] I'm spending enough time with God, family, and others who are important in my life.*
   . . . *my family, which encompasses so much: health, finances, shelter, food, clothing, hoping for college for my children.*
   . . . *the children in our family, that they would not be drawn away from God into the world. [Also] about our family being healthy, and having enough money.*
   . . . *my kids—their future (careers, finances, life skills).*
   . . . *my grown children . . . their walk with God, their finances and health.*
   . . . *being a good mom and not neglecting my children's needs. Raising my children in a way that [they] turn out to be "good," well balanced adults.*
   . . . *whether my husband and I will ever have children of our own.*
   . . . *whether my family is going to be restored back to me as the Lord has promised me.*

What if . . . my finances fail?
Current money woes or, even more often, possible future financial problems top the "worry list" for many Christians. Recurrent concerns included being able to meet present family needs (whether employed or experiencing unemployment), managing the finances of a business, holding down a job so as to continue providing, and planning for college or retirement.

Men and women are equally likely to worry about finances. Frequency of financial worry increases with age, again peaking in the thirty-to-fifty-nine-year-old range (often when financial responsibilities are highest) and declining slightly after age sixty.

Respondents described their money concerns in this way:

"I worry about . . ."

  . . . *supporting a family of eight with one income.*

  . . . *will we have enough money for future needs?*

  . . . *making the budget for home, ministry, and business needs.*

  . . . *paying bills while trying to figure out how to keep my husband from buying more stuff.*

  . . . *paying our bills and mortgage as my husband has lost his job over a year ago.*

  . . . *my job, and if I will continue to make enough money to live on.*

  . . . *money. I'm a single mom with two boys; I worry I won't be able to provide for them.*

  . . . *money. Owning a business, I worry that it has the money to support the families of our employees . . . I also worry that I have the money to support myself and pay for medical bills.*

  . . . *funding my retirement.*

  . . . *always having the money needed to support my family for basic items as well as their college education.*

  . . . *having money to pay daily bills. I have two jobs and I still come up short every month.*

  . . . *finances. I am disabled and the income responsibility rests solely on my husband.*

What if . . . the future doesn't turn out the way I want?

Typically, worry focuses on future events with uncertain outcomes, where at least one possible outcome is negative. With so much future ahead of them, it's not surprising to find that worries about the future are fairly common among young adults. One in five eighteen- to twenty-nine-year-olds said they worry about future events and decisions like what college to attend, what career to pursue, and whether they will marry.

"I worry about . . ."

. . . *the future. I'm a student, always worried about graduating and getting a job.*

. . . *my future, and what I'm going to do with my life, how things will work out.*

. . . *my grades at school, what other people think of me, my future. Will I be able to take good care of myself when I leave for college?*

. . . *what people think of me and [about] my future, specifically who I'll eventually marry.*

. . . *my future. I worry about where I will work after college, will I be doing what I really want in life, will I get married, have kids, complete my bucket list before I die—and those are just the long-term worries. I worry what each day will bring as well.*

. . . *my future. Specifically, how I will balance my career with my husband's and with our desire to start a family. When I have these worries, I try to pray and hand them over to God since I know that He is in charge of my future.*

What if . . . I'm not living my faith as God wants me to?

While younger adults anxiously ponder their future, seniors are more attuned to spiritual matters. On the whole, spiritual issues—whether personal sin, personal spiritual growth, or the spiritual lives of others—don't top many lists of frequent worries. When they do come up, however, they're more likely to be raised by someone sixty or older.

The most common spiritual concern mentioned was personal: Am I following God's will? Am I living in a way pleasing to God?

"I worry about . . ."

. . . *if I'm living according to God's will . . . not that I'm living a life of sin but that am I living for Him in my day to day struggles so that He receives the glory? I feel I should be doing so much more but don't know if there is an area of my life I have not surrendered to Him yet.*

. . . dying before I accomplish the things God needs to do [for me] to become holy.

. . . making sure I'm doing what God needs me to do. Making the most of every opportunity He presents to me to bring Him glory!

. . . whether or not I am having an impact on the world, God's people, and God's kingdom—[whether or not I am] living with purpose.

. . . failing God, going back to the same sins that trip me up.

Where Imagination and Reality Meet

Try a brief memory exercise with me. Think about what you were doing exactly one year ago. What happened that day? Did you go to work? Were you at home? On vacation?

Now, here's the second part: What did you worry about that day?

Can you remember?

I've got nothing. Whatever was setting my heart racing and coursing adrenaline through me last year is gone from my memory now. I could probably guess that it was something related to how my kids' were doing in school, whether we'd have money left at months' end (or month left at money's end), or my parents' health. But the specifics—whether my (Pam's) youngest daughter had a big test that day, I had an important meeting, or the car was making an ominous noise—escape me.

The truth is that most things we worry about either don't happen or, when they do, aren't nearly as bad as we imagined. Certainly there are exceptions, by degree—when a job ends, a biopsy comes back positive, a child doesn't choose to follow Jesus. It's important to remind ourselves that, by definition, exceptions are instances or cases that don't conform to the usual. Thus, most of the "big" concerns pass out of our minds without becoming reality.

So, then, why do we worry? One main reason is that many of us are uncomfortable with uncertainty. Most people find that uncertainty makes them a little uneasy or stressed. And, for about one in four of us, uncertainty produces a great deal of anxiety.

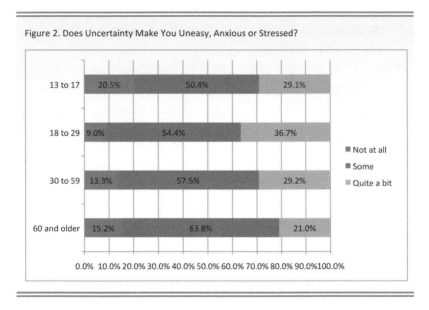

Figure 2. Does Uncertainty Make You Uneasy, Anxious or Stressed?

Linking comfort with uncertainty brings us to the spiritual side of worry. God's Word is filled with encouragement to trust Him in all circumstances. We have His promises to be with us always, and many examples of this promise's guarantee in the lives of the believers who've gone before us. We also have specific examples of God comforting and encouraging His people through uncertainty.

Take Joshua—Moses' right-hand man, groomed for leadership. The prospect of taking charge of the people seems to have set his heart racing, so this is what the Lord said to him:

> Be strong and courageous, for you shall cause this people to inherit the land that I swore to their fathers to give them. Only be strong and very courageous, being careful to do

according to all the law that Moses my servant commanded you. Do not turn from it to the right hand or to the left, that you may have good success wherever you go. This Book of the Law shall not depart from your mouth, but you shall meditate on it day and night, so that you may be careful to do according to all that is written in it. For then you will make your way prosperous, and then you will have good success. Have I not commanded you? Be strong and courageous. Do not be frightened, and do not be dismayed, for the LORD your God is with you wherever you go.[3]

In these sentences, "Be strong and courageous" appears three times. Yet the point isn't that the Lord tells Joshua to buck up; He's telling him *why* he needn't be worried. Joshua can trust God because God has promised that the land is theirs, and God keeps His promises. He has given Joshua the Book of the Law, and He will be with them every step of the way. Essentially, God is saying that what looks uncertain is actually certain, and so Joshua has no need to worry.

Fast-forward a few thousand years: God is telling us the same thing. It's not as specific as a guarantee that a particular piece of land will be ours, but the message's core is still the same.

* * * * *

Again, worry is a matter of the mind, body, and spirit. Now, it's too simplistic and not helpful to say to anyone that "if you have faith, you won't worry." Actually, it's flat-out wrong.

However, worrying does make a spiritual statement. Our beliefs about who God is—His character, abilities, plans—*can* make us more or less prone to worry. We've found that people who trust God more (1) have a higher tolerance for uncertainty and (2) worry less. Similarly, connecting with God through prayer and Scripture also seems to help people accept uncertainty, perhaps by building their trust in Him. Other studies likewise have found similar trends.[4]

Later we'll further explore the intersection of spirituality and worry. But first let's consider some other thought processes that can play into the fear-worry-stress cycle.

A Lie We Believe: "Responsible People Worry"

"Is Gloria worried about starting sixth grade?" asked a well-meaning friend.

"Um . . . no," I stammered. "Errr, not that I've seen, anyway."

"What about you? What about all the peer pressure she'll face and everything?"

There was probably more, but I'd stopped listening at that point. I was too distracted by how unexpected and odd the questions were to me. I hadn't really thought about my usually calm and collected daughter being worried about this. Yes, it was middle school, but she knew almost all the other kids in her grade, was excited about the school, and had breezed through everything academic up to that point.

Then it hit me: mother guilt. Within mere minutes I'd convinced myself that I obviously was a bad mom and should turn in my parent card immediately. I vowed to ask my girl how she was feeling about middle school as soon as we got home. And if she said she was nervous? I'd beg her forgiveness for being clueless.

So how did this happen? One minute I'm relaxing by the pool, soaking in the last bits of summer. The next I'm worried and feeling guilty about not being worried earlier.

Well, unbeknownst to me, lurking in my mind was a positive belief about worry, the belief that responsible people do it. Or, in simpler terms, that worry equals responsible behavior.

I'm not alone in holding this particular belief. Among those we studied (all of them believers), about three of ten saw some truth in the belief that responsible people worry.

This conviction—an obligation to worry, as it were—is just one of several that psychologists have identified that can feed into the fear-worry-stress cycle. For example, some of us believe that fretting is productive. More than two in five of our survey respondents say worrying prompts them to action, helps them know what to do, makes them more effective, and can prevent mishaps from occurring.

Let me briefly illustrate how concern for a problem or situation truly could be productive. When I was leaving our home in Pennsylvania to attend school in Maryland, my parents worried that my car would break down along the road and I'd be stranded. So Dad gave me a full starter box of tools and taught me how to check oil, jump-start the battery, and change a tire. Mom helped me sign up for the American Automobile Association (Triple-A). In short, they turned worry into action. They gave me what I needed both to prevent my car from breaking down (to the extent that I could do so) and to get help if it did break down.

Worry *can*, in such a way, be made productive. It can prompt us to deal with a problem or take some type of preventive action. But problems arise, or keep rising, when we've taken all needful (or even possible) action and still we worry. It's in these types of situations when we may be buying in to what we see as worry's "benefits."

Sometimes we use worry as a type of psychological or emotional protection. On some level we believe that if we worry about something, it's less likely to happen. Because worrisome situations often are rife with uncertainty, we tell ourselves that if we fret about them enough, we'll find a way to fix things, to remove the uncertainty and have it all turn out right.

How much do we buy in to these myths? Adherence is remarkably common. More than 40% of Christians said they believe worry to be effective for problem-solving or avoiding emotional pain at least some of the time. Young people and those who are less spiritually engaged tend more to believe in beneficial aspects of worry than do adults over age thirty and those who are spiritually engaged.

Not surprisingly, seeing positive value in worry can lead to doing it more. And, if we believe that fretting will solve a problem or diminish the pain it's causing, why would we not continue doing it? However, that logic falls apart when we consider other aspects of the matter. For one thing, chronic worrying hurts our bodies and our spirits. For another, most situations we worry about contain factors beyond our control.

"Worry Can Make Me Sick . . .
Which Really Makes Me Worry"

Perhaps the notion that worry can be beneficial sounds to you as wacky as hearing that it's helpful to wear a full-length mink coat for scuba diving. Either way, chances are pretty good that you've picked up this book because you're concerned about the harm that worry causes. Do you believe in the truth of any or all of these statements?

I could make myself sick from worrying.
Worrying puts my body under a lot of stress.
Worry can make it hard to see a situation clearly.

A conviction that worry is harmful or gets in the way of handling a situation represents a negative belief about worry. Worry does indeed affect us negatively (body, mind, and spirit), so it's not surprising that most Christ-followers hold strongly to beliefs like these. We found that 93% affirm that at least one of these three declarations is true.

Understanding the harm of worry can help us if it compels us to reject worrying in the first place or to stop the cycle once it's started. But sometimes the fact of its damaging effects just feels like another thing to worry about. Clinical psychologist Adrian Wells, who refers to this as "Type 2" worry, has found that worrying about worry is a key contributor to anxiety.[5]

The bottom line, then, is to be aware of these effects with-out letting that awareness paralyze you. If reminding yourself that worry is unhelpful and injurious stops you from worrying, then it's a good coping strategy for you, one to keep using. If thinking about how destructive worry can be gets you worrying about worrying, then it's time to remove this from your coping box and find some other, more helpful tools.

What if . . . Worrying Means I Lack Faith?

I know worrying is a sin because it means not trusting that God will work out my life. He holds my future in His hands. I struggle the most with worrying, and I think it keeps me from having a true relationship with God because I don't trust Him like I should. –Brianna (from survey)

Anxiety is not only a pain which we must ask God to assuage but also a weakness we must ask Him to pardon; for He's told us to take no care for the morrow. –C. S. Lewis, *Into the Wardrobe*[6]

We are not necessarily doubting that God will do the best for us; we are wondering how painful the best will turn out to be. –C. S. Lewis, *Letters of C. S. Lewis*[7]

We've mentioned our discomfort with uncertainty and thinking patterns that contribute to worry. We've also noted that another significant piece of the worry puzzle is the spiritual. Most of us are familiar with Jesus telling His disciples to not worry because God will care for them—how would He not do so, when clearly He cares for the sparrows and for lilies of the field? Accordingly, most Christians hold worry to be a sin.

Our study participants identified a number of worry's spiritual effects. A substantial portion feel that worrying indicates a lack of faith, and feel guilty when they worry. Even more believe worry to be displeasing to God and an inhibitor to spiritual growth.

> Uncertainties and beliefs—how do they all fit together? What impact do they have on how much and how often we worry? Check out the discussion of a spiritual-cognitive model of worry in the appendix.

Recognizing that too much focus on our concerns may get in the way of our relationship with the Lord could prompt us to seek him more. Spiritual activities (such as prayer, and worship, and reading God's Word) may then break the worry cycle and provide comfort. But over-focus upon or obsession with how worry is displeasing to God may lead us to fret about whether he still loves us or to anxiously fear that he will abandon us. The goal of focusing on the truth is not to become and remain mired in our faithlessness and insufficiency but rather to remind us of—and root us in—the Lord's faithfulness and sufficiency.

Our Research Says . . .

- Older adults use spiritual coping techniques like prayer and meditating on Scripture more than younger adults and teens do.

- Teens are more likely than older adults to question God's love for them when bad things happen.

- Women worry more than men about family members. Two in five women listed family as their most frequent worry, compared to 28% of men.

Recap and Reflect
Talking Points for Couples or Group Study
• • • • • • • • • • • • • • • • • • • •

Analysis of CBE's research—coupled with findings from other trustworthy national studies—reveals that worry among families is at an all-time high. And the experts we talked to insist our nation is moving toward a related public health crisis. "America is at a critical crossroads when it comes to stress and our health," says the APA's CEO, Dr. Norman B. Anderson. "Worry is also taking a toll on kids. Almost a third of children reported that they had experienced a physical health symptom often associated with stress, such as headaches, stomach aches or trouble falling or staying asleep. And get this: Parents often don't realize their own stress is affecting their children."[8]

- Consider these common worries among parents, kids, and Millennials.[9] Check those that apply to you and your family.

What Husbands Worry About:
- How can I calm the fears of my worried wife?
- How can I protect my family?
- Why can't I connect with my kids?
- Is my job safe?
- Will the economy take another nosedive?
- Am I normal sexually? (Why do I lack energy?)
- Is my marriage okay?
- Is my health okay?
- What if I die? (How will my family survive?)
- Why don't I sense direction for my life?
- Why am I bored with church?
- Why does my spiritual life feel so stuck?

What Wives Worry About:
- How can I help my stressed-out husband?
- How can I protect my kids?
- What kind of a future will my children have?
- Will we ever make ends meet?
- What if a family member gets sick? (Can we afford the bills?)
- Why do I feel so angry and bitter all the time?
- Am I attractive enough to my husband?
- Why won't my husband give me the attention I need?
- Why can't I get along with in-laws?
- What do others think of me?
- How can I help my aging parents?
- Are we pursuing God's will for our lives?

What Kids and Teens Worry About:
- Why do Mom and Dad fight a lot?
- Am I a disappointment to my parents?
- Do my parents love me? (Do they love each other?)
- Does God love me?
- What if I don't make it to heaven?
- Am I safe?
- What if somebody dies?
- Will I fail at school?
- Do the other kids like me?
- Is my body normal?
- Am I smart enough, attractive enough?
- What kind of a future will I have?

What the Millennial Generation Worries About:
- Will I ever have enough money to live on?
- Will I get a decent job—the kind I prepared for in grad school?

- Why do my parents and I disagree on so many issues?
- Am I attractive to the opposite sex?
- How can I hope to ever be married when I'm constantly rejected now?
- Will my marriage survive? (My spouse and I fight all the time.)
- Will I ever figure out who I am and what I believe?
- Does God really love me?
- Why am I so depressed all the time?

- Pick a few statements that you checked and talk about them together.

Here's What's Next

If our stress levels are on the rise and our families are the victims, what should we do about this? One important factor is self-awareness. The next chapter contains a self-assessment quiz that can help provide insight into every member of the family.

4

HOW MUCH OF A WORRYWART AM I?

AN ASSESSMENT QUIZ FOR SELF AND EVERY FAMILY MEMBER

That is why I tell you not to worry about everyday life—whether you have enough food and drink, or enough clothes to wear. Isn't life more than food, and your body more than clothing? Look at the birds. They don't plant or harvest or store food in barns, for your heavenly Father feeds them. And aren't you far more valuable to him than they are? Can all your worries add a single moment to your life?[1]

JESUS

Christ's "Sermon on the Mount" gives an expansive picture of how our lives as His followers should look. He speaks of our being "salt" and "light," of caring for the needy, of prayer and fasting and then money and possessions. On our tendency to worry, He gently reminds us that fretting is just plain pointless. God, our Father, knows what we need, loves us, and will take care of us. Yes, life presents uncertainties. But while we don't have ultimate control, we know who does, and He's always focused on what's best for us. The last question in Christ's words above gets to the heart of why worrying over what we can't change is pointless: *It yields nothing beneficial. It neither improves nor accomplishes anything.*

This is why we're committed to helping you free yourself and your family from worry. It's important early on to take some time to assess how much you actually worry. In this chapter you'll find a few tools to help you gauge not only this but also what triggers might set off a fear-worry-stress cycle and what thought patterns may keep you in it. We call this information your "worry profile." Further, you can help your spouse, kids, and other loved ones complete their own profiles and later in the book we'll show how to use worry profiles to develop each person's own customized action plan for worry-free living.

My Worry Profile: How Much Do I Feel Worried?

Like many college undergraduates, I (Pam) took an intro-to-psychology class to meet my general education requirements and because it sounded interesting. Little did I know I'd get so hooked on the science of human behavior that I'd switch majors and, really, my life course. What I remember most is our discussions of psychopathology and the process of determining an issue is sufficiently severe to be considered a "disease" or, for instance, as Dictionary.com defines pathology, "any deviation from a normal, healthy, or efficient condition."[2]

God created each of us uniquely. Some are naturally "cool cucumbers" who seem to pass through even the most troubling times with little anxiety. Others are racked with worries around the clock, with little relief and few periods of calm. Most experience life somewhere in between these two extremes, with seasons of anxiety and worry and seasons of peace and tranquility.

How does this tie in to those intro-to-psych discussions? One main criterion for psychopathology is that the conditions interfere with a person's life. When moods or behaviors start impacting work or relationships, there is a need to seek help.

* * * * *

Our first worry-profile tool focuses on how much you worry. The goal is to give you a handle not only on the frequency of your worry but also on the extent to which worry is affecting your life. If you are being heavily impacted, it may be time also to get some outside help (for instance, beginning with talking to your doctor and/or pastor).

Please read each question and circle how often it has been true of you in the past month.

	Never	Sometimes	Often	Always
In any situation, I imagine how things can go wrong.	0	1	2	3
No matter what I do, I can't get my mind off my problems.	0	1	2	3
I worry no matter my circumstances.	0	1	2	3
I know I shouldn't worry about things but can't help it.	0	1	2	3
My worries overwhelm me.	0	1	2	3
I find myself worrying about something.	0	1	2	3
I think about how the world is a dangerous place.	0	1	2	3
I avoid certain activities or places because they make me too nervous.	0	1	3	4
My worries hold me back from things I'd like to do.	0	1	3	4
My family complains that I worry too much.	0	1	2	3

	Never	Sometimes	Often	Always
I have trouble going to/staying asleep due to worry.	0	1	2	3
I experience headaches, stomach pain, and/or digestive problems from worry.	0	1	2	3
Add the numbers you circled in each column.				

Add the total from each column to get your score: _____

What does my score mean?

If your score is 12 or fewer, you have a *mild* level of worry. While you may occasionally worry, you don't feel overwhelmed by it; it's not greatly affecting your life. The rest of this book is full of tips that can help you keep worry in check and help you help others with their worry.

If your score is between 13 and 21, you have a *moderate* level of worry. Although it may not always overwhelm you, worry can be a problem for you. It's particularly important that you use the strategies outlined in Part Three to reduce your worry and to prevent it from worsening.

If your score is 22 or more, you have a *severe* level of worry. Still, even if you feel your worry is uncontrollable, there is hope. Part Three will assist you in crafting a customized plan for taming the worry beast. It's also a good idea to consult your doctor to see if any physiological problems are contributing to the troubles you're experiencing.

My Worry Profile:
How Do I Respond to Uncertainty?

As we saw in chapter 3, how comfortable you are with uncertainty plays a big role in your susceptibility to worry. Nearly all of our what-if scenarios contain at least some element of uncertainty, whether it's in regard to the outcome, or the timeline, or both. Our next tool asks you to reflect on how you typically deal with uncertainty.

	Never	Sometimes	Often	Always
Amid uncertainty, I feel nervous, anxious, or unsettled.	0	1	2	3
Unforeseen events greatly upset me.	0	1	2	3
Ambiguity stresses me out.	0	1	2	3
My mind can't relax until I know what will happen tomorrow.	0	1	2	3
I can't stop thinking about a situation when I'm not sure how it will turn out.	0	1	2	3
Add the numbers you circled in each column.				

Add the total from each column to get your score: _____

What does my score mean?

If your score is 5 or fewer, you're comfortable with uncertainty. This means life's unknowns don't generally stress you out, which tends to set you up to worry less.

If your score is between 6 and 11, you're somewhat uncomfortable with uncertainty. Not knowing how a situation will turn out or what will happen next can raise your heart rate a bit and may give you moments or seasons of worry. At those times, or looking back or ahead to those times, it would be helpful to apply some of the strategies you'll find in Part Three.

If your score is 12 or more, you're very uncomfortable with uncertainty. Life's unknowns create high anxiety and leave you worrying over a long list of what-ifs. Actively working to strengthen your ability to deal with uncertainty, including reminders to yourself of God's presence and power, will help you lower your daily stress and weather future uncertainties.

My Worry Profile: How Do I Think About Worry?

Your profile is almost complete! We hope that as you've gone through the previous sections you've learned about your worry tendencies and levels of comfort with uncertainty. How you think about worry—whether it's ever helpful, to what degree it's harmful, etc.—provides the third segment. In chapter 3 we broached some of these beliefs and how they can feed the cycle. Now it's time to reflect on your own beliefs. Read each statement and indicate how it does or doesn't reflect your convictions.

	No	Yes
I worry in order to know what to do.	0	1
If I've already worried about a situation I'll be able to handle it better if it goes badly.	0	1
Worrying can prevent mishaps from occurring.	0	1
I know I shouldn't worry about things but I can't help it.	0	1
Worrying motivates me to do the things I must do.	0	1
Worrying helps me find solutions to my problems.	0	1
Responsible people worry.	0	1
Count how many of these you answered with "yes."		
I could make myself sick with worrying.	0	1
Worrying puts my body under a lot of stress.	0	1
Worry can keep me from seeing a situation clearly.	0	1
Count how many of these you answered with "yes."		
My worrying is a sign that I lack faith.	0	1

	No	Yes
Worrying is a sin.	0	1
I feel guilty when I worry.	0	1
My worrying is displeasing to God.	0	1
Count how many of these you answered with "yes."		

What do my scores mean?

The first seven statements reflect positive underlying beliefs about worry. The more you agree with these, the more likely you are to accept or even embrace worry.

The next three statements focus on negative beliefs about worry. If you agree with them, you're at risk of getting tied up in secondary worry. That is, you may find you start worrying about a situation and then become more and more anxious as you start worrying about being worried. An important facet of your worry-wise strategy (see chapter 8) will be learning how to stop the cycle of fear and worry and stress before it escalates.

The last four statements concern spiritual beliefs about worry. If they prompt you to seek God through prayer and His Word, they're productive. However, if you find that they feed your worry, causing anxiety about your spiritual life, addressing them should be part of your strategy.

Worry Level
Mild Moderate Severe

Comfort with Uncertainty
Comfortable
Somewhat Uncomfortable
Very Uncomfortable

How I Think About Worry
Worry is good: ____ / 7
Worry is good: ____ / 3
Worry is good: ____ / 4

A Worry Profile for My Young Child

As we'll talk about later, many young children also struggle with worry, but it can be hard for them to verbalize what's troubling them. Depending on your child's age, maturity, and reading ability, you might have him/her read and answer the questions, or you may need to read and explain or illustrate the items. (In chapter 10 you'll be able to consider and—hopefully, if need be—ascertain whether your child is showing signs of anxious behavior.)

In the past two weeks, how often have you been bothered by these problems?

	Not at all	Several days	More than half the days	Nearly every day
Not being able to sleep or control worrying	0	1	2	3
Becoming easily annoyed or irritable	0	1	2	3
Feeling nervous, anxious, or on edge	0	1	2	3
Feeling as if something awful might happen	0	1	2	3
Worrying too much about various things	0	1	2	3
Having trouble relaxing	0	1	2	3
Being so restless that it's hard to sit still	0	1	2	3
Add the numbers circled in each column.				

Add the total from each column to get your child's score: _____

What does his/her score mean?

If your child's score is 9 or fewer, he/she has a minimal anxiety level. Worry is not a big issue right now. Together you can use the tips in chapter 10 to keep worries at bay as he/she navigates toward the teenage years.

If your child's score is between 10 and 14, he/she has a moderate level of anxiety—even if he/she isn't feeling overwhelmed, worry is starting to become a problem. You can help reduce worry and prevent it from worsening by adopting strategies outlined in Part Three.

If your child's score is 15 or more, he/she has severe anxiety, experiences worry that feels out of control, and needs you to help him/her to break free from the fear-worry-stress cycle. The strategies in Part Three will help you craft a plan together. Also, consult your pediatrician to evaluate whether or not a medical condition might be contributing to the anxiety.

* * * * *

Knowledge is the first step toward finding relief from worry. The basic helps in this chapter are meant to provide you with specific knowledge about how much your family members worry and what thoughts may be contributing to that worry.

However, a word of caution: Because our beliefs about worry and faith can contribute to the cycle, many of us can be tempted to think that "it's all in my head." That is not the case. When working through our struggles or helping a loved one who's suffering, the last things anyone should hear are messages like, "Get over it and have more faith," "Stop being so self-absorbed and start thinking about the needs of others," or "Worry is nothing short of idolatry."

Our Research Says . . .

- Chronic worrying can interfere with your appetite, sleep, job performance, and relationships.
- It's estimated that more than six million Americans suffer from panic attacks. Panic attack symptoms

like shortness of breath and a pounding heart are often mistakenly seen as evidence of a heart attack.[3]

• One in three people with a panic disorder subsequently develops agoraphobia. However (good news!), early diagnosis and treatment can shorten the disorder's chronicity and reduce a person's chances of developing agoraphobia.

Recap and Reflect
Talking Points for Couples or Group Study

Family life can be turbulent, and we'll all have our share of troubles in a given day—including worrisome thoughts that invade our minds. Being concerned won't hurt us; the problem arises when we allow anxiety to paralyze our thinking.

• Share what you learned from your worry profile.

How did my family and I score? Is this what I anticipated? Am I surprised or concerned?

As we said earlier, becoming self-aware—learning about what's bugging us and examining how we react to stress—can move us toward worry-free living. Our intent here is *not* to dispense a medical diagnosis. (That's a conversation we hope you'll have with a medical professional.) Rather, now is the time to think about your next steps. With knowledge on your side, you're better able to pray, plan, and plot a realistic course toward healing.

- Identify at least two issues you want to work on . . . and help with in the lives of those in your care.

  How does a commitment to progress make me feel? (e.g., motivated, nervous, hopeful, overwhelmed, inspired . . .)

Here's What's Next

While Christians definitely hold the keys to meaningful change and real transformation through our faith in Jesus, we also must consider physiological and emotional factors that are unique to each one of us. The next chapter is intended to help us to do just that.

THE TRUE CULPRITS REVEALED

By the End of Part Two You'll Be Able to:

- Identify physical and emotional processes in the fear-worry-stress cycle
- Catch and correct triggers to worry and anxiety
- Understand the adrenaline connection and take steps to re-regulate it
- Take comfort in what God's Word says about His provision
- Use the Worry-Wise Plan to de-stress and calm down

Ten Little-Known (But Real) Social Phobias

- Anthropophobia: The fear of people (or of human company)
- Aphephobia: The fear of being touched
- Autodysomophobia: The fear of emitting a bad or vile odor
- Ecclesiophobia: The fear of church buildings and/or of religious practices

- Gamophobia: The fear of getting married or of making a relational commitment
- Nomophobia: The fear of being out of cell phone contact/losing service
- Sociophobia: The fear of being judged harshly or embarrassed in social situations
- Soteriophobia: The fear of becoming dependent on other people/another person
- Syngenesophobia: The fear of relatives and/or in-laws
- Venustraphobia: The fear of beautiful women

IT'S NOT JUST A LACK OF FAITH

PHYSICAL AND EMOTIONAL PROCESSES AT WORK

You're blessed when you're at the end of your rope.
With less of you there is more of God and his rule.
JESUS CHRIST[1]

Briana Beckworth dangles helplessly from the driver's side window of her crumpled pickup. She gasps for air, tries to scream, but struggles just to breathe.

Pain surges through every inch of her body—especially her left leg. *It feels stuck,* she thinks. *Am I caught on something?*

The lean twenty-two-year-old blinks a couple times and then squints. Smoke and dust rise from the ground. Acrid smells fill the air. Everything has the odor of gasoline and burnt wires.

I'm outside—must have been thrown from my truck. But why am I upside down? She turns her head and strains to look up: The mangled roof of what was once her 1995 Toyota is crushed around her leg. *I AM trapped!*

She glances frantically to her left, then to her right. *And I'm alone.*

On one side is the steep embankment Briana's truck had rolled down. On the other is a plowed cornfield with long furrows of black dirt stretching endlessly away.

She listens intently. Apart from the sound of her own labored breathing there's *nothing*; no cars crunching on gravel, no barking dogs in the distance—not even a lone cricket's chirp.

Suddenly reality presses in: *I'm stranded in the middle of nowhere, on a country road nobody ever uses. I'm gonna die.*

She gasps for another breath—and coughs. She pushes against the truck with her hands and tries to pull herself up with her free leg, but her strength is gone.

"Somebody! Anybody!" she screams. "Help! Please! Please..."

* * * * *

Briana throws off the covers and bolts upright, her heart racing. She rubs her eyes, then focuses on a photo of her fiancé, Steve, on the nightstand. Sweat rolls down her neck.

I'm at home, she consoles herself. *In my own room. It was just a—*
She trembles. If only it were just a dream.
Why, God? Why?
Will I have a normal life?
Will I get to do the things I love?
Will I ever walk again?

When Life Gets Messy

It's frightening to consider how everything can change in a moment.

You're heading to a friend's house, laughing at what's on the radio, enjoying a sunny afternoon—*living*—and making plans for the future: *a fall wedding; one day a few children; dogs in the yard; a home of our own . . . maybe that little farmhouse I've always had my eye on . . . even horses in the pasture?*

And then in an instant the unthinkable happens.

Before you know it, you're facing challenges you never imagined enduring. Everyday activities you once took for granted—grabbing milk from the fridge, hugging a loved one, or even just *walking*—take on much more meaning.

That's how it was for Briana.

In 2004, a freak accident just two miles from her home in Beatrice, Nebraska, changed her whole world. As she rumbled down an old one-lane road that cut through rolling farmland, a speeding pickup appeared in her path. She twisted her steering wheel, narrowly missing the oncoming vehicle—and launching her own truck into a ditch.

"Here's the hardest part," explains Briana, now thirty-one. "I never lost consciousness as it was happening. I remember every second—every detail of something I wish I could forget. And when my pickup stopped rolling, I heard the other truck drive away. At that point, I knew I was in the middle of nowhere . . . stranded."

Injured, alone, and left for dead on the roadside is more trauma than most people think they can handle. Yet Briana was both physically and emotionally strong. In fact, she worked as an Emergency Medical Technician (EMT) and was trained to keep her cool during stressful moments. It was the heartless act of two men fleeing the scene that really shook her up.

To add insult to injury, her obstacles went from bad to worse in the days that followed. Once she was stabilized, doctors explained that her back had been broken and her spinal cord injured. She needed multiple surgeries, would endure months of rehab . . . and faced the strong possibility of spending the rest of her days in a wheelchair.

"I was young and in the prime of my life," she says. "I had no clue anything like that could happen to me. I had tested for the fire department the week before. It was crazy. The thought of never walking again . . ."

Briana soon spiraled deep into the fear-worry-stress cycle. At night, horrific images stole the rest she desperately needed. During the day, catastrophic thoughts gripped her mind: *What if*

Steve stops loving me? What if I can't pay all these medical bills? What if I have to depend on others to do everything for me? WHAT IF?

It had all begun with a pair of split-second mistakes.

* * * * *

For EMTs, there's no such thing as an ordinary day. Hours of boredom and tedious chores can change with a single heart-pumping call. Today, though, would catch Briana by surprise. Little did she realize that all attention was about to be focused on her.

She glanced at her watch. 1:30 p.m. *Better get a move on.*

It was her day off, and she was headed to a friend's house, a mere couple of miles from where she lived. She was a seatbelt fanatic—never going anywhere without buckling up—yet on this fateful day when leaving her driveway Briana somehow forgot to snap in.

That was her first error. Her second was making a wrong turn. "I ended up on one of those roads no one ever takes," she remembers. "If you don't live on this route, you have no business driving on it. To this day I have no idea why I made that turn."

Halfway down the road, she noticed another truck in the distance, moving toward her. *Hunters?* she thought. *It's the start of deer season.* As she held her course, she didn't realize how fast the other vehicle was speeding along. The moment she crested a hill, the trucks met head on.

Briana instinctively swerved, dodging aside by mere inches.

"But my truck lost control, and I rolled two or three times," she says. "Unrestrained, I was thrown out of my seat and partially ejected out the driver's-side window. And once I stopped rolling, my truck landed on all four tires—with me hanging out."

When she realized the other truck was gone, she knew she was in trouble. She struggled to breathe and was pretty certain that at least her leg was broken. She attempted several times to pull herself up and break free but couldn't. She needed help, quickly. "I just sort of let go and hung there—probably for ten minutes," she says. "And that's when God intervened."

Another driver who'd also taken a wrong turn that day—a middle-aged man looking for his sister's house—happened to show up.

"When I heard his car coming, I used my leg that was free and threw it up over the driver's door, because I was on the back side," she explains. "I knew he wouldn't be able to see me down in the ditch. Yet he stopped when he saw my foot moving. He didn't have a phone, and mine was gone—we couldn't find anything . . . everything was just scattered everywhere."

Her EMT training quickly kicked in, and she talked him through triage procedures: he removed her from the wreckage and carefully placed her on her side so she could breathe a little better. "Tell the police to get a helicopter here quickly," she told him. "I'm in critical condition—I need to go straight to the hospital."

As for the other vehicle, "those guys were long gone by the time authorities arrived," she says. They were never found, though she'd given the police an extensive description. "Yet I never stopped wondering what ever happened to them."

* * * * *

In the weeks and months that followed, Briana found herself struggling with a wide range of difficult emotions—everything from anger and bitterness to fear and worry.

"I just didn't realize what I had to live for anymore," she reflects. "I was constantly looking back at what my 'normal' used to be—and I wanted it again. I wanted to reclaim the life I'd known. I was just so terrified of the *un*known."

Even though she'd been freed from the wreckage and her body was on the mend, she hadn't left the accident emotionally. She often felt as if she were still dangling helplessly from a twisted mess.

Would she ever trust again?

* * * * *

During critical moments in the ER, doctors worked feverishly. Once they'd stabilized Briana's vital signs they bombarded her with questions:

"What medications do you take?"

"Do you feel pain?"

"Where does it hurt?"

Her body ached indescribably. "My back," she groaned, trying to point to her midsection. And then it was off to surgery.

Hours later a surgeon delivered troubling news to Briana's mom: "Your daughter's vertebra was shattered, at L4, and her spinal cord is mostly severed. We've repaired the damage, and she's in stable condition. But there's a chance she'll never walk again."

After enduring an induced coma for a week those same words were on replay in Briana's brain like a broken record.

As she lay in a hospital bed, staring at ceiling tiles, her mind began racing with catastrophic possibilities. *The REST of my LIFE? Are they serious?! No more work. No more hiking or riding horses. And absolutely no chance of—*

She stopped the thought in midsentence and glanced at her fiancé's photo.

No chance of walking down the aisle. Why would he want to marry a cripple?

Tears rolled down her cheeks.

* * * * *

Rapid heartbeat, tightness in the chest, hyperventilation, dizziness, sweating, tension headaches . . . the effects of stress are easy to detect. Nearly all of us have been there. But for those who've been traumatized like Briana, the symptoms are hyper-intense:

sometimes the thoughts of helplessness and self-consciousness ("everyone is looking at me") and the fears of forever "losing control" and also of being alone are relentless.

In addition to the long battle to regain the use of her legs, Briana faced two other big challenges: Frequent panic attacks and post-traumatic stress disorder.

"My life had taken such a dramatic turn, and I wasn't coping very well," she says. "I was always so upbeat, so easy-going. Now I was a nervous wreck. The flashbacks, the fear, the panic—none of it would go away. I would cry out to God. Yet there I sat in a prison of worry, constantly asking *What if—*"

When You Can't Simply Pray Away Worry

Fifty-five-year-old Brian can relate. "If people knew about all the things that worry me, they'd think I'm crazy and that I lack what it takes to be a true Christ-follower," he says.

For this Oklahoma City native, anxiety moves from an occasional nuisance to a daily trial that binds his natural ability to cope in this world. "I worry about having a heart attack or think that something terrible might happen to my wife," he shares. "I worry about countless small things: *Did I lather up enough when I washed my hands? Do the cats like the food I bought?* And then I feel guilty about worrying—and fret about that too. *Lord, what's happening to me?!*"

Kathy, fifty-nine, of Redding, California, has asked herself these questions as well.

"The types of emotions I've dealt with all these years relate to apprehension, worry, stress, and anxiety," she says. "They can range in severity from mere twinges of uneasiness to full-blown panic attacks marked by rapid heartbeat, trembling, sweating, queasiness, and terror."

Sometimes her feelings are connected to everyday worries and strike out of the blue (called "free-floating anxiety"). Sometimes they're a bit more out of proportion, even unrealistic—and are triggered by specific struggles (called "situational anxiety").

"People who suffer from anxiety are especially prone to engage in fearful self-talk," explains Dr. Edmund Bourne, who specializes in the treatment of anxiety disorders. "Anxiety can be generated on the spur of the moment by repeatedly making a statement to yourself that begin with the two words: 'what if.'"[2]

Briana, Brian, and Kathy aren't alone.

They, like millions of Americans, struggle daily with anxiety. And their reasons for struggling are as varied as the issues bugging them . . .

- *Long-term, Predisposing Causes:* heredity, dysfunctional parenting, childhood trauma
- *Recent Circumstantial Causes:* loss, life change, trauma in adulthood, increased stress levels at work and at home, recreational drug use
- *Maintaining Causes:* attitude and lifestyle choices, low self-confidence and self-worth, fearful *what-if* thinking, avoidance of fear or fearsome situations, development of a "worry habit," neglect of exercise, consumption of large amounts of caffeine, sugar, or junk food
- *Neurobiological Causes:* deficiencies or imbalances in certain neurotransmitters, particularly serotonin, norepinephrine, GABA, and excessive levels of adrenaline; excessive reactivity of certain brain structures, especially the amygdala and locus coeruleus; insufficient inhibition or "braking" of excessive reactivity by higher brain centers such as the frontal or temporal cortex[3]

"Sometimes we become stressed as we deal with this often messy thing called *life*," explains Dr. Eric T. Scalise. "Regardless of the cause, it does set into motion certain processes within the body and within the brain that affect mood. So just telling someone, 'Pray more, read your Bible more, be in church more,' shouldn't be a Christian's only solution. There may be other things that are going on inside that need immediate attention."[4]

How about you and your family?

Could it be that the problem is more physiological than spiritual? Instead of being afraid of what's stressing us, let's learn more about it . . . and find some solutions.

The Many Faces of Anxiety

My long career as a behaviorist has taught me (Arnie) three key things about stress: It's a normal emotion, it's increasing rapidly in contemporary society, and it has many "faces."

While we all misread circumstances and get caught up in a worry cycle from time to time, prolonged fear, worry, and stress can lead to anxiety disorders—problems that go way beyond ordinary, everyday stress. These types of disorders are more intense, interfere with our lives, cause unnecessary distress, can develop in to phobias, and are a definite health hazard.

Let's take a closer look at some common anxiety disorders. The definitions and descriptions I've presented here are based on what the American Psychiatric Association has published in the *Diagnostic and Statistical Manual of Mental Disorders, Fifth Edition (DSM-5)*, its current guide for therapists and medical professionals.[5]

Don't worry—this isn't crammed with psychobabble. Instead, you'll see a lot of different faces in this section. Study them closely. Listen to their stories. And, as you read, think about the loved ones in your world:

In what ways can you empathize with their struggles?
How can they better understand your worries?

What steps can you take to help free your family from fear, worry, and anxiety?

Panic Disorder

Key Issues
- Recurrent, unexpected episodes of panic without any obvious situational cause
- Worry about having more attacks
- The concern that "I will lose control, go crazy—even die."

Common Triggers
- Crowded places, such as shopping centers, busy streets, and concert halls
- Enclosed spaces, such as tunnels, elevators, and airplanes
- Perceived threats, such as spiders, heights, and public speaking
- Internal triggers, such as a feared sensation or a negative thought

What Happens
Sudden episodes of acute, intense anxiety appear to come from nowhere. Sufferers have at least one panic attack per month and often worry about when the next one will strike. Frequently the attacks are accompanied by irrational fears and repetitive thoughts. For example, someone may fear they'll be stricken with a life-threatening illness, such as cancer, or are about to have a heart attack. Panic attacks can be terrifying.

The Face of Panic: Allison's Circular Struggle
Allison, thirty-five, has a tendency to get stuck on—locked into—certain fears, thinking and rethinking the same negative thought. Even as a child her family labeled her a worrier: "You're obsessing

again, Ali," her mom would say. "Just let it go and stop worrying so much."

Allison couldn't then—and she still can't today. This wife and mother of three gets so worked up about stress, both real and imagined, she finds herself gripped in full-blown panic as often as two or three times a month. The attacks rise out of the blue and usually involve irrational fears: *Will something bad happen to my kids? Is my husband okay? Does he still love me?*

Her heart races, breathing turns to gasping, and she usually feels tightness in her chest. While the physical reactions peak within a few minutes, the repetitive negative thoughts hang on and constantly circle through her mind. The more she tries to control them, the more powerful they become.

Maybe I'm just going crazy. I simply can't live this way. Something has to give.

Agoraphobia

Key Issues

- Fear of having a panic attack
- Fear of the physical sensations that occur during panic
- The concern that "I may have a panic attack while in public and be helpless and humiliated," or "An episode could hit while I'm alone, meaning I won't receive any help if my life is threatened."
- Fears lead to self-imposed restrictions on activities

Common Triggers

- The same as panic attack: crowds, being alone, driving, enclosed spaces
- Situations in which escape is difficult or impossible
- Situations in which help is unavailable

What Happens

Many sufferers ruminate about having panic attacks, and they continually wonder when the next one will strike. Yet agoraphobia goes beyond the fear of *having* another attack; there is worry about *where* it will happen—specifically the kinds of places that could impair their safety or be difficult to escape: *Maybe it will happen in a car on a crowded freeway or in a check-out line at the store.* Such fear can lead to avoidance of a wide range of activities and public places.

The Face of Agoraphobic Fear: Mildred's Regimented Life

Mildred won't set foot on an airplane or a train . . . and she won't travel long distances by car. In fact, since retiring a few years back, she rarely goes anywhere.

The sixty-seven-year-old widow can't seem to get a handle on her frequent panic attacks. When she's not chained into a terrifying episode, she worries about the next: *When and where will it strike?*

So she sticks with what's safe: short drives to the pharmacy or the grocery store—during off-hours, of course; always keeping her anti-anxiety meds within reach in case of emergencies; never straying too far from her sister, who moved in after her husband died. Mildred's life is structured and predictable—and that's exactly how she likes it.

Social Anxiety Disorder (SAD)

Key Issues

- Fear of social settings in which public attention is drawn to the individual
- Exaggerated concern about being embarrassed or humiliated
- Extreme fear of situations where the individual is exposed to the scrutiny or judgment of others or must perform

Common Triggers

- Public speaking or performing

- Interpersonal communication: meetings, interviews, parties, dating
- The concern that "I may embarrass myself in front of others and end up looking foolish, making a bad impression, or being rejected altogether."

What Happens

Those with this phobia freeze up at the thought of speaking or performing in front of an audience—whether a large group or a small group or an interview setting, for example. Those who suffer with SAD often go out of their way to avoid situations where they might be the center of attention: meetings at work, social gatherings, speaking up in class, job interviews, meeting new people, eating in public, interacting with those in authority.

The Face of Social Anxiety: David's Commitment to Being Invisible

During meetings, David avoids eye contact with his boss. *Don't call on me to answer questions,* he thinks—almost pleads, inwardly. *If I can blend in I can remain stealth.*

Even as others at the table speak nonsense about issues within his expertise, he remains quiet. *I'll correct it later by email.*

The fifty-two-year-old executive panics when public attention turns to him, especially in a room full of supervisors and vice presidents. His tongue gets tied, and his heart races.

But remove the spotlight, and David suddenly shines.

Specific Phobia

Key Issues

- A strong fear and avoidance of a certain particular object or situation
- Excessive or unrealistic fear of that specific object or situation
- The concern that "I may be threatened by this specific object or situation."

Common Triggers

- The range of objects and situations that can trigger fear are endless—everything from *enclosed spaces* (elevators, tunnels, cramped rooms, crowded places) to *animals* (spiders, snakes, dogs) to *stormy weather* (thunder, lightning, rain, snow) to *heights* (tall buildings, looking down from a railing, balconies, rooftops, rides at amusement parks), and a vast array of other things
- Just the thought of these objects and situations can trigger uneasiness

What Happens

Sufferers grow fearful (and often panic) when they encounter an object, situation, or environment that makes them uncomfortable. *DSM-5* includes four main types of specific phobias: (1) *Animal type*—these can include fears of any animal or insect. The most common include dogs, cats, mice, spiders, snakes, bugs, moths, cockroaches, birds, and lizards. (2) *Natural environment type*—these include fears of heights, water, storms, and the dark. (3) *Blood / injection / injury type*—these include fears of the sight of blood, watching surgery, receiving a shot, having blood tests, having dental procedures, and many other related fears. (4) *Situational type*—these include specific fears of flying, driving, enclosed places, and related situations.[6]

The Face of Specific Phobia: Stephanie's Irrational Avoidance

Stephanie, forty-four, hates elevators—or any tight space from which she can't easily escape.

Even just the thought of such places makes her knees weak and her heart skip a beat. As an elevator door closes, Stephanie grows tense: her heart begins to race, her hands tremble, beads of sweat roll down her neck, and she experiences instant shortness of breath. All of this is followed by nausea, lightheadedness, and feelings of detachment.

She squeezes shut her eyes—concentrating on each gasp of air—and a minute or two later, she's back to normal. The familiar "ding" of the elevator and the sound of doors opening assure her that everything's okay again.

It makes no sense at all. Why am I so afraid of elevators? she asks herself, then shivers at the thought of stepping into one.

Generalized Anxiety Disorder (GAD) and Worry

Key Issues
- Extreme worry (about a variety of issues) that lasts six months or longer
- Individuals often experience such physiological symptoms as muscle tension, rapid heartbeat, insomnia, fatigue, anxiety, irritability, anger, constantly feeling jittery, often being "on edge"
- Panic attacks and phobias usually aren't present with GAD
- The general concern that "I may be facing a threat—at work, at home, at the doctor's office" and a tendency to anticipate disaster.

Common Triggers
- Worries about finances: making ends meet, spending money
- Worries about the workplace: deadlines, meetings, pleasing the boss
- Worries about family: parenting challenges, disagreements with spouse, communication
- Worries about health issues: neglecting exercise, poor diet, physical pain, illnesses among family and friends, hearing negative medical reports via media.

What Happens
Constant worry: this is what occupies the minds of GAD sufferers. According to Martin M. Antony, PhD, "They worry about a wide range of topics: work, school, their family, their health, money, the world, and minor matters that arise from day to day."[7] Dr. Antony is president-elect of the Canadian Psychological Association and professor and director of graduate training in the Department of Psychology at Toronto's Ryerson University. He explains that three factors lead to a GAD diagnosis:

> First, it needs to have been a long-standing problem . . . Many people with GAD describe themselves as having been worriers for as long as they can remember. Second, the worry must be about many different things. If a person only worries about work, that's not GAD. Third, the worry must be excessive, out of proportion to the actual situation.[8]

The Face of Generalized Anxiety: Ron's Treadmill of Worry
Ron is worried.

The forty-eight-year-old missed a deadline at work, and even though he has his boss's full support, he's convinced his reputation has been critically damaged. *I'm the go-to guy,* he tells himself. *I NEVER miss one! These younger execs are going to eat me alive—and go after my job. Got to do better, got to work harder.*

He grabs his cell phone and punches his wife's number. No answer. *That's the third try this hour. Why won't she pick up? Is she avoiding me?*

Ron tilts back in his office chair and puts his hand on his heart. *It's racing again. Better check my blood pressure; better calm down. Definitely my numbers are bad.*

Worry, worry, worry. It's what Ron does—all throughout the day, every day. It's become his identity: "Hey, stop being

'Ron the Worrywart,'" friends say with a wink. "Life's too short to be so stressed. Relax!"

He cringes when he hears these comments. The problem is, he simply doesn't know how to let go of worry.

Obsessive-Compulsive Disorder (OCD)

Key Issues

- Unreasonable thoughts and fears (obsessions) lead to repetitive behaviors (compulsions)
- Obsessions often center on a theme such as irrational fears of bringing harm to a loved one or fear of coming into contact with germs and being contaminated
- Compulsions may include constantly checking to see if a task has been completed (e.g., the stove has been turned off and the doors are locked) or repeating actions, words, and prayers over and over
- The concern that "I may not be okay, therefore I must double-check my actions or follow a particular thought process in order to work through the anxiety."

Common Triggers

- Touching objects that are feared to be "contaminated"— for example, shaking another person's hand, touching an elevator button, coming in contact with "toxins," such as gasoline or insecticide
- Irrational fears about hurting others or acting aggressively toward them; being near objects that could be used to hurt others, such as a hammer or a knife
- Fear triggered by certain words or images; hearing, seeing, and talking about them
- Fear associated with making a mistake; taking part in activities in which mistakes may occur

What Happens

Recurring obsessions (repetitive thoughts, for example) won't leave a person's mind, so he/she often engages in compulsive behaviors (rituals) to dispel the anxiety. Sometimes these thoughts and behaviors are severe enough to be time-consuming or cause marked distress.[9] Persistent hand-washing or constantly checking that a door is locked are two common types;[10] the obsessions are usually irrational—in the form of thoughts, images, urges—and often upset the individual, who sees them as intrusive, inappropriate, or frightening. The compulsions sometimes follow a rigid, self-imposed set of rules that he/she believes will prevent bad things from happening.[11] According to *DSM-5*, other obsessive-compulsive and related disorders are characterized primarily by recurrent body-focused repetitive behaviors (e.g., hair-pulling, skin-picking) and repeated attempts to decrease or stop behaviors.[12]

The Face of Obsessive-Compulsive Disorder: Connie's Troublesome Thoughts

Connie loves her teenager's contagious excitement.

She sips her orange juice, leans on the kitchen counter, and listens intently as her daughter downloads about another busy day. Yet right in the middle of the story—*ping!* An unthinkable thought races through her mind: an image of her daughter somehow being hurt.

What if something bad happens to her at school?

Ping! Another irrational fear swirls through the forty-nine-year-old mom's brain: It's a sickening feeling that she herself could bring harm to her child. Connie takes a deep breath and swallows, nodding her head every now and then—signaling that she's following the details. But internally she's trying to shake off the disturbing thoughts. The same frightening scenarios replay over and over—they just won't go away.

She takes another deep breath and looks down briefly: *These thoughts are irrational,* she tells herself. *They are not real; they do not have power over me. Trust Jesus . . . he is in control.*

The ugly scenarios dissipate, for now, after she recites a "script" that has helped in the past. She then reengages in her daughter's story. Yet she's weary, and left with a knot in the pit of her stomach. *Why do I* constantly *battle these thoughts?*

Post-Traumatic Stress Disorder (PTSD)

Key Issues

- An anxiety disorder following an intense trauma in which a person's life or safety was threatened
- Victims experienced extreme fear, helplessness, or horror during the trauma
- Possible causal events include natural disasters, a serious accident, assault, sexual abuse, combat, witnessing an event that involves death or injury to another person

Common Triggers

- Repeated disturbing memories of, flashbacks to, or nightmares about a traumatic event
- Situations, places, conversations, activities, and people that remind of the trauma

What Happens

Victims often battle disturbing memories, flashbacks, and nightmares following such an experience. The images can be intense, causing sufferers to feel as if they are reliving it. This sometimes causes them to go out of their way to avoid situations that remind them of the trauma; they attempt to cope by numbing their emotions. (He or she can seem detached, disinterested in important activities, or unable to be happy.) Victims also have a heightened awareness of their surroundings and can battle difficulty sleeping, anger issues, an inability to concentrate and hold a thought, and the sense of frequently feeling startled and on guard for repeated danger.

The Face of Post-Traumatic Stress Disorder:
Tanya's Living Nightmare

Tanya bolts out of bed, then nudges her husband. "Did you hear that?"

He stretches to click on a lamp. "Yes. Same sound we heard thirty minutes ago. It's just the cat." Then he touches her hand and smiles. "It's the ongoing battle—'Feed me, humans, or suffer the consequences!'—but we're not going to; Mr. Whiskers is already way too fat."

Tanya nods. Slowly she sits down and then lies back on her pillow.

"You okay?" asks her husband.

"Will be."

"Same nightmares?"

She looks up and nods again. But the truth is, she isn't okay. Things haven't been the same for her ever since the break-in.

Tanya, twenty-eight, was alone in their condo that night—her husband was away on business. It started with a loud *THUMP.* And then the sound of broken glass. Before she could pull on her bathrobe, her bedroom door flew open, and a huge man in a black mask pointed a gun at her head. She was so stunned she couldn't even scream.

Just as the man put his finger on the trigger, sirens blared in the distance. He turned and fled the house. (Apparently he broke into two other units in the complex and later was spotted.)

Tanya is thankful to be alive, yet the memories won't go away.

"I close my eyes at night and the horrible scene replays over and over," she says. "I just cannot get over it. It's as if my life has been immobilized. I'm stuck on 'what if.' I can't seem to move forward again."

Separation Anxiety Disorder

Key Issues

- Fear of separation from home or from primary figures in a person's life
- Extreme anxiety when away from home or from close attachment figures (e.g., parents or other family members)

- Worry about losing, or harm coming to, a person the individual is attached to
- In children: "clinging" behavior; "shadowing" a parent around the house

Common Triggers
- In children: being separated from key people in the child's life and from home; going to school for the first time; being away from parents for the first time
- In adults: fear of being alone; uncomfortable physical sensations associated with being separated from loved ones and from home; being separated for an extended period of time from a spouse (e.g., when he or she is deployed overseas)

What Happens
The disorder's primary feature is excessive fear or stress concerning separation from home or from attachment figures (spouse, parent, close friend, pet). The anxiety exceeds what may be expected given the person's developmental level. According to *DSM-5*, individuals with separation anxiety disorder have symptoms that meet at least three of the following criteria: (1) recurrent excessive distress when separation from home or major attachment figures is anticipated or occurs; (2) worry about losing, or harm coming to, close attachment figures; (3) worry about something bad happening to them—e.g., getting lost, being kidnapped, or having an accident—that would keep them from ever being reunited with key attachment figures; (4) refusal to go anywhere for fear of separation; (5) extreme fear of being alone, even at home; (6) reluctance (or refusal) to sleep without the attachment figure nearby; (7) repeated nightmares about being separated; (8) physical symptoms—e.g., headaches, abdominal complaints, nausea, vomiting—whenever separation occurs or is anticipated.[13]

The Face of Separation Anxiety: Mike's Terror of Losing His Mother
Five-year-old Mike stands by the door of his kindergarten class, sobbing uncontrollably.

Moments earlier—while the boy's teacher distracted him—his mom slipped out quietly. But the second he couldn't find her, waves of fear began to sweep over him.

It all started after his parents divorced, and his mom was forced to go back to work. The boy simply won't tolerate being separated from her: he follows her to the bathroom, sleeps in the same room with her, lugs every Matchbox car into the kitchen . . . anything to be near her.

Mike even worries that something bad might happen to his mom—especially that she might die and leave him alone. Whenever the two drive past a local cemetery, he grows tense. "I don't like that place," he says. "It's scary. You won't have to go there . . . right, Mom?"

His separation anxiety is severe, and his mom is at her wit's end. "There's so much stress in our lives now," she says, "and I fear that my son is scarred for life."

Substance-Induced Anxiety Disorder

Key Issues
- Anxiety caused entirely by a medication, illegal drug, or other substance
- Panic attacks, extreme mood swings, or excessive worry brought on by use of medications, stimulants (tea or coffee), alcohol, or illegal drugs

Common Triggers
- Certain medications
- Illegal drugs
- Alcohol
- Coffee or other stimulants

What Happens

A substance/medication-induced mental disorder is potentially severe but usually temporary. Problems in the central nervous system (CNS) are triggered by the effects of alcohol, drugs, medications, or other toxins. "They are distinguished from the substance use disorders, in which a cluster of cognitive, behavioral, and physiological symptoms contribute to the continued use of a substance despite significant substance-related problems."[14] For accurate diagnosis, the problem must have persisted during or within one month of a substance intoxication or withdrawal, and the involved substance/medication must be capable of producing a disorder.

The Face of Substance-Induced Anxiety:
Ann's High-Octane Dilemma

Ann, twenty-six, can't start the day without her extra-large, triple-shot coffee concoction. The problem is, large doses of caffeine bring on severe physiological reactions: extremely rapid heartbeat, sweating, shaking, gasping for air, *and* full-blown panic attacks.

I think I'm having a heart attack, she tells herself during an unusually severe episode. *But how can that be? I'm much too young.*

Still, events like these have landed her in the ER more than once. Her physician then got tough with her: "Lay off caffeine," he said. "Or limit yourself to a cup or two in the morning."

Ann scrunches her forehead. That advice makes sense . . . and her therapist also identified the coffee-panic connection. *Maybe a compromise,* she thinks. *Maybe I can cut back and reduce the stress. My busy life would not be the same without coffee!*

Anxiety Due to Another Medical Disorder

Key Issues
• Predominant panic attacks or anxiety

- Medical investigation proves that the disturbance (anxiety) is the direct pathophysiological consequence of another medical condition.
- Doctors and psychiatrists make this diagnosis when they are certain that the medical condition preceded the onset of anxiety.

Common Triggers

- A variety of medical illnesses: cardiovascular disorders (e.g., congestive heart failure, arrhythmia), respiratory illness (e.g., asthma, pneumonia), metabolic disturbances (e.g., vitamin B-12 deficiency), etc.
- OCD symptoms might be triggered by a brain tumor, for instance, or panic attacks might be triggered by an overactive thyroid.[15]

What Happens

Sufferers become anxious or have panic attacks after being diagnosed with another medical condition. Perhaps their health concerns cause them to worry about quality of life, ability to function normally—even possibility of death. Yet medical professionals aren't quick to make this diagnosis. Before it's officially classified as Anxiety Due to Another Medical Disorder, they make certain the disturbance causes "clinically significant distress" and that it's interfering with a person's life on many different levels: relationships, work, ability to concentrate, overall well-being, and many other factors.

The Face of Anxiety Due to Another Medical Disorder: Mary's Quest for Peace

Mary's stroke changed everything.

She's making a full recovery, and she's thankful to be alive and increasingly well at seventy-four—but now she worries all the time.

It's a new reality for her; she's generally happy. She's thankful for her loving husband and large family (with six grandkids), loves her church, and, overall, is satisfied with her life experiences—which includes extensive global travel.

But the stroke . . .

"It has rattled me," she told her doctor. "I'm so scared about my blood pressure, and frightened that I'll have another one; the kind that could leave me paralyzed."

And lately, she feels keyed-up, irritable, constantly on edge. She's even had a couple of panic attacks.

"I want my life back," she continues. "I want to be the happy person I once was."

* * * * *

Did you see your face among any of these other sufferers?

Take comfort in being reminded that you're not alone. While only a medical professional can accurately diagnose your condition (and the conditions of loved ones in your care), there are steps we all can take, including lifestyle changes, to calm down and worry less. (Chapter 8 contains extensive details, including our Worry-Wise Plan.)

But before we move along, let's check back in with Briana to see the progress she has made. Extensive physical training and emotional support *is* paying off.

Briana's Healing Path

One year after being admitted to the Madonna Rehabilitation Hospital in Lincoln, Briana took her first step.

Gradually she learned to bend her knees and lift her feet. She began with tiny steps and worked up to more difficult challenges. At first it seemed silly to her: walk from the bed to the door and then back to the bed. Then, it was to the door and back twice.

Yet each success was a big accomplishment, especially considering how doctors feared she might never walk again.

And, eight months later, Briana walked down the aisle and became Mrs. Briana Bartlett.

"I married the love of my life," she says. "Steve never left my side, coaching me with each step . . . and holding me when the panic would strike."

Today, the panic attacks are gone, even though PTSD is still an issue.

"Medicine, prayer, and the support of those I love has made all the difference in the world," she says. "I'm on a healing path, and that's a good place to be."

* * * * *

Our goal in this chapter was to raise awareness about what to look for when you're concerned that worry has crossed over to an anxiety disorder. These are the most commonly diagnosed mental illnesses in the United States, affecting forty million adults (about 18% of the adult population, or more than one in six).[16]

We found similar rates among the believers in our study, with 17% sharing that they've been diagnosed with an anxiety disorder. If you or a loved one finds yourself in a similar situation, take heart: anxiety disorders are highly treatable. Armed with the strategies outlined in this book and the assistance of your doctor, you can break free of the fear-worry-stress cycle.

Our Research Says . . .

- As with many mental illnesses, anxiety disorders are underdiagnosed. For example, we included screening questions for Generalized Anxiety

Disorder in our study. Based on these questions, an estimated 17% of teens and adults likely have an anxiety disorder that has not been diagnosed (and therefore treated).
- Teens and young adults had higher rates of undiagnosed anxiety disorders than adults over thirty.
- Christ-followers who receive and reflect on Scripture most days of the week struggle less with anxiety than those who do not.

Recap and Reflect
Talking Points for Couples or Group Study

The many worrisome thoughts that have held Briana hostage—especially the fear of the unknown—aren't caused by a lack of faith. For her, an unthinkable event changed everything. Now she faces a new question when she wakes up each morning: Will I be immobilized by my pain today . . . or will I learn the patience to let God heal the root causes and show me how to get moving again?

What do I think is the root cause of worry for me and for others in my life?

- Consider the many things that worry us all: financial troubles, a difficult relationship, health concerns . . . According to medical professionals, there can be countless physical and emotional processes behind the fear-worry-stress cycle.

*Is all this stress in my life really "punishment from God"?
Is it the result of weak faith? Could there be other issues
that are causing me to suffer: trauma from my past, a
stressful lifestyle, physiological processes inside my body?*

Here's What's Next

The rushes of adrenaline that surge through us—regardless of
whether they're produced by excitement over good news or from
a crisis—are all the same to the brain. Adrenaline causes stress.
It's also addicting. This is exactly what a group of father-son ad-
venturers discovered on a canoe trip through Colorado: adrenaline
is best suited for excursions . . . not for the home front.

FACING DOWN A MONSTER

HOW ADRENALINE FUELS THE FEAR-WORRY-STRESS CYCLE

Joshua 1:9: "Have I not commanded you? Be strong and courageous. Do not be terrified; do not be discouraged, for the LORD your God will be with you wherever you go." We are called to be bold and brave, not because of our own power, but because of God's perfect power and strength. His awesome presence is what allows us to face challenges without fear.[1]

KERI WYATT KENT

"Rough water ahead—paddle left!" Jeffery shouts to fifteen-year-old Jonathan.

"No, Dad, let's go left, so paddle right."

"Son, listen to me," Jeffery says, sternly. "There are big rocks and strong rapids on the left. We need to veer right. Quickly!"

Jonathan points downstream. "But do you see that?" he asks. "There's junk in the water. Maybe it's a fallen tree or something."

"We'll take our chances," Jeffery responds, digging his paddle and stroking harder. "We'll flip if we hit the rapids."

"But, Dad—"

"Don't argue. Paddle left. *Now!*"

In just another instant, *THUMP! BUMP!* The canoe strikes a mound of twisted branches clogging a narrow strip of Colorado's Gunnison River. The vessel begins to rock violently but doesn't tip over. Seconds later the water is calm again.

Jonathan turns around and grins. "Okay, you were right—this time!"

Jeffery high-fives his son, then slumps back in the canoe. "I think we're getting the hang of this adventure thing," he says. "Now if we could just figure out some challenges back home."

The Twists and Turns of Family Life

Hurried, hassled home lives. Overextended schedules. Days, weeks, and months—hours, minutes, and seconds—all set on fast-forward.

Navigating life can seem very much like a perpetual ride over wild and torrential rapids. Our safe passage depends upon our faith in God, the strength of our connections with loved ones, our physical, mental, and emotional health . . . and how we manage stress.

During my (so far) twenty-seven-year ministry to teens and their families, I've found that life-changing lessons are best learned experientially—especially when they're taught with the great outdoors as a backdrop. A few years ago, Jeffery, Jonathan, and a dozen other father-son pairs—including me (Michael) and my son, Christopher—took a four-day adventure through Colorado's canyon country. In the end, we had faced the rapids head on, and we'd come away stronger. Our mission that week was to break through barriers that tear families apart.

It takes cooperation and communication to keep canoes stable, making these ideal vessels for bringing families together in shared adventure and toward deepened relationships. Even so, the most powerful moments happened back on shore. Each evening the men and boys gathered around a campfire, discussing the lessons they'd learned on the river. Inevitably, they pulled off their masks and shared what was inside.

"I'm so proud of you, Jonathan, for trusting me today," Jeffery told his son one night. "We were a solid team, which is how God wants us to be."

Jonathan smiled and put his arm around his father. "My heart was racing, and I felt so scared when I saw the rapids," he said. "But you stayed calm. That really helped. And when we came through okay, it gave me more confidence."

The teen paused, thought carefully about his words, and then continued. "I wish it could be this way at home. It's like, there's so much stress. Your job; Mom saying we have more bills than money; pressure at school; the way we fight sometimes. Maybe we can start handling troubles like we did today."

Another father, Paul, vowed to spend more time with his seventeen-year-old son David. "We get busy, with each of us moving fast and in so many different directions," he said. "We've got to slow down and stay connected. We've got to do a better job of being a family."

David then opened up for the first time about his biggest fears. "The other kids are brutal," he said. "The constant teasing and bullying, the stupid cliques, the struggle to fit in—I get so sick of it all. I just want to live a normal life."

"I didn't realize that life has been so tough for you," his father responded. "But we're going to work through these troubles—together."

As I sat back and watched the generations bond, I began to see clearly how, in one family after another, (1) worry and stress are dealing heavy blows and (2) our high-octane lifestyles seem to be making things worse.

While adventure and adrenaline go hand-in-hand, our *homes* need to be peaceful environments; safe havens from the hectic world around us. Yet the medical doctors and psychologists I've talked to say the average American family could make Indiana Jones seem boring. Many if not most have become adrenaline junkies, zooming through activities, and taking on more and more projects and tasks to the point of over-commitment and then exhaustion.

It's not surprising that so many feel helpless throughout their plunges down the rapids of fear, worry, and anxiety.

What's primarily fueling it all, doctors insist, is *adrenaline* itself.

What Indiana Never Mentioned

Navigating a twisting, churning river through the mountains will get your chest pounding—but so will deadlines at work and pressures at home. Most of us are all too familiar with the feeling: As an adrenaline rush surges through us, our breathing accelerates, our heart rate jumps, our senses become heightened, and we receive an instant burst of energy. We even feel stronger. But if we remain too long in this supercharged state, we crash. (What goes up must come down, right?) That's when we end up feeling all kinds of highly unwanted emotions: vulnerability, uncertainty, insecurity, doubt, fear, worry, stress.

Fact: *Adrenaline causes stress, and stress produces anxiety.*

"People feel scared and helpless when experiencing so much emotional turmoil because they don't know what is happening in their brains," says Dr. Archibald D. Hart. "It seems so mysterious, and this lack of understanding only causes more anxiety."[2]

Hart, licensed psychologist and board-certified diplomat fellow in psychopharmacology, has basically written the book on the adrenaline-stress connection—at least twenty-six of them, in fact, to date. He's convinced families can achieve more peace in their lives (and ultimately learn to worry less) once they're able to reduce the production of adrenaline in their bodies. "Indisputably, there is a strong connection between the overuse of our adrenal system and stress disease. But just as living high on adrenaline causes stress disease, it also causes anxiety problems. The mechanism is very simple. Stress depletes our natural brain tranquilizers."[3]

Adrenaline is one of the most powerful chemicals either man-made or naturally occurring. *Adrenaline is pure speed!* According to Dr. Eric T. Scalise, anytime we feel excited or anxious, the brain tells the adrenal glands—which sit on the back of our kidneys—to release adrenaline to manage that stress. But our brain doesn't distinguish between a joyful moment and a life-threatening crisis. Adrenaline rushes through us as we encounter *any* kind of excitement, from the loss of someone we love to the birth of a child.

On the upside, an adrenaline rush can be exhilarating and can give us the energy and clarity we need to achieve whatever is needed. On the downside, the exhilaration can be addicting, and it can plunge us into a cycle of fear, worry, and stress.

Let's take a closer look.

The Neurobiology of Stress

Our brain is part chemical factory, part German autobahn.

Information is transmitted from one nerve cell to the next by chemical messengers called *neurotransmitters*. They race through the nerves, giving orders: "Full alert—get moving," or "Be calm and slow down." They tell the brain to be happy, sad, anxious, or tranquil. They warn of emergencies and indicate when it's safe for us to rest.

How—by what process? Through *stress hormones*, pumped into the bloodstream.

Each nerve cell (or neuron) releases small amounts of neurotrans-mitters, some of which trigger a reaction in the next neuron; others are reabsorbed by the original neuron (in a process known as re-uptake).[4] The subsequent effects on our body depend on factors including the type of neurotransmitter released, the amount that's produced or reabsorbed, the sensitivity of the receptors on the receiving neuron, and the location in the brain where the process is occurring.[5]

Two hormones play a big role in the adrenaline-stress connec-tion: GABA (gamma-aminobutyric acid), or what Hart calls a "happy messenger," and cortisol, which he calls a "sad messenger."[6] We need both neurotransmitter types to coexist and work in tandem inside our brains. When we're ill, sad messengers tell the body to rest. When our lives are endangered, they act as lifesavers, sending our body into action to prevent harm. And happy messengers help us to cope with pain and remain tranquil; they energize us, and make us feel vital, and optimistic.

Excessive worry and anxiety, however, cause the body's sympathetic nervous system to release large amounts of cortisol. This can boost blood sugar levels and triglycerides (blood fats) that the body can use for temporary fuel. "Cortisol is kind of like the after-burner," Scalise explains. "It gives everything a good kick. But too much can be a problem."[7]

GABA
- *chief inhibitory neurotransmitters in the central nervous system (CNS)*
- *regulates neuronal excitability and helps us to calm down*
- *includes brain chemicals such as serotonin, dopamine, norepinephrine (noradrenaline)*

Cortisol
- *partners with adrenaline*
- *is released in response to stress*
- *depletes GABA*

Adrenaline triggers the fight-or-flight reaction.

Every time adrenaline is released in the body, the brain signals the blood supply to go to our major muscle groups. Why? To help us determine if we should engage or disengage from a given situation—in other words, should we fight for our lives or head for the hills? But, as blood is pumped to our muscles, think about where it isn't going: to our brains. Or, in a sense, messages are being steered from its thinking portion to its feeling realm. That's why a stressful situation often sparks emotions that can include *fear, panic, anger, distrust,* and *insecurity.*

From "high alert" to "system crash"

When our adrenaline hormones are exhausted from overuse, our bodies crash; adrenaline is then under-produced in an attempt to recover from its overproduction. With under-production of adrenaline during such times, we can feel so vulnerable that even the smallest stressor might seem overwhelming. Each of our physiological systems interacts with the others and is profoundly influenced by our coping style and our psychological state.

When the GABA and cortisol hormones are in balance, we usually feel pretty good—relatively peaceful, happy, tranquil. But when the sad messengers outnumber the happy ones, we end up depressed, panicked, worried, and/or anxious. Says Dr. Hart:

> I am truly amazed by this process. Proper communication between our brain cells is all wonderfully complex and vitally essential to our sanity. Normal human emotions are determined by whether these neurotransmitters are successful in communicating their messages to your brain cells. On a typical day in the life of your brain, literally trillions of messages are sent and received by these neurotransmitters.[8]

* * * * *

So, with this neuro-snapshot in mind, let's approach the process of how to manage it. The first step involves asking a key question: *Why is my life, and/or the life of my family, being supercharged with so much adrenaline?*

Then, look around. (Go on—try it.) What do you see . . . at home, at the office, at school, at church?

Perhaps you'll discover what the guys and I saw so clearly on the river.

"Stuck in the Crosscurrents"

That's how Jeffery described his life back in Grand Rapids, Michigan. And it took huge doses of adrenaline on Colorado's Gunnison River to help him see it.

"Everything is so upside-down in my world," he says. "I work endless hours to pay for a big mortgage and all the things that go with it: electronic toys and gadgets that end up keeping us apart even when we're under the same roof. Most of the time we're on the go, sort of stuck in the crosscurrents—constantly moving but not really connecting. And that has to change."

Even some in the mainstream media are waving a white flag. As Tim Kreider said in the Op-Ed section of the *New York Times*:

> Busyness serves as a kind of existential reassurance, a hedge against emptiness; obviously your life cannot possibly be silly or trivial or meaningless if you are so busy, completely booked, in demand every hour of the day . . . I can't help but wonder whether all this histrionic exhaustion isn't a way of covering up the fact that most of what we do doesn't matter.[9]

I think these observations are dead on.

Our lives are moving at a frantic pace. Most of us are *busy being busy*. And here's another sad reality: Even our kids' lives often are scheduled down to the half-hour. School activities, clubs, other extra-curricular commitments, sporting events, daycare, play dates . . .

Along the way, we're becoming more and more disconnected—from our families, friends, coworkers, even from God.

We spend countless hours supposedly plugged in: surfing, emailing, posting, texting, tweeting . . . staring at screens, typing quickly but not meaningfully interacting. We rarely talk to our neighbors, let alone know their names. Even in church we press through the crowds, slide into a pew or chair, and become spectators. We blend in . . . but we don't truly connect.

When we stop connecting with someone or something outside ourselves, we become anxious. When we start feeling that way, we frequently try to cope by escaping. More and more, the felt need for relief from anxiety and worry is leading us into addictions of a thousand kinds.

We're flooded with messages exhorting us toward this or that sort of "perfection"—things will be ideal if we buy this or acquire that. The values of consumerism, materialism, and instant gratification serve only to amplify the void many of us feel day after day after day.[10] Again, as our busyness escalates and we come under more stress, we're turning *from* the connections that offer help (with God and with others) and *toward* thought patterns and actions that just leave us more worried and anxious. More and more we have been losing our compass.

> Faced with a barrage of inconsistent world views and standards presented by the media, we are left with the responsibility of having to create our own meaning and moral order. When we are unable to find that meaning, many of us are prone to fill the gap with various forms of escapism and addiction. We tend to live out of tune with ourselves and thus find ourselves anxious.[11]

From Escapism to Solutions

We've identified many worry- and anxiety-related problems. Now it's time to shift our conversation toward meaningful solutions.

We touched on the issues of escapism and addiction; let's take an honest look at the role of pharmaceutical medications and various natural remedies.

As a professional in the mental health field—and someone who's seen lives torn apart by the misuse of drugs, prescription and otherwise—I (Arnie) advise extreme caution and plain old common sense. *Abuse medicine and you're playing Russian roulette with your life.*

God did not create us to be addicts. But because we live in a fallen world that has not yet been restored, and because until Christ returns or calls us home we all will battle against sin, the same psychological, neurological, and spiritual dynamics of full-fledged addiction are actively at work in every human being. In the words of Dr. Gerald G. May: "The same processes that are responsible for addiction to alcohol and narcotics are also responsible for addiction to ideas, work, relationships, power, moods, fantasies, and an endless variety of other things. We are all addicts in every sense of the word."[12]

Accordingly, viewing medication as a cure-all for worry and stress is a mistake. I believe we must do much more than relieve the symptoms of what's bugging us; we must get to the causes, addressing the problem at its source. In addition to adrenaline over-saturation, we must evaluate five key aspects of our lives:

Our Diet—Are we getting the nutrition we need?
Our Aerobic Health—Are we getting regular aerobic exercise?
Our Need for Relaxation—Are we making ample time for rest and restoration?
Our Need for Sleep—Are we getting what we need every day?
Our Overall Lifestyle—Are we pursuing a less driven, more balanced life?

Now, though, for this issue's flipside: While anxiety meds aren't a cure-all, they're often a *must* for those who struggle with severe anxiety—especially at the beginning of a wellness program. (So I am not replacing medication with a cup of herbal tea—and neither should you!) Those battling panic disorder, agoraphobia, obsessive-compulsive disorder, and post-traumatic stress disorder, for example, often can benefit tremendously from the right pharmaceutical help.

My advice: Talk with your family physician and with a licensed therapist. Get a complete physical and full mental health evaluation. To help you take that step, I've asked a couple of medical professionals to offer their perspectives on the question of anxiety meds and/or natural remedies. My intention here is not to present a debate, with one side seeking to prove the other wrong, but rather to raise awareness of multiple solutions for combating and defeating worry.

"Pharmaceutical Drugs Should Be a Last Resort"
Nanette Gingery, Therapist / Addiction Specialist

Frankly, I believe there's a too cavalier attitude toward anxiety meds. We often hear, "Oh, yeah, I'm on my Prozac, my Valium, my Xanax" . . . pick the pill of choice and fill in the blank. Some even treat an anxiety drug like a status symbol. But to care for our body we must be careful about what we put into it.

The best solution: Pursue a natural route first. Sometimes, taking pharmaceutical drugs for anxiety treatment is simply unavoidable. But we'd be wise to make this our last resort. Why? In addition to being addictive, over time—and depending on the dosage—some anxiety meds can cause *increased* anxiety as well as depression, digestive disturbances, sleep problems, loss of sex drive, nervousness, and other effects that should not be a result of a health aid.

Herbs are plant-based medicines that are safer and healthier. Did you know that more than 25% of current prescription drugs are based on herbs? Here are three of my favorites.

HERB	MEDICAL USES	PRECAUTIONS
Kava *Available Forms:* concentrated liquid extract, capsules, tablets	• A natural tranquilizer • Treats mild to moderate anxiety • Performs as well as the benzodiazepine class of drugs (Valium, Xanax) • Small doses produce a sense of well-being • Large doses produce drowsiness and reduce muscle tension • Non-addictive	• If you have liver problems, do not take kava • Avoid combining with tranquilizers like Xanax or Klonopin • Avoid alcohol while taking kava
Passionflower *Available Forms:* liquid extract, capsules, tablets	• A natural tranquilizer used for nerve-calming purposes • As effective as valerian • Relieves nervous tension and relaxes muscles • Higher doses can be used to treat insomnia	• That this is a natural herb does not mean it is risk-free • Consult your physician before using
Lemon Balm *Available Forms:* liquid extract, capsules, tablets	• Improves mood and boosts both calmness and alertness • Enhances sleep when used with other herbs (valerian, hops, or chamomile, e.g.) • Taken in tea form, imparts a tranquil feeling in minutes	• Use with caution • Seek the advice of your physician, and tell him or her about other medications you are taking

Nanette's Notes

Some extreme cases of anxiety are non-responsive to either synthetic or natural remedies. But for many people who suffer from mild to moderate anxiety, these natural remedies can make a real difference. Before you escalate to drugs that may impart effects that you don't want, give these a try. If you explain your symptoms to your family physician and he or she instantly pulls out a prescription pad and begins jotting down a pharmaceutical drug solution, speak up, and ask: "Do you have any other intervention ideas that are organic and natural; solutions I can try at home?" If there's simply no way around taking an anxiety drug, ask about using a medication as a temporary solution, and try it until you can incorporate other stress-relieving strategies.

Perhaps because of past trauma or physiological issues, for some people only medication proves to be effective. If this describes your situation, don't feel guilt and shame for taking it. Follow your physician's advice, and incorporate strategies that make sense to you from this book. In all cases, beware of merely treating the symptoms and not getting to the root of what's bugging you.[13]

"Pharmaceutical Drugs Are Sometimes the Best First Option"
Tess Cox, Physician's Assistant / Counselor

In treating stress and anxiety, I definitely recommend implementing a complete wellness program that includes proper diet, exercise, and relaxation techniques—along with a physical and mental evaluation.

From experience I'm convinced that if you suffer from high anxiety, there is only one long-term answer: You must make some significant life changes. This is not to say anti-anxiety medications don't have their place—they do, and in some cases they should be prescribed. But long-term changes must follow these interim solutions if you want to be free of the trouble.

Here's a sample of the types I recommend for anxiety.

DRUG	INDICATIONS	POSSIBLE REACTIONS
Alprazolam *Trade Name:* Xanax, Niravam Pharmacologic Class: Benzodiazepines Dosages (tabs): 0.25, 0.5, 1, or 2 mg	• Anxiety • Panic disorders	• Central Nervous System: insomnia, irritability, dizziness, headache, anxiety, drowsiness, depression, suicide • Cardiovascular: palpitations, chest pain, hypotension • Genitourinary: dysmenorrhea, sexual dysfunction, premenstrual syndrome, difficulty urinating
Citalopram *Trade Name:* Celexa Pharmacologic Class: SSRIs Dosages (tabs): 10, 20, or 40 mg	• Depression • Premenstrual disorders • Obsessive-compulsive disorder	• Central Nervous System: insomnia, somnolence, suicide attempt, anxiety, agitation, dizziness, depression, fatigue • Cardiovascular: tachycardia, orthostatic hypotension, hypotension • Genitourinary: dysmenorrhea, amenorrhea, ejaculation disorder, erectile dysfunction
Clomipramine *Trade Name:* Anafranil Pharmacologic Class: Tricyclic Dosages (capsules): 25, 50, or 75 mg	• Obsessive-compulsive disorder • Panic disorder	• Central Nervous System: somnolence, tremor, dizziness, headache, insomnia, nervousness, myoclonus, fatigue, seizures, EEG changes • Cardiovascular: orthostatic hypotension, palpitations, tachycardia • Genitourinary: urinary hesitancy, UTI, dysmenorrhea, ejaculation failure, erectile dysfunction

Continued on page 119

DRUG	INDICATIONS	POSSIBLE REACTIONS
Clonazepam *Trade Name:* Klonopin/ Rivotril Pharmaco- logic Class: Benzodiazepines Dosages (tabs): 0.5, 1, or 2 mg	• Lennox- Gastaut syndrome, atypical absence seizures, akinetic and myoclonic seizures • Panic disorder • Bipolar disorder • Tic disorders	• Central Nervous System: amnesia, aphonia, choreiform movements, coma, confusion, depression, dysarthria, dysdiado- chokinesis, "glassy-eyed" appear- ance, hallucinations, headache • Cardiovascular: palpitations • Genitourinary: dysuria, enure- sis, nocturia, urine retention, colpitis, dysmenorrhea, delayed ejaculation, erectile dysfunction, urinary frequency
Diazepam *Trade Name:* Valium Pharmaco- logic Class: Benzodiazepines Dosages (tabs): 2, 5, or 10 mg	• Anxiety • Acute alcohol withdrawal • Muscle spasm	• Central Nervous System: drowsiness, dysarthria, slurred speech, tremor, transient am- nesia, fatigue, ataxia, headache, insomnia, paradoxical anxiety, hallucinations • Cardiovascular: hypotension • Genitourinary: incontinence, urine retention

Continued on page 120

DRUG	INDICATIONS	POSSIBLE REACTIONS
Duloxetine *Trade Name:* Cymbalta Pharmacologic Class: SSNRIs Dosages (delayed-release capsules): 20, 30, or 60 mg	• Major depressive disorder • Generalized anxiety disorder • Fibromyalgia • Neuropathic pain • Chronic musculoskeletal pain • Stress urinary incontinence	• Central Nervous System: dizziness, fatigue, headache, insomnia, somnolence, suicidal thoughts, fever, hypoesthesia, irritability, lethargy, nervousness, anxiety • Cardiovascular: hot flashes, hypertension, increased heart rate • Genitourinary: abnormal orgasm, abnormally increased frequency of urinating, delayed or dysfunctional ejaculation erectile dysfunction
Escitalopram *Trade Name:* Lexapro/Cipralex Pharmacologic Class: SSRIs Dosages (tablets): 5, 10, or 20 mg	• Major depressive disorder • Generalized anxiety disorder • Post-traumatic stress disorder	• Central Nervous System: suicidal behavior, fever, insomnia, dizziness, somnolence, paresthesia, lightheadedness, migraine, tremor, vertigo, irritability, fatigue • Cardiovascular: palpitations, hypertension, flushing, chest pain • Genitourinary: ejaculation disorder, erectile dysfunction, anorgasmia, menstrual cramps, urinary frequency
Fluoxetine *Trade Name:* Prozac Pharmacologic Class: SSRIs Dosages (tabs): 10, 15, 20, or 60 mg	• Depression • Obsessive-compulsive disorder • Panic disorder • Post-traumatic stress disorder	• Central Nervous System: nervousness, somnolence, anxiety, insomnia, headache, drowsiness, tremor, dizziness • Cardiovascular: hypotension • Genitourinary: sexual dysfunction

Continued on page 121

DRUG	INDICATIONS	POSSIBLE REACTIONS
Lorazepam *Trade Name:* Ativan, Lorazepam Intensol, Novo-Lorazem, Nu-Loraz Pharmacologic Class: Benzodiazepines Dosages (Tabs): 0.5, 1, or 2 mg	• Anxiety • Insomnia from anxiety • Preoperative sedation • Status epilepticus	• Central Nervous System: drowsiness, sedation, amnesia, insomnia, agitation, dizziness, weakness, unsteadiness • Cardiovascular: hypotension
Paroxetine *Trade Name:* Paxil Pharmacologic Class: SSRIs Dosages (Tabs): 10, 20, 30, or 40 mg	• Depression • Obsessive-compulsive disorder • Panic disorder • Social anxiety disorder • Generalized anxiety disorder • Post-traumatic stress disorder	• Central Nervous System: asthenia, dizziness, headache, insomnia, somnolence • Cardiovascular: palpitations, vasodilation, hypertension, tachycardia • Genitourinary: ejaculatory disturbances, sexual dysfunction, urinary frequency

Continued on page 122

DRUG	INDICATIONS	POSSIBLE REACTIONS
Sertraline *Trade Name:* Zoloft Pharmacologic Class: SSRIs Dosages (tabs): 25, 50, or 100 mg	• Depression • Obsessive-compulsive disorder • Panic disorder • Post-traumatic stress disorder • Premenstrual dysphoric disorder • Social anxiety disorder	• Central Nervous System: fatigue, headache, tremor, dizziness, insomnia, somnolence, suicidal behavior, paresthesia, hypesthesia, nervousness, anxiety, agitation, hypertonia, pain • Cardiovascular: palpitations, chest pain, hot flashes • Genitourinary: male sexual dysfunction
Venlafaxine XR *Trade Name:* Effexor XR Pharmacologic Class: SSNRIs Dosages (tabs): 25, 37.5, 50, 75, or 100 mg	• Depression • Generalized anxiety disorder • Panic disorder • Social anxiety disorder • Hot flashes • Diabetic neuropathy • Premenstrual dysphoric disorder	• Central Nervous System: asthenia, headache, somnolence, dizziness, nervousness, insomnia, suicidal behavior, anxiety, abnormal dreams • Cardiovascular: hypertension, tachycardia, vasodilation, chest pain • Genitourinary: abnormal ejaculation, impotence, urinary frequency, impaired urination

Tess's Notes

Any anxiety disorder also has a strong underlying biochemical disturbance and responds well to medication. Except in relatively minor cases, effective use of medication is essential for effective treatment in the early stages of panic and other anxiety disorders.

Proper medication, combined with cognitive-behavioral psycho-therapy, will ensure a complete cure in most cases.

For those with moderate to severe anxiety disorders, an SSRI (selective serotonin re-uptake inhibitor) is an excellent medication to consider; brand names are Paxil, Zoloft, Celexa, and Luvox. These medications are not habit forming and have had excellent results in treating depression, OCD, panic disorder, PTSD, and social anxiety disorder.

However, regardless of whether you treat your anxiety with med-ication or natural remedies, the most important healing comes from knowing, serving, and following God.[14]

Time to Get Out of the Canoe

What steps can we take toward change? Try the following.

Unplug. The average US household has three TVs (each with dozens of channels), three computers, two gaming systems, and multiple smart phones and tablets and MP3 players as well as count-less other devices and "connections." While life in front of the screen can distract from anxiety, it likewise can (and very often does) have the reverse effect. What's more, it's a hindrance to building deeper connections with the ones we love.

Slow Down. Instead of having the necessary resources to pro-cess things cognitively and spiritually (in a meditative way), we're constantly on the go—and constantly we feel stressed (if not also anxious and worried). This is happening because our bodies are pumping adrenaline and cortisol. The key: force yourself to step back and slow down. (More on this in chapter 8.)

Further, there's a secret to survival that's exercised by EMTs like Briana—not to mention disaster-relief workers, lifeguards, police officers, and fire-rescue personnel. Ask them, "Why did this person survive, while that person didn't?" and often they'll say: "Survivors keep their wits about them." In other words, people who can manage their adrenaline levels under stress put themselves in a better position to handle what life brings. It's something we all need to learn.

Get Some Sleep. God doesn't want us to push through the day feeling weary and worn out. The fact is, too little shut-eye can drain our brain. "Sleep is absolutely vital to your health and well-being," explains Dr. Don Colbert. "During sleep, you actually recharge your mind and body. It allows your body to recuperate and restore itself from exhaustion."[15]

In addition, Dr. Colbert says sleep enables our cells to regenerate and rejuvenate because our bodies secrete growth hormones that repair tissues and organs. Conversely, a lack of sleep can lead to serious health consequences and jeopardize our safety and the safety of individuals around us. For example, short sleep duration is linked with:

- Increased risk of motor vehicle accidents
- Increase in body mass index—a greater likelihood of obesity due to increased appetite caused by sleep deprivation
- Increased risk of diabetes and heart problems
- Increased risk for psychiatric conditions including depression and substance abuse
- Decreased ability to pay attention, react to signals, or remember new information.

Says Dr. Maiken Nedergaard, co-director of the Center for Translational Neuromedicine at the University of Rochester Medical Center:

We have a cleaning system that almost stops when we are awake and starts when we sleep. It's almost like opening and closing a faucet—it's that dramatic. The brain has different functional states when asleep and when awake. In fact, the restorative nature of sleep appears to be the result of the active clearance of the by-products of neural activity that accumulate during wakefulness . . . You can think of it like having a house party. You can either entertain guests or clean up the house, but you can't really do both at the same time.[16]

* * * * *

Dr. Hart points to the solution: "You must come down from the 'hills' of stress and into the 'valleys' of rest on a daily basis." He explains that our bodies are designed not for continuous fear, worry, and anxiety but for ongoing tranquility with short bursts of adrenaline.[17]

And the apostle Paul gives us the most important solution of all:

Here's what I want you to do, God helping you: Take your everyday, ordinary life—your sleeping, eating, going-to-work, and walking-around life—and place it before God as an offering. Embracing what God does for you is the best thing you can do for Him. Don't become so well-adjusted to your culture that you fit into it without even thinking. Instead, fix your attention on God. You'll be changed from the inside out. Readily recognize what He wants from you, and quickly respond to it. Unlike the culture around you, always dragging you down to its level of immaturity, God brings the best out of you, develops well-formed maturity in you.[18]

Our Research Says . . .

• We're wired to worry first and to think second. According to neuroscientist Joseph LeDoux, connections from the limbic (emotional) systems to the cortex (cognitive) systems are stronger than connections from the cognitive systems to the emotional systems.[19]

- It's possible to retrain yourself to let your mind override your limbic system. In fact, research reveals that cognitive-behavioral therapy changes the neural circuits involved in regulating worry and anxiety.
- Worry has been shown to increase heart rate and decrease heart rate variability. These effects are still evident up to two hours after the worrying episode.

Recap and Reflect
Talking Points for Couples or Group Study

Adrenaline is a major culprit for stress—and can be addicting.

- Evaluate your lifestyle (and those of others in your care).

  Would I describe my day as a triple shot of espresso, a cup of chamomile tea, or sort of a "green tea" combo of the two? Am I constantly revved up, or (as Dr. Hart recommends) am I able to "come down from the mountain" at some point during the day?

- Imagine climbers clinging to a jagged overhang—ropeless, and high up. An adrenaline rush surges through their bodies as they defy death and climb to safety. In this context, adrenaline is vital . . . and a very necessary physiological factor.

- Based upon what you learned in this chapter:

Can I identify some instances in my life in which adrenaline is triggering the fear-worry-stress cycle? Do I feel there's an excess of adrenaline in my family's life?

- Arnie identified five key areas we must evaluate: diet, health, need for relaxation, importance of sleep, overall lifestyle. (Flip back to mid-chapter to review.)

- Share how you've assessed these areas.

Are there changes I need to make?

Here's What's Next

Constant rushes of adrenaline rob Barbara in a different way: She simply can't shut off her brain at night and get the rest she desperately needs. As it happens, for her the issue is more spiritual than physiological. She struggles greatly to trust God and surrender to His will.

SLEEPLESS NIGHTS, ANXIOUS DAYS

WHEN A STRUGGLING FAITH IS THE ISSUE

"It is quite true that the way up to the High Places is both difficult and dangerous," said the Shepherd. "It has to be, so that nothing which is an enemy of love can make the ascent and invade the Kingdom. The inhabitants of the High Places do need 'hinds' feet.' I have them myself," he added with a smile. "But, Much-Afraid, I could make yours like hinds' feet also, and set you upon the High Places." [1]
HINDS' FEET ON HIGH PLACES

Home—that was Barbara's favorite place.

It didn't matter that her 1960's rancher wasn't anybody else's idea of a dream home . . . or that the carpet and paint showed some wear and tear . . . or that her elderly mother, three dogs, and four cats had to manage with cramped quarters . . . not to mention a toilet that wouldn't stop running. The place was definitely rough around the edges—*a little like me,* she thought—yet it was stout. It had heart and a solid foundation.

Most of all, it was *home.*

Before turning in for the night, ending another hectic day that bounced from working in retail to managing her "zoo" (Barbara[2] had a weakness for stray pets), she stole a few quiet moments on her back patio. Besides, she couldn't sleep anyway, couldn't shut off her anxious mind. Nothing new. So she settled into a comfy chair and pressed a steaming mug of decaf to her lips. The strong aroma of French roast coffee beans never failed to carry away the usual smells of the horse ranch across the field: leather, hay, smoldering fire pits, musky stables.

She took a long, slow sip, and then gazed at the Idaho sky. "Perfect," she whispered. Endless blue had given way to countless stars. Intense white lights skipped and danced around milky clusters of yellow and purple. Shooting stars raced across the horizon.

For Barbara, this nightly treat had a way of captivating her thoughts . . . resetting her focus . . . reminding her, "God is in control." The middle-aged mom thought about how our heavenly Father never leaves things as they are. He's always at work . . . creating, perfecting, regenerating—*reclaiming what's His.*

She took another sip and began talking aloud to her Savior: "You've given me so much, and I deserve none of it. You know my stubborn heart, my thoughts, my hang-ups—my past."

Barbara regretted so many decisions and actions from her younger years: racking up so much debt that she and her family could barely make ends meet; eventual divorce that all but crushed her daughter's heart; more over-spending; putting selfish needs first; coveting; worrying. *Stupid,* she thought. *I did a bunch of stupid things. I lived in darkness, wasting precious time.*

Even after she'd prayed and committed her life to Jesus, Barbara could not let go of the past. Day after day she hobbled along spiritually as if her heart were in shackles. And for more than a decade she hid behind a mask, letting the world see a tough, steady lady. But on the inside she was grieving—beating herself up, constantly feeling immobilized and neutralized by fear.

How often do I not feel worried, Lord? I know I should let go. I know I need to trust you more. Yet when I'm anxious I fear you won't catch me; when I'm panicked I wonder if you'll abandon me.

One day, right in the middle of her muddy back yard, something remarkable happened: Barbara came clean with Christ. She found the courage to release every festering memory, to surrender every vile choice . . .

* * * *

It was a mundane chore, but just as she'd always done, day in, day out, she walked around her yard, watering trees, shrubs, grass . . . even the bare ground her dogs had trampled. As she tugged on the hose, moving it mechanically, rhythmically . . . drenching every clump and pebble . . . her mind began to flood with thought after thought. Most were painful.

Child of God? Disciple? Loving wife and mom? *Liar.* That's who I really am.

She took a few more steps and sprayed the yard's center. Fool—that's *what* I am. Forgiven? How can I ever be forgiven for my idiocy? My lack of common sense?!

"Let it go."

Barbara froze in her tracks and looked around.

"Release it."

She nearly dropped the hose. God had her attention. She sensed Him compelling her heart, extending a hand that would pull her from her emotional pit.

"Trust me."

But she was afraid to take His hand. "I can't, Lord . . . I just can't. *I'm* the captain of my ship. I know right from wrong, and *I* made all those decisions. That's why I just—"

"No, Barbara. This is wrong. I am God, and I've forgiven you, yet you haven't forgiven yourself."

This time she dropped the hose. She began to weep.

There she stood—alone with her Creator. Water gushing everywhere, puddles rising in the mud . . . and tears rolling down her cheeks. And then, she began to laugh, and cry, all at the same time.

"Yes. It's true. You're right."

She paused and scrutinized the truth staring her in the face. "I have not forgiven myself. But are you the Lord, or am I? It's wrong for me to shout no in your face when you say yes. I can let go—I will. I'll do as you say, forgive and be free. I *am* free."

She felt like jumping and dancing in the mud. She wanted to scream from the bottom of her lungs.

"Thank you, God! I get it now. Thank you, Thank you—"

Suddenly, the Cross made sense. Salvation through Christ—her redemption—was real. Though she'd beaten herself up day after day, her Savior had been mending broken pieces; taking apart the mask, releasing the shackles, and wiping away the tears. The words of John 14:27 flooded her mind:

I give you peace, the kind of peace that only I can give. It isn't like the peace that this world can give. So don't be afraid or worried.[3]

* * * * *

Back in the present, Barbara continued to talk with the Lord: "I'm a prodigal, and I love being back home. To think I was once so lost, so alone—yet you loved me and pursued me! I can't begin to comprehend this. All I can do is thank you."

Even now, as a mature believer, Barbara knows she still doesn't have it all together. Just when she thinks she's finally mastered this whole cycle of fear and worry and stress . . . another anxious thought pops into mind. Before she knows it, she's fretting again. First it's an excessive preoccupation with life's uncertainties. Then it's constant "what-if" thoughts that seem to stab at her stomach. Then it's panic—even anger.

Is this just how it is in life—all the way to the end?

She took a deep breath and pictured the faces of her family today—from the perfect smile of her beautiful daughter (now married, with kids of her own) to her sweet ninety-two-year-old mother, now in her care. Even her "zoo" of scruffy pets soothed her heart. "Lord, thank you for my home—my little bit of heaven on earth. Thank you for your grace. You forgive . . . and then give, and give, and *give*. Help me to trust fully . . . to change what needs to be changed. Amen."

She slipped back indoors—ready to end another routine day. She knew tomorrow would bring a new batch of challenges. "We *will* face tribulation in this world," she reminded herself.

Barbara was ready.

Uncertainty, or Surrender?

Sometimes the scariest places to be are in the safety of our warm beds, especially when our minds are reeling with countless what-ifs, robbing us of needed rest and tranquility.

Twelve hundred miles away, in Omaha, Peg can't shut off the catastrophic thoughts racing through her mind. After tossing and turning half the night, she heads to her bathroom. Inside the medicine cabinet is a temporary when-most-needed relief from insomnia: a 10-milligram capsule of Zaleplon that her doctor prescribed. Lately, though, the when-most-needed for this forty-year-old mother has become a nightly ritual. "When my head hits the pillow, I simply cannot shut off my mind," she says. Fearful thoughts take over:

> *Will my husband weather the storms at work . . . and get to keep his job?*
> *Can we get back on track with our mortgage payments?*
> *Why is my ten-year-old getting into fights at school?*
> *Can my dad survive his stroke—or is a fatal one imminent?*
> *Will a move to Maine give us the fresh start we need?*

* * * * *

Three hours south, in Kansas City, Mark is dealing with an impossible situation at the office. His job description clearly says he must be at his desk by 8:45 every weekday morning. It also says he must unlock all side doors at the beginning of his shift. But his card key won't let him until precisely 8:45. There is no physical way he can make all this happen at the exact same time. He has requested to have the access times changed so he might enter the building earlier. But these requests are handled over at corporate, which has continued to deny his request.

To Mark this seems such a no-brainer. Give him the tools to do his job, or change the requirements. But his boss, a real jerk, continues to give him bad reports for not accomplishing his duties on time. If he gets one more, he'll go on probation. The folks on probation are always the first to go when layoffs start. He can't afford to be out of work. He can barely pay his bills now. Living paycheck to paycheck is stressful, but it's better than not having a paycheck at all.

Mark spends his lunch breaks surfing online for job openings. *Seems like lots of possibilities for nurses out there.* But he knows that even if he found a job for which he's qualified, his boss would never give him a good recommendation. He's stuck. Stuck in an impossible job with no hope for a better future. He works hard. He goes over and beyond. Yet coworkers who goof off and just do enough to get by continue to be promoted over him.

Frustration wells up inside as he sits at his desk. *There's no way out. I am STUCK.*

* * * * *

Barbara, Peg, and Mark aren't alone. Each evening, their brains go into fight-or-flight mode, shifting from "tranquility" to "survival." Their thoughts become imbalanced, literally overloaded with stress hormones. The physiological presence of stress, in turn, causes body and mind to stress out about feeling stressed, leading to a downward spiral.

As we saw in chapter 6, the spiral's outcome can be trouble sleeping, fatigue, depression, and even physical aches and pains. Each day the struggles are left untreated, their bodies weaken and their anxiety levels grow. Fear/worry/stress/anxiety can become a health killer.

But for Barbara, the anxiety stemmed from a lack of surrender to Jesus Christ; a lack of trust in His plan and provision for her. God makes clear that such worry displeases Him.

Watch yourselves lest your hearts be weighed down with dissipation and drunkenness and cares of this life, and that day [of Christ's return] come upon you suddenly like a trap. For it will come upon all who dwell on the face of the whole earth. But stay awake at all times, praying that you may have strength to escape all these things that are going to take place, and to stand before the Son of Man.[4]

. . . [Says] the God who made you in the first place, Jacob, the One who got you started, Israel: "Don't be afraid, I've redeemed you. I've called your name. You're mine. When you're in over your head, I'll be there with you. When you're in rough waters, you will not go down. When you're between a rock and a hard place, it won't be a dead end—because I am GOD, your personal God, The Holy of Israel, your Savior. I paid a huge price for you: all of Egypt, with rich Cush and Seba thrown in! That's how much you mean to me! That's how much I love you! I'd sell off the whole world to get you back, trade the creation just for you."[5]

If you decide for God, living a life of God-worship, it follows that you don't fuss about what's on the table or whether the clothes in your closet are in fashion. There is far more to your life than the food you put in your stomach, more to your outer appearance than the clothes you put on your body. Look at the birds, free and unfettered, not tied down to a job description, careless in the care of God. And you count far more to him than birds. Has anyone by fussing in front of the mirror ever gotten taller by so much as an inch?[6]

The Key: Becoming "Worry-Wise"

Passages like these aren't suggesting that Barbara (and all of us) are condemned because we worry, or that we should never be concerned about anything. Paul tells us to *stop perpetually worrying about the same things—ruminating on the same things over and over.* (See Philippians 4:6, and flip back to our discussion in chapter 3 for a refresher.) And he gives us the prescription for curing our worries: We're to bring our requests to God with an attitude of thanksgiving, expecting that what awaits us is God's peace, which surpasses all understanding.

The very serious spiritual problem is that our lives become filled with fear and worry when we refuse to surrender all to Jesus. When we decline to be joined to our Creator, even when He has provided us a way back to Himself through Christ, we settle down into the bog of our own anxiety.[7]

We need to embrace the big picture. Every moment is only a sliver when you take time to step back and look at your life as a whole. And yet these slivers aren't insignificant at all. They're the building blocks of our lives. The small decisions we make daily build the foundation of our own big picture. If we dwell on the mistakes, then we're reinforcing them. If we decide daily to start fresh and move forward, then we're building a stronger base for our future.

Know this: Positive thinking can only go so far without being challenged by reality. We must dig deeper and identify the source of our motivation. *Who am I in the sight of my Creator? Why am I here? What am I to do with my life?* The answers to these questions cannot be found on the surface of our lives. They do not begin with our job titles or accomplishments. They come from a much deeper place. It's a place that gives birth to our self-identity and worldview. And once we go deep down and wrestle with our inner selves, then we can begin to identify who we are and why we're here.

It's often a messy battle as we sift through our beliefs and our past. But as we emerge on the other side, we begin to see how the puzzle pieces fit together. As the big picture begins to take shape, we're able to find our place. And suddenly the worries found in the slivers of time seem so very small. Our focus shifts from the problems to our responses. And from this view we're able to give thanks to God for all the opportunities we have to trust Him. He is just waiting for us to release our burdens and worries into His care.

Our Research Says . . .

- Our survey respondents rated seeking God's love and care, reading or listening to Scripture, and looking for a stronger connection with God as "most helpful" for coping with worry.
- Adults and teens who engage Scripture most days of the week are more comfortable with uncertainty, are able to trust God more, and worry less than those who do not.

Recap and Reflect
Talking Points for Couples or Group Study

- Consider this observation from C. S. Lewis:

> The almost impossible thing is to hand over your whole self—all your wishes and precautions—to Christ. But it is far easier than what you are trying to do instead. For what we are trying to do is remain what we call "ourselves," to keep personal happiness as our great aim in life, and yet at the same time be

"good." We are all trying to let our mind and heart go their own way—centered on money or pleasure or ambition—and hoping, in spite of this, to behave honestly and chastely and humbly. And that is exactly what Christ warned us you could not do.[8]

Am I able to give up control and surrender my will to God's will? If not, what's keeping me from doing so? If so, in what practical ways will this bring relief from worry?

• Read Romans 8:38–39:

I am convinced that neither death nor life, neither angels nor demons, neither the present nor the future, nor any powers, neither height nor depth, nor anything else in all creation, will be able to separate us from the love of God that is in Christ Jesus our Lord.

Do I believe this? In what ways can this truth free me from worry?

Here's What's Next

Relief from worry must happen on three different but interrelated levels: (1) in our mind, (2) in our body, and (3) in our spirit. In the next chapter we'll share a biblically based, easy-to-follow solution for "coming down from the 'hills' of stress and into the 'valleys' of rest."

TOWARD RIGHT THINKING

A MIND-BODY-SPIRIT APPROACH TO DE-STRESSING AND CALMING DOWN

*By sheer grace, God will not permit us to live even for a brief
period in a dream world. He does not abandon us to those
rapturous experiences and lofty moods that come over us like a
dream. God is not a God of the emotions but the God of truth.
Only that fellowship which faces such disillusionment, with all
its unhappy and ugly aspects, begins to be what it should be in
God's sight, begins to grasp in faith the promise that is given to it.
The sooner this shock of disillusionment comes to an individual
and to a community the better for both.[1]*

DIETRICH BONHOEFFER

Not everyone gets to wake up with a clear head and a calm heart.
The fact is, most of us struggle with emotional and physical pain
of some kind, and we're often distracted and dismayed by the many
what-if questions that worry us. Nevertheless, relief is within reach—
for every age, for every stage of life . . . for every member of the family.

In this chapter, I (Arnie) want to help you either get on or
continue along that road toward healing. My goal is to walk with
you through a practical and effective *mind-body-spirit* approach to
handling worry—what we call the Worry-Wise Plan.

Straightaway, let's be clear about what this plan is and isn't. It could be that the second you noticed the chapter's subtitle, you thought, *Uh-oh—is this book suddenly taking a New Age turn?* Or, maybe "A Mind-Body-Spirit Approach" sent you in the opposite direction: *Here come the impossible standards that normal people can't live up to.* Rest assured—you'll find no crazy concepts here.

I don't follow the "Transcendentalist's Metaphysical Playbook for Enlightenment and Holistic Happiness" any more than I see myself as a poster child for Christianity. I'm merely a Christ-follower who's also a behaviorist and researcher, and during my six decades on planet earth I have learned it's a big mistake to turn to other people or to manmade philosophies in an effort to quench a thirsty spirit or to find emotional healing and wholeness. Those who attempt this are always deluded, ever disappointed. We can find life only in God's Living Spirit. Right thinking and emotional wellness don't come about via mechanistic rituals or by filling our minds with positive thoughts or correct theology. This is nurtured through relationship with a Person.

Theology doesn't save. Manmade philosophies can't save. *Only Jesus Christ saves.*

"The first-century disciples were totally involved with a Person," explains Richard Halverson in *No Greater Power.* "They were followers of Jesus. They were learners of Jesus. They were committed to Jesus."[2] Our faith grows as we encounter Jesus in the Bible. Scripture's message is the message of Jesus, who said, "I am the way and the truth and the life."[3] Therefore, our Worry-Wise Plan is grounded in the guidance we can trust: The commonsense principles found in God's timeless, holy Word.

The Bible makes plain what medical professionals are now echoing: our mind, body, and spirit are interconnected. For example, obviously I inhabit a physical body, and my body's health is connected to my feelings and thoughts. So from a behavioral health perspective, I know I need to treat my entire being. Obsessive thoughts—the judgmental ones and the negative self-talk that goes on inside my head—can affect how I feel. This, in turn, can affect my body.

Consider the stomach, which can act as a "second brain" when it comes to worrying. According to Dr. Mehmet Oz, like our brains, "our stomachs have their own nervous systems, called the enteric nervous system. When we worry, millions of receptors embedded in the gastrointestinal tract react to fear by speeding up or slowing down our digestion, which can lead to nausea, diarrhea and heartburn."[4]

Elouise Renich Fraser says this about our physical bodies and the effects of worry:

> My body, once ignored and despised, has become an ally in the reorientation of my internal and external life. It lets me know when I'm running away, avoiding yet another of God's invitations to look into my past and the way it binds me as a theologian. I can't trust my mind as often as I trust my body. My mind tries to talk me into business as usual, but my body isn't fooled. Insomnia, intestinal pain, and diarrhea let me know there's work to be done.[5]

Remember what we learned in chapter 6, about the adrenaline connection to worry? (If you need to, flip back and review it before continuing.) While our *sympathetic nervous system* (SNS) turns on the fight-or-flight response, our *parasympathetic nervous system* (PNS) promotes the relaxation response. Big deal, right? Yes, it is! Understanding this is the first step toward breaking the fear-worry-stress cycle and learning to relax. The SNS and PNS maintain metabolic equilibrium by making adjustments whenever anything disturbs this balance. So our goal is *homeostasis*—the state of metabolic equilibrium between our body's stimulating and tranquilizing chemical forces. Another way to state our goal is, "Let's find balance again."

The question is, *how*? Once worry triggers an anxious state, how do we get our bodies to return to normal, that is, get the tranquilizing parasympathetic nervous system to calm things down? The answer is not stress *elimination* but stress *management*. This means learning how to take steps that will effectively help our brains to activate the relaxation response.

Let's dig in and discover how to apply the Worry-Wise Plan to our own circumstances. Remember, we want to unravel wrong thinking/negative thoughts and begin managing worry. We'll need to accomplish this on three interrelated levels: our mind, our body, and our spirit.

Your Mind's Worry-Wise Plan

We can break the fear-worry-stress cycle by calming our thoughts. We need to clue in to the neurological processes at work and then take steps to help us quiet our brain and worry less. First, understand that worry is much more than a "feeling." Dr. Oz explains that deep inside our brain is an almond-shaped structure called the amygdala, which acts as our fear-and-anxiety center. "When we experience a potential worry, the amygdala sends warning messages to the cortex, the rational part of our brain, which can assess whether that worry is of true concern. As the rational cortex is flooded with more and more warning signals from the amygdala, however, it is unable to process them all, leading to worry loops or anxiety."[6]

Here's where to start:

Identify Your Degree of Stress

From a clinical perspective, anxiety and worry are on a continuum: On one end is someone who may be nervous and upset about an issue but can think rationally about it. On the other end is someone in the grip of a full-on panic attack: her heart is racing, and she feels as if she can't breathe.

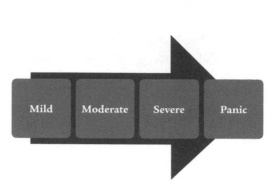

Anxiety Continuum

Here's a look at four different levels of anxiety.

1. Mild: This is the stuff of everyday life—a pang of worry here, a surge of stress there. No one is immune, and it isn't necessarily a negative experience. Again, a little bit of adrenaline and stress can motivate us to take action, run for safety, complete a task—and because our perception is increased, mild anxiety can enhance creativity and out-of-the-box problem-solving.

What Happens at This Level
- Slight Shortness of Breath
- Elevated Pulse and Blood Pressure
- Stomach Discomfort

Recommended Action: Follow the steps presented in this chapter, emphasizing diet changes, aerobic exercise, and relaxation techniques.

2. Moderate: At this point our minds get increasingly stuck on worried, what-if thinking. *What if I look foolish in front of my coworkers? What if the doctor gives me really bad news? What if I fail the test?* Yet a moderate anxiety level is still considered normal by healthcare professionals. Despite having a narrowed perceptual field, we're still able to solve problems and work through what's bugging us.

What Happens at This Level
- Sweating
- Shaky Voice
- Headache
- Trouble Sleeping

Recommended Action: Follow the steps presented in this chapter, emphasizing diet changes, aerobic exercise, and relaxation techniques.

3. Severe: This degree of anxiety begins to interfere with our lives. Often we feel overwhelmed by fearful thoughts, and awareness of our surroundings is significantly narrowed; we simply can't take our mind off what's stressing us. *I can't handle this alone,* we think (and increasingly believe). *I just don't know what to do.*

What Happens at This Level
- Muscle Tension
- Hyperventilation
- Talking Fast in a High Tone
- Pacing
- Trembling

Recommended Action: Follow the steps presented in this chapter and seek the advice of a healthcare professional, as well as a Christian counselor or pastor.

4. Panic: This degree of anxiety—the highest and most dangerous—can be a terrifying experience. Sufferers often sense impending doom, and they may be unable to speak logically or hold a thought (can't think rationally). Some pace uncontrollably and become increasingly active without a purpose. Intervention is crucial, as prolonged panic can be harmful to one's health.

What Happens at This Level
- Extreme Muscle Tension
- Pronounced Shortness of Breath; Often, Gasping for Air
- Rapid Pulse and Elevated Blood Pressure
- Aimless and Haphazard Actions
- Shaking

Recommended Action: Seek medical attention (both from your family physician and from a licensed therapist), gain some spiritual advice from a pastor or church leader, and consider following the steps presented in this chapter.

My Worry-Wise Plan: The Degree of Anxiety in My Life

Here's how I would rate my degree of anxiety:
❏ **Mild** ❏ **Moderate** ❏ **Severe** ❏ **Panic**

Here's how I feel when anxiety strikes:

_____

_____

Get Grounded

Whenever our degree of anxiety maxes out, we must talk ourselves down from a "panic cliff." And then we can get moving toward truth, and more constructive thinking. Remember therapist Nanette Gingery, from chapter 6?

"I strive to walk patients step-by-step through these kinds of circumstances," she explains. "I tell them something like this: 'You're in my office. Grab on to the arm of the chair and look around. You're safe. Everything is okay. Take a deep breath, and let's work on slowing the breathing.' I get them to the point in which the anxiety is manageable."[7]

As Nanette suggests, getting grounded is a technique that an individual can do on his own. I've used this exercise after waking in the middle of the night, panicked about something. When my heart is racing and my head is swirling with all kinds of anxious thoughts, I stop, and I remind myself that it's the middle of the night. *Everything seems worse when it's dark out. Let's take some time to breathe, to relax, and then go back to bed.* And then I do that, as needed.

My Worry-Wise Plan: Attacking Panic

1. Take deep breaths and slow your heart rate.
2. Hold on to something—the edge of a chair, your Bible, a photo . . . anything.
3. Examine your surroundings. What do you see?
4. Remind yourself to be still and to trust God. Tell yourself that everything is okay, you're not in danger. Jot down a few thoughts to remember when panic hits:

_____

_____

Change Your Thoughts

Let's say we have a friend who's obsessing and is extremely worried because her son is overseas in the military—a fairly common concern. She could just go about her day, constantly ruminating about his circumstances, endangering her own health, jeopardizing other relationships—and having a miserable time in the process. Or she can take some steps that will enable her to refocus her thoughts and break the fear-worry-stress cycle. Consider these eye-opening insights from Dr. Daniel Amen (*Change Your Brain, Change Your Life*):

> Thoughts are very powerful. They can make your mind and your body feel good, or they can make you feel bad. Every cell in your body is affected by every thought you have. That is why when people get emotionally upset, they frequently develop physical symptoms, such as headaches or stomachaches. Some physicians think that people who have a lot of negative thoughts are more likely to get cancer. If you can think about good things, you will feel better . . . You can train your thoughts to be positive and hopeful, or you can allow them to be negative and upset you . . . One way to learn how to change your thoughts is to notice them when they are negative and talk back to them. When you just think a negative thought without challenging it, your mind believes it and your body reacts to it. When you correct negative thoughts, you take away their power over you.[8]

So much anxiety in our lives is caused by self-condemning thoughts. Whether we realize it or not, we wrongfully judge ourselves. A thought enters my mind, I become worried, and then right away I'm thinking, *What's wrong with me?* And then that voice of judgment spirals me downward. "Instead," suggests Nanette, "this should be my reaction: *Oh, I'm worrying again. There's that thing I do.*"

In other words, have a sense of humor as you combat the cycle. It really is about choosing; it's about getting to a mental place where you're aware of your thoughts—your meta-cognitions—so you can stop them in their tracks. You *can* shift your thinking to what is far more interesting and even far more peaceful.

My Worry-Wise Plan: How I Will Change My Thoughts

Sometime this week, use the chart below to document your thoughts, worries, and stressors within a twenty-four hour cycle. Whenever anxiety strikes—whether mild or severe or inbetween—jot down (1) what you're thinking, (2) how you feel, and (3) what struggles are affecting you. Then (below), tell what you've observed about yourself during this exercise . . . along with some verses and truths to tell yourself when you feel worried and stressed.

24-Hour Cycle	What I'm Thinking When Anxiety Strikes	How I Feel	What I'm Struggling With/Worried About
Early Morning (Night): 12–3 a.m.			
Early Morning (Night): 3–6 a.m.			
Early Morning (Day): 6–9 a.m.			
Mid-to-Late Morning: 9a.m. -12 p.m.			
Noon Hour: 12–1 p.m.			

24-Hour Cycle	What I'm Thinking When Anxiety Strikes	How I Feel	What I'm Struggling With/Worried About
Early Afternoon: 1–3 p.m.			
Midafternoon: 3–5 p.m.			
Early Evening: 5–7 p.m.			
Mid-Evening: 7–9 p.m.			
Late-Evening: 9 p.m.–12 a.m.			

What I've observed about myself when I feel stressed:

_____

_____

Scriptures I will read when I'm anxious and worried:
- 1 Corinthians 13:4–8
- Philippians 4:8
- 1 Peter 5:7
- Additional Passages:

_____

_____

What I'll tell myself when I find I'm caught up in fear and worry and stress:

_____

_____

_____

As I unravel wrong thinking, here's how I'll pursue "right talking" (for some clues, read Mark 11:23; Exodus 15:26; Isaiah 53:3-5; Matthew 8:17; 1 Peter 2:24):

_____

_____

_____

_____

Reframe and Refocus

When I begin to feel overwhelmed by my circumstances—especially from worry and stress—I go outside and simply take a walk. As I take in deep breaths of fresh air, I study my environment: the horse arena in the middle of our property, the pastures that surround our house, a pond in the distance. On other occasions, I listen to my favorite tunes as I sweep the stables—anything to put my attention on something different and enjoyable. Very therapeutic, and I've done something productive to boot! My point is this: As negative and worrisome thoughts begin to take over, disconnect them by focusing on your environment. Find something that's not threatening you. Find one thing at a time, and really look hard at it. Then find another thing that's not threatening you. Do this, or these, until you feel better.

My Worry-Wise Plan: How I Will Refocus

Here are some hands-on, practical things I can do when anxiety strikes:

_____

_____

_____

_____

_____

Tap the Power of the Pen: Journal Those Nagging Thoughts
Grab a blank notebook or journal and spend fifteen minutes a day acknowledging your worries in a tangible way. Listing your biggest worries and creating a calendar of stressful upcoming activities will enable you to face and deal with each concern so they don't collectively balloon and press you toward panic.

As you write down what you're worried about, include the thoughts and observations you completed above, as well as your imagined worst-case scenarios. In the case of the worried mom, I would encourage her to write a daily letter to her son. Not only will this serve as a release during specific moments, but she also can go back and review what she's written. In the heat of the moment, when anxiety has taken over, you're often not thinking clearly. You may feel as if you're trapped in an all-or-nothing scenario. _I can't take this any longer. It's always going to be this way._ Before you know it, you're overwhelmed within a downward spiral of worry and fear. But if you're not having a full-on panic attack—and if you can journal during those moments—you'll be able to go back and reflect on what you've written.

My Worry-Wise Plan:
How I Can "Journal Away" My Stress

Get started with these simple steps:

(1) First, find a comfy place at a time that's relatively distraction free, if possible, and then begin in prayer. As you talk with God, reflect on the issues in your life that you feel stressed about. (Again, feel free to use the completed exercises above as a guide.)

(2) Do the "look around and find something that's not threatening you" action, if needed. The purpose is to help you step back and more precisely identify sources of stress. When I get worked up, things seem to mush all together and appear to be one massive blob. When I can look at one thing at a time, then I can work on handling one thing at a time. While you're doing this, you might feel upset or angry at first—keep at it until you feel better. Don't run away—take a break, maybe, but come back to it.

(3) Next, write out your worries. Don't waste your time with an "Oh, poor me, how can I possibly handle this" scenario, or allow yourself to ruminate on the worries. Stay above that. When you identify something, write it down and move on. Still, please don't rush these steps.

(4) Finally, strive to gain some perspective on your fears, worries, and stresses. Say to yourself, "How is my day today? I was so worried earlier, yet I survived that tough situation. And look at my environment—nothing has changed. I'm okay!" As you do so, you'll eventually have some "a-ha" moments— those healing points when you're able to view your circumstances through the lens of reality: The what-if thoughts that swirl through our heads are often of our own making and sometimes aren't even real. Gaining a better perspective enables

you to better handle what's worrying you. You just might look at some of these things and realize they're really not problems or worth the stress. And, as you engage these steps, you will definitely be doing something positive to manage stress more effectively.

Get Off Your "Can't" and Begin Walking Toward Change

In order to reduce worry in your life, change what's within your control. This can involve a range of steps both big and small: For example, consult a debt consolidation service that can help you establish a workable budget; meet with the school's principal about the bullies harassing your daughter; talk to your spouse about moving closer to work so neither one of you is spending half your life stuck in traffic.

Next, look over the worrisome thoughts that you feel you can't take any action on. Consider which are excessive or distorted and have very little basis in reality. Take each of these worrisome thoughts and write down an alternative thought that is more realistic, as a believable challenge to the worry. (See the exercise directly below.) Finally, try to catch yourself when worries began to mount. Stop, and tell yourself the alternative thought.

My Worry-Wise Plan:
How I Can Take Steps Toward Change

Referring back to your journal, jot down three worries, along with three realities and solutions: For example, if you're worried about public speaking, write that in the first column.

In the second column, add something that's true about you and your abilities: *I'm prepared, I know my material, I will be okay.*

Worries

1. _____
2. _____
3. _____

Realities / Solutions

1. _____
2. _____
3. _____

At-a-Glance Steps to Calming Your Mind

Identify—your degree of anxiety, as well as worrisome thoughts and what's behind them: insecurity, the constant need for approval, fear of confrontation, etc.

Discern—fearful thoughts that are excessive or distorted and have little basis in reality.

Change—what's within your control.

Let Go—of what's out of your control, and learn to be okay with this.

Catch—negative thoughts, and replace them with positive ones.

Remind—yourself that God is the Shepherd who guides, the One who provides, the Lord of peace during life's trials, the Physician who heals the sick, the Banner that guides the soldier. "Be still, and know that I am God."[9]

Accept—yourself as you are, knowing that it's perfectly acceptable to perform at your own level instead of at someone—anyone—else's.

Face—tasks that push you out of your comfort zone, but release those that are distractions or that just aren't necessary.

De-Shame—the fear of failing, of being blamed for something, of making a mistake, of having a life-controlling struggle, etc.

De-Clutter—by reducing busy schedules and striving to simplify life.

Your Body's Worry-Wise Plan

I must be blunt about a serious matter: Inactivity and stress are a deadly mix. If our body is constantly overloaded with adrenaline, yet we're not working off the nervous energy, then we're putting a lot of stress on our heart and other vital organs. And the worst thing we can do is fill an inactive, anxious body with depressants, stimulants, and fat: sugary or caffeinated drinks, fried foods and desserts, salty canned or prepared foods, nicotine, alcohol . . .

On the positive side: Exercise is a powerful stress reducer, and our age or inexperience shouldn't hold us back. Everyone *can* take steps to improve his/her physical condition. What's more, getting active will benefit our mood and help us to be happier, healthier Christ-followers!

Of course, we must be smart, and start out slowly, gradually increasing the amount and intensity of our workouts. Once we have combined exercise with a balanced diet, we'll be well on our way toward a worry-free lifestyle. The fact is, stress and worrying provoke some people to eat too little, others too much, or to eat unhealthy foods. Keep your health in mind whenever worrying nudges you toward the fridge.

* * * * *

Ready to continue building the new you? Begin by talking with your primary care physician. Get a thorough physical exam to make sure other health problems are not fueling your feelings of anxiety. Your doctor may prescribe medication such as anti-anxiety drugs or anti-depressants to help you self-manage anxiety and excessive worry.

Once you get the green light, try the following.

Stretch and Relax
Michael's wife, Tiffany, incorporates a variety of stretching routines into her daily exercise regimen. For example, she does stretches for her back, for her legs, feet, and ankles, and for her shoulders and arms. Tiffany often ties in a spiritual element with each maneuver: She meditates on Scripture, and she prays to Jesus during her workouts. Her focus is on relaxing through proper stretching and breathing and also endeavoring to set her mind on God's peace.

"[Stretching] is peaceful, relaxing, and noncompetitive," writes fitness expert Bob Anderson, in Stretching.[10] "The subtle, invigorating feelings of stretching allow you to get in touch with your muscles . . . It relaxes your mind and tunes up your body, and it should be part of your daily life." (Tiffany highly recommends his excellent book.)

Breathe Deep
When that pang of anxiety strikes and your heart begins to race, take a simple step that can help quiet your mind and calm your

emotions and body. Breathe in slowly to the count of six, then breathe out slowly to the count of six. Do this for five minutes; gradually increase to twenty minutes over time. The point is to slow your heart rate and reduce the pace at which stress hormones are flying through your system. While focusing on each breath, remind yourself that the anxiety you're feeling is a chemical response.[11] Repeat some phrases, verses, or prayers: "Relax, and live in truth, not fear"; "Be at rest; know that God is in charge"; "Lord Jesus, calm my mind and my body. Please grant me peace."

Deep breathing is helpful in interrupting irrational thoughts. But the key is to take long, steady breaths from the diaphragm. This slows down your heart rate, lowers blood pressure, and helps your body use oxygen more efficiently. It also has a calming effect. Our lungs supply red blood cells with fresh oxygen—enabling normal cell function and proper metabolism—and they also rid our bodies of harmful waste products like carbon dioxide.

Exercise Daily

God designed our body to be active. The harder we work it, and the better the nutrients we put into it, the leaner, stronger, and more energetic it will become. In fact, the chemicals produced during moderate exercise can enhance the function of the immune system and train our bodies to deal with stress under controlled circumstances.

Here are the two types of exercise we need to incorporate into our daily lives:

Aerobic Activity—the technical definition is "training with oxygen." In other words, an activity that gets your heart pumping and air flowing through your body: walking, hiking, jogging, swimming, bicycling, cross-country skiing. The benefits are indisputable:

- Our heart is strengthened
- Blood pressure is lowered
- Metabolism is improved

- Fat stores are burned after twenty to thirty minutes of sustained activity
- Endorphins and other "feel good" hormones are released

Anaerobic Exercise—this means "training without oxygen," and it involves all forms of high-intensity activity engaged for short periods of time. Examples include sprinting, resistance training (working out with weights), powerlifting, tennis, racquetball, and any other sport you can think of that causes fatigue to the muscles with harder but shorter bursts of energy. During anaerobic exercise, our cardiovascular system has a challenging time delivering the necessary levels of oxygen to our muscles fast enough. And since muscles require air to maintain prolonged exertion, anaerobic exercises can only continue for brief stretches. Why is this important for overall good health? Resistance training provides benefits like these:

- Improves muscle strength, which enhances other athletic pursuits
- Builds and maintains a lean, toned body
- Enhances weight loss
- Fights stress through vigorous exercise

Checklist of Family-Friendly Exercises

- Take a twenty-minute walk each evening around your neighborhood
- Go for a Saturday-morning bike ride
- Play "adults vs. kids" football or soccer in the backyard

- Engage in a once-a-week hike at a local park, the mountains, the beach
- Swim and work out at the YMCA (or other family-oriented health club)
- Take a karate class together
- Get up early three days a week and stretch together—followed by family devotions
- Host a laser tag or paintball marathon
- Pop an aerobic-style game into the Wii or Xbox and work out together
- Jog three nights a week at a local park or on an indoor track

My Worry-Wise Plan:
Weekly Stretching, Deep Breathing, and Exercise Routine

Day	Aerobic and Anaerobic Exercise	Stretching & Breathing	My Fitness Goals	Fitness Goals for My Family
Sunday				
Monday				
Tuesday				
Wednesday				
Thursday				
Friday				
Saturday				

Know That Eating Smart Can Promote Worry-Free Living

A well-balanced diet is crucial to good health and will enable you to reduce the fear-worry-stress cycle. Certain foods and drinks can stimulate our bodies and actually trigger anxiety. In other words, that daily run to your favorite coffee spot is a fun vice, but in the long run it might be taking a toll on your health: Think about the caffeine, sugar, and fat you put into your body. Think about how you feel after your body crashes. More stressed—right?

Here are some dietary steps I guarantee will reap profound benefits:

Cut Back on Caffeine. You're probably getting more of this than you think, especially if you consume daily doses of coffee, tea, chocolate, energy drinks, and many soft drinks.

What happens inside our body: Caffeine stimulates the nervous system, which—as you know—triggers the release of adrenaline, making you feel nervous and jittery. Some medical professionals claim there is a link between caffeine intake and high blood pressure, as well as high cholesterol levels.[12]

My advice: Consume caffeinated beverages in moderation. For example, no more than two cups of coffee in the morning. This will provide more than enough caffeine to increase your alertness and increase activity in your muscles, nervous system, and heart. In excess, caffeine can increase our stress levels.

Limit or Eliminate Alcohol. It's ironic, really. Some people drink beer or wine to calm their nerves. But in reality, large amounts of alcohol make us feel more stressed out.

What happens inside our body: Alcohol stimulates the secretion of adrenaline, which affects nervous tension. The result: When the buzz wears off, we end up feeling irritable, and we may even struggle to fall asleep. Excess alcohol can increase fat deposits in the heart, decrease immune function, and limit the liver's ability to remove toxins from the body.

My advice: A glass or two of red wine with a meal can be very useful and has even been shown to benefit the cardiovascular system. But use common sense: alcohol is addictive and can be easily abused. Moderation is the key.

Reduce Sugar Intake. Our craving for sweets starts at an early age, yet sugar has no essential nutrients. It gives us a quick boost of energy, and then we crash.

What happens inside our body: Our adrenal glands become exhausted—i.e., the crash—and we begin feeling irritable and have difficulty concentrating. We may even feel depressed. In addition, much sugar is bad for the pancreas and increases the possibility of developing diabetes.

My advice: Keep your blood sugar constant, and never use sugar as a pick-me-up.

Use Salt Sparingly. We need salt (or sodium chloride) to help our bodies function properly, but most of us are getting way too much of it. Check the labels of processed foods and you'll probably find sodium chloride in the list of ingredients. Order a meal from your favorite restaurant and more than likely you'll be served a dish that's high in sodium. According to the Mayo Clinic, the average American should limit salt to less than 2,300 milligrams a day—or 1,500 if you're fifty-one or older and/or have high blood pressure, diabetes, or chronic kidney disease.[13] Most of us consume more than 3,400 milligrams of salt per day.[14]

What happens inside our body: Sodium chloride aids nutrient absorption and transport, and when salt breaks down into its two chemical components, then one of them, chloride, becomes part of the acids in our digestive tract.[15] These absorb nutrients from our food. Sodium, the other component, influences the volume of liquids retained by our body outside of our cells.[16] This determines our blood volume, which in turn regulates blood pressure. In excess, however, it can deplete adrenal glands and cause emotional instability. Even worse, it can increase our blood pressure and can put us at risk for heart disease.

My advice: While salt plays an important role in our body's proper functioning, we must use it sparingly. Consider a salt substitute that has potassium rather than sodium. Avoid junk foods (e.g., potato chips) and foods cured with salt (e.g., bacon and ham); cease using table salt.

Cut Back on Fatty Foods. According to medical professionals, there are three main types of dietary fats: unsaturated fats (which include monounsaturated and polyunsaturated fats), saturated fats, and trans fats. Most of us are all too familiar with the immediate effect of fatty foods—tummy discomfort, gas, bloating, acid reflux, and heartburn. But somehow we overlook the most lethal risk: *heart disease.* Some fats are necessary for wellness, but others should be limited or avoided as much as possible. Let's take a closer look at the good, the bad, and the ugly risks associated with a diet high in fat.

What happens inside our body: Monounsaturated and polyunsaturated are the good fats that actually improve cholesterol levels and decrease our risk for cardiovascular disease. These fats are found in nuts, avocados, and olive oil. Polyunsaturated fats include omega-3 and omega-6 fatty acids, essential to our body's needs. The saturated fat-type comes primarily from animal products, such as meat and dairy products, as well as from coconut and palm oils. This fat-type is unhealthy and may increase our risk of type 2 diabetes as well as heart disease by increasing our LDL ("bad") cholesterol. Trans fat (the most unhealthy kind) is a major enemy to our body; it can increase our LDL cholesterol and decrease our HDL ("good") cholesterol, increase our risk of cardiovascular disease and type 2 (adult-onset) diabetes, and lead to insulin resistance.

My advice: Avoid eating foods full of saturated fats. As fat accumulates in our body, we end up gaining weight and risk becoming obese. An unhealthy weight gain can lead to chronic illnesses like diabetes, heart disease, and arthritis. It also adds unnecessary stress on the cardiovascular system and puts us at a greater risk for a heart attack. In addition, a high-fat diet is believed to cause breast, colon, and prostate cancers.

My Worry-Wise Plan:
Weekly Menu and Dietary Goals for My Family and Me

Day	Weekly Menu	Portions and Calories Per Serving	My Nutrition Goals	Nutrition Goals for My Family	Food and Beverages to Limit or Avoid
Sun.	Fruits: Vegetables: Whole Grains: Healthy Protein:				
Mon.	Fruits: Vegetables: Whole Grains: Healthy Protein:				
Tues.	Fruits: Vegetables: Whole Grains: Healthy Protein:				
Wed.	Fruits: Vegetables: Whole Grains: Healthy Protein:				
Thur.	Fruits: Vegetables: Whole Grains: Healthy Protein:				
Fri.	Fruits: Vegetables: Whole Grains: Healthy Protein:				
Sat.	Fruits: Vegetables: Whole Grains: Healthy Protein:				

Foods to Eat

- **Healthy Carbs** (also known as good carbohydrates): whole grains such as whole wheat, brown rice, millet, quinoa, and barley; beans, fruits, and vegetables. Whole grains help the brain produce serotonin, which increases our sense of well-being.

- **Green, Yellow, and Orange Vegetables:** These are all rich in minerals, vitamins, and phytochemicals, which boost immune response and protect against disease. Eating more vegetables can increase our brain's serotonin production. Also, vegetables contain the natural, safe form of L-Tryptophan.

- **Seafood:** Foods from the ocean are high in selenium, and, according to Dr. Reginald B. Cherry, "studies have determined that people who do not get enough selenium tend to suffer more depression, fatigue, and even anxiety. When enough selenium is available, mood changes improve significantly."[17] David Zinczenko, author of the popular book series *Eat This, Not That*, recommends these fish choices: Wild Alaskan salmon, farmed rainbow trout, Pacific halibut, farmed catfish, farmed tilapia, yellowfin tuna, mahi-mahi.[18]

- **Flavonoids and Resveratrol:** These can be found in grapes—specifically in red wine. Flavonoids have been effective in fighting diseases ranging from cancer to heart disease to circulatory problems. Resveratrol inhibits tumor growth at three different stages: initiation, promotion, and progression. Both are available in supplements as well as in certain juices and teas.

Foods to Avoid

- **Fried Foods:** Steer clear of foods rich in fat. These are immune-depressing, especially when stress is taking its toll on our bodies.

- **Unhealthy Carbs:** These are foods like white flour, refined sugar, and white rice that have been stripped of all bran, fiber, and nutrients. Unhealthy carbs digest quickly and cause spikes in blood sugar levels and energy.[19]
- **Foods High in Sugar:** According to *Men's Health,* the average American is consuming 460 calories from added sugars every day—more than 100 pounds of raw sugar per person per year (enough to make 3,628 Reese's Peanut Butter Cups).[20] All this sugar excess is leading to an epidemic of obesity and other illnesses, including type 2 diabetes and cancer. So as you make your way through the supermarket, check labels closely. Sugar is often defined as monosaccharides (galactose, glucose, fructose) and disaccharides (sucrose, lactose, maltose). All such foods should be limited or avoided.

At-a-Glance Steps to Calming Your Body

Exercise—weekly at the least, daily if possible. Without question, the chemicals produced during moderate exercise can enhance the function of the immune system, as well as train your body to deal with stress.

Breathe—do it slowly to the count of six, and then breathe out slowly to the count of six. Do this for five minutes; gradually increase to twenty minutes over time.

Stretch—this keeps our muscles supple, makes our bodies feel more relaxed, prepares us for motion, and helps us to stay fit.

Eat—a healthy, balanced diet. Stress and worry provoke some people to skip meals or to eat too little, and others to consume too much and/or to attach to unhealthy foods.

Drink—an appropriate amount of water every day. This flushes toxins from vital organs and carries nutrients to your cells. How much? That depends on your health, how active you are, and where you live.

Engage—take up relaxing and enjoyable hobbies.

Connect—with family and friends every day.

Laugh—it lifts your spirits, especially if you feel run-down. It's a good idea to avoid taking yourself too seriously and to laugh at your shortcomings.

Savor—a moment with your spouse, a walk in the park, a piece of art, a song, time spent outdoors, etc. What's more, getting sunshine and fresh air daily can be good for your emotions and your overall health.

Detox—avoid or limit substances such as caffeine, nicotine, and alcohol.

Sleep—get seven to nine hours of rest every day for adults; more for teens and kids. Lack of sleep can inhibit productivity, trigger anxiety, and lead to serious health consequences.

Your Spirit's Worry-Wise Plan

Prayer, praise, and meditation on God's Word are three basic disciplines that can have a profound impact on every believer's life. I (Michael) have observed that people of faith are better able to handle the stressors of life if they're practicing their faith. So to have that spiritual connection and to take it a step further is pragmatically utilizing your faith in daily life. This could mean ten to fifteen minutes of prayer and meditation. Not only will this help you in the moment, and throughout the day, but this kind of spiritual practice will have a physiological cumulative effect on your life, one that will help you deal with the fear-worry-stress cycle.

Prayer

Instead of worrying over our problems, which simply fuels anxiety and stress, God's Word recommends taking everything to Him in prayer. Paul's letter to the Philippians (the first two chapters, specifically) reveals that as we pray, our minds will be protected by a peace that goes beyond our ability to understand.

Through prayer, we can open a window that allows God's eternal love and healing power to shine into our lives; we can open our hands to receive His many blessings; we can open our hearts to let His presence fill and strengthen us.

In the words of R. C. Sproul,

> The Lord God of the universe, the Creator and Sustainer of all things . . . not only commands us to pray, but also invites us to make our requests known . . . In the act and dynamic of praying, I bring my whole life under His gaze. Yes, He knows what is in my mind, but I still have the privilege of articulating to Him what is there. He says, "Come. Speak to Me. Make your requests known to Me." And so, we come in order to know Him and to be known by Him.[21]

God hears and answers our prayers. But we must be proactive. We must open the window by kneeling before Him in prayer. Jesus says that we have not because we ask not. James tells us a righteous person's effectual, fervent prayer accomplishes much. Again and again, God's holy Word reveals to us that prayer is an effective tool. That is, prayer works.

God delights in our prayers. He longs to demonstrate His power in the tremendous trials that shake the foundation of our lives as well as in the tiny troubles that annoy us. Giant needs are never too great for His power; small ones are never too insignificant for His love.

God answers prayer because he is the supreme ruler of all. He governs both world events and our individual lives, ready at our request to act, to intervene, to overrule for our good, for His glory, and for the progress of the gospel.

God moves through prayer. Not only are we called to this activity,[22] we're also assured of God's action in response. As His Word clearly states,[23] God promises results if we pray. He has assured us that prayer is the way to secure His aid and move His mighty hand. Even in sickness, failure, rejection, or financial distress, we can pray and experience His peace.

> Embrace this God-life. Really embrace it, and nothing will be too much for you. This mountain, for instance: Just say, "Go jump in the lake"—no shuffling or shilly-shallying—and it's as good as done. That's why I urge you to pray for absolutely everything, ranging from small to large. Include everything as you embrace this God-life, and you'll get God's everything. And when you assume the posture of prayer, remember that it's not all asking. If you have anything against someone, forgive—only then will your heavenly Father be inclined to also wipe your slate clean of sins.[24]

Our Lord Jesus often slipped away to be alone and to pray. Margaret Magdalen writes:

> Jesus needed the silence of eternity as a thirsting man in the desert needs water . . . He longed for time apart to bask and sunbathe in His Father's love, to soak in it and repose in it. No matter how drained He felt, it seems that this deep, silent communion refreshed Him more than a good night's sleep.[25]

Meditation on the Word of God

If I'm so busy being worried all the time, then my heart isn't focused on God's Word. The Bible is filled with incredible promises from him. Meditating on these words of assurance can dispel our worry, doubt, anxiety, fear, and stress.[26] Here are just three more examples:

> The Lord will keep you safe from secret traps and deadly diseases. He will spread his wings over you and keep you secure. His faithfulness is like a shield or a city wall. You won't need to worry about dangers at night or arrows during the day. And you won't fear diseases that strike in the dark or sudden disaster at noon.[27]

> Don't worry about anything; instead, pray about everything; tell God your needs, and don't forget to thank him for his answers. If you do this, you will experience God's peace, which is far more wonderful than the human mind can understand. His peace will keep your thoughts and your hearts quiet and at rest as you trust in Christ Jesus.[28]

> Let the peace of Christ keep you in tune with each other, in step with each other. None of this going off and doing your own thing. And cultivate thankfulness. Let the Word of Christ—the Message—have the run of the house. Give it plenty of room in your lives. Instruct and direct one another using good common sense. And sing, sing your hearts out to God! Let every detail in your lives—words, actions, whatever—be done in the name of the Master, Jesus, thanking God the Father every step of the way.[29]

Praise and Worship

Someone once said: "I find it to be almost impossible to be stressed and praise God at the same time. When I'm anxious, I just start praising and the worry just seems to go away."[30]

Wise advice.

Praising and worshiping God is an interactive experience. It's both private and public. It involves our heart and our head. And, as we linger in God's presence, praising Him, we connect with the divine—the very Source of life. "Come near to God and He will come near to you."[31]

Praise is the spontaneous response of a grateful child of God in His presence. That's how Henry Blackaby describes it.

> The person who knows God and experiences Him intimately sings to the Lord with deepest praise! Mary was overwhelmed by the Lord's goodness to her. In response, she sang one of the most beautiful and profound songs of praise found in Scripture. Trying to stop the praise of a thankful heart would be like trying to arrest the flow of a mighty waterfall! God created us to praise Him; praise will be our activity when we are gathered around His throne in heaven.[32]

My Worry-Wise Plan: Steps Toward Peace

Study John 14 and 16. Jesus tells us, "Do not let your hearts be troubled. Believe in God, believe also in me."[33] He also says, "If you love me, you will keep my commandments. And I will ask the Father, and he will give you another Advocate, to be with you forever. This is the Spirit of truth."[34] And, "When the Spirit of truth comes, he will guide you into all the truth."[35]

Why are these messages from Jesus crucial to combating anxiety and overcoming worry?

_____

_____

Share how you believe God's truth will deliver you and your family from worry.

_____

_____

Memorize Scriptures that emphasize God's power, protection, and provision.

Here's one to consider:

Humble yourselves therefore under the mighty hand of God, so that he may exalt you in due time. Cast all your anxiety on him, because he cares for you. Discipline yourselves, keep alert. Like a roaring lion your adversary the devil prowls around, looking for someone to devour. Resist him, steadfast in your faith, for you know that your brothers and sisters in all the world are undergoing the same kinds of suffering. And after you have suffered for a little while, the God of all grace, who has called you to his eternal glory in Christ, will himself restore, support, strengthen, and establish you. (1 Peter 5:6–10 NRSV)

Make a list of twelve verses/passages you plan to memorize during the next year.

1. _____
2. _____
3. _____

4. _____
5. _____
6. _____
7. _____
8. _____
9. _____
10. _____
11. _____
12. _____

Pray for release from the weight of worry—and trust that God WILL answer you!

Reflect on these prayers:

Cleanse our mind, O Lord we beseech thee, of all anxious thoughts for ourselves, that we may learn not to trust in the abundance of what we have, save as tokens of thy goodness and grace, but that we may commit ourselves in faith to thy keeping, and devote all our energy of soul, mind, and body to the work of thy kingdom and the furthering of the purposes of thy divine righteousness; through Jesus Christ our Lord.[36]
      —Euchologium Anglicanum

Strengthen me, O God, by the grace of Thy Holy Spirit; grant me to be strengthened with might in the inner man, and to put away from my heart all useless anxiety and distress, and let me never be drawn aside by various longings after anything whatever, whether it be worthless or precious; but may I regard all things as passing away, and myself as passing away with them. For nothing is lasting under the sun, for all things are vanity and vexation of spirit. Oh, how wise is he who thus regards them.[37]

—Thomas à Kempis

Share what you see to be the common spiritual thread woven into these two prayers.

_____

_____

_____

How would you pray, in this same vein? Write your prayer in any words you choose.

_____

_____

_____

For help with standing against fear and worry, consider starting either an accountability group or an accountability relationship with one other person.

Which people would I like to talk with about this?

How often would I prefer to meet?

What would be my expectations?

Tonight, and again anytime, consider expressing this prayer by Dietrich Bonhoeffer:

O Lord my God, I thank you that you have
  brought this day to a close;
I thank you that you have given me peace in
  body and soul.
Your hand has been over me and has protected
  and preserved me.
Forgive my puny faith, the ill that I this day
  have done, and help me to forgive all who have
  wronged me.
Grant me a quiet night's sleep beneath your
  tender care.
And defend me from all the temptations
  of darkness.
Into your hands I commend my loved ones
And all who dwell in this house;
I commend my body and soul.
O God, your holy name be praised. Amen.[38]

At-a-Glance Steps to Calming Your Spirit

Confess—tell Jesus everything that's bottled up inside: sins, mistakes, fears, worries, disappoint-
  ments . . . absolutely *everything!*
Talk—to Jesus during uninterrupted prayer times
  and continually throughout the day, especially
  during stressful moments. "No one can pray
  and worry at the same time."[39]
Praise—express your love to Jesus as you give him
  your worship and your heart.

Receive—God's Word into your mind by reading, listening to, and "spiritually consuming" the words of the Bible. Consistently be asking, *What does God say about giving up control and surrendering everything to Him?*

Reflect—actively, on God's Word, thinking, meditating, and pondering the message of the Bible into your heart. *How can surrendering my life bring more peace into each day?*

Respond—to God's Word, looking for ways to live out the truth. *What are some steps I've decided I will take in order to let go of worry?*

Worship—again, this is to be an interactive experience.[40] *When we're close to Jesus, praising and worshiping Him, what happens to worry?*

Rest—in His promises, in His protection, in His love. "There is no fear in love. But perfect love drives out fear, because fear has to do with punishment. The one who fears is not made perfect in love."[41]

Trust—for the one whose hope is in God will never be put to shame.[42] "Worry does not empty tomorrow of its sorrow. It empties today of its strength."[43]

Go—and face tomorrow, because He is constantly at our side, loving us and encouraging us. When we hurt, God hurts. And we're to do the same for our friends.[44]

Our Research Says . . .

- Recording your worries and then reviewing how many really come true can help you appreciate how few, and how relatively rarely, bad things actually do happen.

- Practicing deep breathing and relaxation techniques "ahead of time," before anxiety hits, makes it easier to use them when you need them most.
- A good belly laugh can lower the level of stress hormones in the blood and also make us feel more hopeful.

Recap and Reflect
Talking Points for Couples or Group Study

• • • • • • • • • • • • • • • • • • • •

We can break the fear-worry-stress cycle by attaining *homeostasis—* balance between stimulating and tranquilizing chemical forces in our bodies.

How will I work toward accomplishing this in our home?

The Worry-Wise Plan is a mind-body-spirit solution that helps people unravel wrong thinking and negative thoughts. Consider again these words: "Don't copy the behavior and customs of this world, but let God transform you into a new person by changing the way you think. Then you will learn to know God's will for you, which is good and pleasing and perfect."[45]

Do I and my family fit right in with the world's ways, or are we becoming new people as we learn to change our thinking and as those thoughts become our choices and actions?

- Explain. Then, from one area of the Worry-Wise Plan—for example, "mind"— share two changes that you and your family will make.

Managing worry can be lasting and successful when we learn to let go of yesterday's troubles and stop ruminating about tomorrow. We are to find peace with God today . . . in this moment.

Do I believe this? Why, or why not?

Here's What's Next

Now that we've completed Part Two and are armed with practical, biblically based techniques, let's look at ways of helping those we love. In the next section we'll specifically consider the worries, anxieties, and stresses of spouses, children, and Millennials, and examine how the Worry-Wise Plan can be applied to their lives as well.

PART THREE

HAPPY, HOPEFUL, AND WHOLE

By the End of Part Three You'll Be Able to:

- Get to the root causes of worry in your life
- Have more empathy for your loved ones
- Incorporate the Worry-Wise Plan
- Plot some steps that will help you move further into worry-free living

Stress-Relieving Suggestions

- *Singing can make you happy.* Scientists say that singing with a group (e.g., a choir) can help reduce stress and release feel-good endorphins. It boosts the anti-stress hormone hydrocortisone and also immunoglobulin A proteins, antibodies that keep us healthy by fighting off infections.[1]
- *Green apples cure claustrophobia?* Well, sniffing one might help, at least! A study from the Smell and Taste Treatment and Research Foundation found that the scent given off by green apples can actually relieve symptoms of claustrophobia. The same study found benefits for migraine sufferers too.[2]

- *Laugh your way to a worry-free life.* Not only does it benefit us emotionally, but doctors also say that laughing stimulates our organs (heart, lungs, and muscles, for example), increases the brain's release of endorphins, activates and relieves our stress response, and soothes tension.[3]
- *Aromas are powerful memory triggers and mood enhancers.* Our sense of smell is processed through the limbic system, which governs emotion and memory. That's why sizzling bacon, freshly perked coffee, or crackling logs in an outdoor fire pit can trigger memories of a camping excursion. Best of all, some scents can help ease tension as well. Which work best? Try jasmine, lavender, vetiver, tangerine, chamomile, or grapefruit.[4]
- *Pets help us reduce stress.* Petting your cat or dog, or even watching fish in an aquarium, lowers cortisol (a stress hormone) and raises production of the feel-good chemical serotonin.

RX FOR A WORRIED SPOUSE

PRACTICAL WAYS MARRIED COUPLES CAN SUPPORT EACH OTHER

My life has been filled with terrible misfortune,
most of which never happened.[1]
MICHEL DE MONTAIGNE

Robin glances quickly at the clock as her fingers fly across the keyboard. *Already 4:42 p.m.* Three more letters to finish before she can call it a day. She grabs her phone and texts Andy:

Please pick up Sarah @ daycare, take her to dance, & then we'll meet at Logan's game (Wright Park).

Her husband responds within a few minutes:

Sorry, can't. In critical meeting. Meet you at soccer later.

Robin sighs.

REALLY NEEDED YOU TO DO THIS. I have to get Logan at Jake's, stop @ home for cleats & make it across town for the game. No time to get Sarah before we pay late-pickup rate.

She quickly finishes her letters. As she's racing out the door she's mentally planning the fastest route across town, calculating what she can fix quickly for dinner with what they have on hand— there's no money in the budget for eating out—and reminding herself to mail the electric bill before it's *really* late. Her racing heart and pounding head combine with weighty fatigue to make her dread the rest of the evening. *When will we ever relax? Is rushing all there is to life?*

* * * * *

Exhausted—again.

It's no different than any other random day of Tiffany's life. The alarm's annoying buzzing began at 6:30 a.m., and she started her stretching routine to make it shut up. Every nine minutes her arm peaked out of the warm covers and hit her clock—which is also her cell phone.

Of course it is. She won't sleep more than three feet from her lifeline. This young mom needs something to do at 2:34 a.m. when she's wide awake. She can return email, check the weather, send a birthday text, add items to her shopping list, take notes for the novel she's been working on more than three years, review her prayer list, search for her dream vacation, transfer funds between accounts . . . even play a round of Mahjong (her favorite game). Tiffany usually stops when her wrists begin to ache from what she's sure is a near-future case of carpel tunnel.

If she's still awake, she can always get up and fold laundry or unload/reload the dishes. But most often she's on her pillow, frustrated because she can't sleep. Tiffany finally gets around to talking to God. Even though her usual prayer begins with, "Why can't I sleep?"

Yet then she finds herself remembering how amazing He is and how lucky she is.

After several minutes of praise and reflection, she frequently falls back into deep slumber. So she shouldn't be surprised when she stretches out her arm to hit the snooze. Then she's on her feet in sheer panic. *NO—overslept again.* She quickly starts deleting chores off her to-do list so she can get out the door in time. *Microwave breakfast, skip washing hair, throw on some clean clothes (just folded two hours ago), turn the ringer to "on," clean snow off the car and head out for the day.*

And Tiffany's days are no different than her nights. She guzzles caffeine and power foods as she multitasks through the hours. She sends out detailed status reports at the office. She hits the gym several times a week. She compares prices and finds the best deals in town before buying. She volunteers at church. She invests much time and energy landscaping her front yard. She goes to lunch with friends. She gets the oil changed every three thousand miles. She takes the cats to the vet. She does it all! When she tries to slow down, she just feels guilty.

Why would I do less than I'm capable of?

She works so hard trying to achieve the life she wants—the one she feels she deserves from all the hard work. But lately she's been wondering if it's what she's supposed to be striving toward. She often feels so burned-out, stressed-out, on a treadmill of never-ending worry. *Something's* wrong *with this picture.*

Tiffany's early-morning conversations with God have been leading her to reexamine her goals. *Could things be different? Should they be? I know the life of a believer is supposed to be better, more peaceful, surrendered to God—more fulfilling. But what does that mean?*[2]

* * * * *

Do these scenarios sound like your typical day and night? The current reality in America, regardless of age or family structure, is that we're overextended. And at times it feels there isn't a calendar big enough to hold all we have planned.

When we first began talking to people about their spiritual lives, a common theme was feeling "too busy" to spend time with God between Sundays. In fact, it seems that much of our day is spent trying to make our hectic lives work *without* God in the center. Sure, we may say a quick prayer before we rush out the door in the morning or as we're falling into bed at night, but during the inbetween hours, the Lord is in our "God compartment."

Tweens are echoing a desire to slow down their lives a bit too. Laura, a quiet blue-eyed twelve-year-old, said busyness makes it hard to follow Jesus: "With clarinet, piano, and Girl Scouts, I have something almost every day after school. Sometimes I don't even think about God unless I'm in church." Surprisingly, a slower pace in Sunday school was one way they said life could be improved. More than another game, a fun craft, or tastier snacks, they want time to ask questions and have conversations with their teachers about what's going on in their lives.

Rushing from activity to activity crowds God from our lives. Yet we still expect Him to cooperate with us—relating to us on *our* terms, revolving around *our* plans, solving problems so we can live the way *we* want to live.

Other consequences come from not allowing any margins. We can see it when something unexpected throws a wrench into the works. What happens when turmoil hits? *More turmoil.*

We panic when things go wrong.

We fight with our loved ones—kicking aside anything that remotely resembles love.

We medicate ourselves with impulses, with compulsions, with chemicals.

We grow weary, we grow dull, we grow even more stressed . . . and we blame God, even as we're blaming each other.

It doesn't have to be this way.

* * * * *

If you're married, you've been given a partner with whom to share life's journey—someone to share joyful, beautiful moments as well as trials and concerns. Unfortunately, busy family life can get in the way of spouses working together. Harried schedules crowd out time to connect meaningfully—relationally, spiritually, and physically. Conversations stick to administrative details: who's picking up the kids, who forgot to empty the dishwasher, which bills must be paid on Friday. We can lose sight of who our spouse is, what makes them smile, what they may be struggling with inside, and how we can support each other.

Think a moment about where you are in your marriage right now. Do your days feel like you're in an endless spin cycle? Are you troubled by worries and stress? Are you seeing your spouse struggle with anxiety and aren't sure what to do? If you answered yes to any of these questions, this chapter was written for you. We'll start by sharing the signs that reveal whether or not your spouse is struggling with worry. Then we'll hear from men and women on their worlds and about how their spouses can help them break free. We'll end with tips and techniques for couples.

Clueing In to Signs of Worry

Research has consistently found that women worry more and experience more symptoms of stress than men. In fact, women are twice as likely to have panic disorder, agoraphobia, post-traumatic stress disorder, or Generalized Anxiety Disorder during their lifetime. But men are not immune from worry. In our study, nearly one in four men said he worries frequently, compared to just about one in three women.

Whether the worrier is the wife, the husband, or both, the resulting stress can affect our marriages, our parenting, and our children themselves. That's why it's important to be alert to signs that you or a loved one is having a problem. Look for signs such as:

- Being constantly tense, worried, or on edge
- Irritability and angry outbursts
- Skipping meals or overeating because of stress
- Neglecting intimacy
- Neglecting time with God

- Withdrawal from social interactions
- Shortness of breath, rapid heartbeat, and lightheadedness
- Increased muscle tension or shaking
- Problems falling asleep or staying asleep
- Self-medicating with alcohol or other substances

How Wives Can Help Their Husbands

Jack pulls into the driveway, turns off the engine, and sits back in his seat. He thought this workday would never end. It began with the report on horrible weekend sales and only went downhill from there. The office buzzes with talk of layoffs. *If that happens, what will we do?*

He combs his fingers through his hair and tries to slow his breathing. He looks through the window and sees Lexi moving around the kitchen. He knows she's had a long day too, chasing a pair of toddlers while dealing with awful morning sickness that just won't go away. *I can't let her know I'm worried. She has enough to deal with already.*

* * * * *

Though a man is not immune to the fear-worry-stress cycle, pressure to "be strong" often keeps him from showing it (or trying not to show it), even to his wife. His self-image is tied to toughness and to his ability to provide for and protect those he loves. Acknowledging anxiety or worry runs counter to these facets. He may try to protect his wife by concealing his concerns.

Unfortunately, hiding worries can worsen the situation. With highly developed emotional and relational radars, wives pick up that something is off. Jack's wife, in the story above, can sense that he's quieter than normal, doesn't seem interested in the kids, and feels distant. Without any information from Jack about his work worries, Lexi will start to fill in her own story: *Did I somehow upset him? Maybe he's not attracted to me anymore. What if he's met someone else?*

A primary challenge for wives is not to get carried away by what-ifs. Instead, focus on communicating your love and support to your husband. Take time to pray together as a couple. If this isn't something you've been doing, it may feel awkward at first. Once you get comfortable, though, you will find it a great way to share your worries and burdens with each other.

When he begins to open up, listen and acknowledge his concerns. Remind him that whatever curveballs come your way, you two are in it together. There will be ups and downs: lost jobs, health crises, and other unexpected trials. You are much stronger facing them together than trying to go it alone (literally or emotionally).

Money is a frequent marital tension point and, for husbands, can be a big source of worry; most see it as their duty to provide for the family. Approaching your finances as a team and using biblical principles can go a long way toward relieving money worries.

What about those situations in which a husband cannot financially provide because of unemployment or disability? A wife can help by acknowledging the other ways he does provide, such as giving spiritual leadership, caring for the children, praying for their (and her) well-being.

Another concern he may have is not accomplishing what he's wanted to do, that he's wasting his life. This is the core struggle for George Bailey in *It's a Wonderful Life*. Young George desired adventure and the most exciting sounds in the world: "anchor chains, plane motors, and train whistles." Life's curveballs led him to stay in the little town where he grew up, marry the girl next door, settle into an old fixer-upper, and work in the business his father started.

Then financial disaster sets off an existential crisis, leaving George feeling that he's squandered his whole life. Yet all hope is not lost: Clarence, an angel just trying to earn his wings, shows George what would have happened if he'd never been born, noting: "Each man's life touches so many other lives. When he isn't around, he leaves an awful hole, doesn't he."

When a husband is worrying that he's wasted his life, a wife can help by being his own Clarence. She can reflect with him on what they've accomplished together—both the "big" and the "little." Also, couples can spend time talking about their future goals and aspirations. Maybe he'll never pitch a no-hitter in the World Series, but he can still complete that 5K, and together they might visit the Baseball Hall of Fame.

How Husbands Can Help Their Wives

The alarm goes off; Cassie's eyes immediately pop open. It's Monday morning, time to get everyone up, dressed, fed, and out the door. She slips quietly out of bed to avoid waking David. *He's been working so much. He needs his rest.*

Her body goes through the motions of letting out the dogs, making coffee, packing lunches . . . but her mind is all over the place. She wonders if her son had another nosebleed last night and whether the new medicine is causing the problem. She frets over her daughter's continuing struggles with reading. Making a mental note to call her mother this afternoon to find out what the doctor said, she sadly remembers how much older Mom sounded on the phone yesterday. At the very back of her thoughts is the nagging concern for the boy her daughter accidentally rejected at the middle-school dance. *Are his feelings still hurt?*

* * * * *

Cassie's Monday morning mindset is not unusual for women in today's busy world. Much of her energy (and worry) is focused on her husband, her kids, and the rest of her family. Often she puts herself last on her own priority list—and then worries that she's not exercising enough, not interesting or pretty enough, not putting enough effort into her appearance . . . enough, *enough*, *ENOUGH!*

For a man who tends to want to fix things, his wife's wide and vast worry list can be frustrating. With all of the different what-ifs, easy fixes aren't readily at hand.

Remember: often when your wife shares her concerns it's not because she's looking to you for a solution. She may just want you to hear her, to empathize with her, to comfort her. You can help by providing her with words of reassurance and encouragement. Remind her that she is not alone and that together you can face life's challenges. Gently remind her of God's promises and the certain hope we have in Him.

My (Pam's) husband has a great way of doing this when I'm feeling overwhelmed by a situation. He reminds me of the times when we've faced other such situations. So far in our marriage we've had four children, moved seven times across three states, and grieved the loss of several dear family members. Like most couples, we've faced our share of worrisome situations. When a new one comes up, he talks about how we prayed through and sweated over these circumstances. Sometimes they turned out better than we expected. Sometimes the worst happened. Through it all we've grown closer together and closer to our Lord. In essence, he gives me a personalized "this too shall pass" message that helps me breathe deeply and relax.

In addition to providing comfort and reassurance, a husband may also help his wife combat stress through problem-solving. He can learn what fears and worries trouble her most. Then, together they can work to help her avoid those. For example, if she's concerned that he may suffer a heart attack, he can help her worry less by having regular medical checkups and following the doctor's advice for managing his health.

Wives worry about their loved ones' emotional and spiritual health as well. As mentioned above, she may worry more when she senses that her husband is worried or withdrawn. A husband can lessen these worries by sharing what's going on inside emotionally and spiritually. Praying together helps to build intimacy and connection as well, between you *and* with God.

De-Stressing As a Couple

Every marriage experiences its seasons of stress and worry. Through the previous sections we've tried to give wives and husbands the briefest of glimpses into each other's worries. In addition to the specific suggestions peppered throughout those paragraphs, here are some general stress-management techniques that can help you become a Worry-Wise couple.

Prioritize your goals and activities as a family. Overpacked schedules contribute to family stress, leaving little time to connect with God and with each other. It's important to prioritize your goals and activities as a family. Start by listing your shared values and goals. Then review your schedules to see how they line up with those goals and values. Are there activities you can adjust or eliminate?

Break down emotional walls and keep talking. Even within our families, the desire to appear as though we have it all together can keep us from being open and honest about our struggles. Add crammed schedules, and our fascination with tech toys, and the result is a lack of meaningful conversation and connection. To be worry-wise, couples need to be purposeful in setting aside time for real conversation.

Communicate your love and support. Worry and anxiety can take a heavy toll on a couple. When one spouse is struggling with worry, it's key that the other spouse continues to convey love and support. It's also crucial to look beyond the worry— that is, to not let your spouse's struggle with anxiety define who he/she is.

Pray together and connect with God as a couple. In our study, praying was one of the most common ways of coping with worry.

Praying together allows you to share your concerns with each other and come together to set them before your heavenly Father. This draws you closer to each other and to your Lord.

Exercise together. Physical activity is a wonderfully effective stress reliever. Whether you prefer an easy stroll around the park or a hard-hitting game of racquetball, exercise pumps up endorphins, clears the mind, and can leave you with a renewed sense of optimism.

Bring calm back to your house. Together you and your spouse set the tone in your home. One foundational Worry-Wise strategy is to consciously work toward calm. Understanding each family member's worry profile, forging a toolbox of de-stressing techniques, and having those ready for when worries surface, set the stage for restoring and maintaining a peaceful home.

Consider seeing a Christian therapist or talk to your pastor. As we said in chapter 6, severe fears and anxieties—those that interfere with daily life—may require outside intervention. At those times, consulting your pastor and a Christian therapist is the best Worry-Wise strategy.

* * * * *

Sometimes, when a spouse is worried, what he/she needs most is reassurance and comfort. It might come in the form of a hug, some heartfelt words, or time spent together. It helps a worried loved one to know that, whatever happens, you will be there with love. On other occasions, a spouse needs to be shown how to let go of worry rather than dwell on it—and this may involve the help of a professional. Regardless, strive to look on the bright side of a struggle and to voice optimism. Responding with hope and confidence can remind your mate that problems are temporary and that tomorrow is another day. Bouncing back with a can-do attitude will help him or her to do the same.

Worry-Wise and Live Well:
Action Steps for Helping Your Spouse Manage Worry

This chapter gives us a lot to think about. At this point, do you feel hopeful, or discouraged? If the latter, consider these words from Bernard M. Baruch: "The art of living lies less in eliminating our troubles than in growing with them."[3]

It could be that you and your spouse are on the verge of a new stage of spiritual growth—for you *and* your whole family. Sometimes the only way God can bless us is by breaking us. It's not easy, and it's not fun. We feel alone, wrestling and questioning, feeling fragile and full of doubts—unaware that we might actually be very close to an amazing encounter with God.

Let's explore some practical ways you can nurture peace in your spouse's life.

STEP 1: Review Yours and Your Spouse's "My Worry Profile" (see chapter 4). Did you fill out one for the two of you? If not, flip back and do so now. Considering what we've discussed in this chapter, and with your completed profile(s) in mind, it's time for the next step.

STEP 2: Apply the Worry-Wise Plan to Your Spouse (see chapter 8). Remember: Our goal is *homeostasis*—helping our loved ones move from cyclical, adrenaline-driven fear and worry and stress to a balanced mindset that's much more peaceful. And we accomplish this on three interrelated levels: our mind, our body, and our spirit. With your profiles in hand, and armed with some skills you learned in the last chapter, fill in the blanks that follow.

MIND: Identify worries plaguing your spouse's thoughts and plot a course of action.

My wife / husband, _____, often frets about _____
_____.

Here's what I will communicate as often as needed:

_____

_____

_____

_____

This is a message your spouse may need to hear repeatedly:

- An encouraging phrase that will help him or her dispute a false thought or irrational fear: e.g., "'Tension is who you think you should be. Relaxation is who you are.'[4] *Everything* will be okay. *You* will be okay."
- A Bible verse: e.g., "Do not be afraid. I am with you. Do not be terrified. I am your God. I will make you strong and help you. My powerful right hand will take good care of you. I always do what is right."[5]
- A reminder about how much God values us: e.g., "We can trust Him. He has not abandoned us; he's with us and loves us more than we can fathom."

Here are some negative behaviors I will lovingly encourage my spouse to work toward changing and some positive ones he or she can start doing:

Change: _____.
Do: _____.
Change: _____.
Do: _____.

BODY: List key ways in which you'll strive to improve your relational health.

Diet: _____.
Exercise: _____.
Healthcare Visits: _____.
Ways to Relax: _____.
Family Connections: _____.
Sleep: _____.

SPIRIT: Consider how you can encourage your spouse to turn to God when troubles hit and so avoid spiraling into the fear-worry-stress cycle.

Begin by taking to heart this verse:

> I am leaving you with a gift—peace of mind and heart. And the peace I give is a gift the world cannot give. So don't be troubled or afraid.[6]

As a spouse, here's how I'll endeavor to model these words:

_____
_____
_____
_____

Here are some biblical lessons I'll share with my spouse:

_____

_____

_____

Here are some practical steps we can take together that will help build our trust in God and decrease stress in our relationship:

_____

_____

_____

STEP 3: De-stress as a couple. Refer back to this chapter's advice (under "De-Stressing As a Couple," p.188), then examine each point below. Which do you and your spouse need to begin doing or improve?

- Prioritize your relational goals and activities.
- Break down emotional walls and keep talking.
- Communicate your love and support.
- Pray together and connect with God as a couple.
- Exercise together.
- Bring calm back to your household.
- Talk about seeing a Christian therapist or talk to your pastor.

STEP 4: Learn and prioritize your spouse's communication style. This is a crucial step in helping—not pushing away—your spouse. Ask yourself this: What kinds of conversations, words, or phrases cause walls to go up between us? (How can I avoid these things—and work on tearing down existing walls?) How can I improve communication with him/her?

Consider this advice from Dr. Phil:

> Be honest but diplomatic in communicating what you think are your partner's needs. Remember to characterize them in an uncritical way . . . Explain to your partner that the needs you've discerned are merely a starting place for further discussions. Allow your partner to disagree and replace your interpretation of a need with one of his/her own. Stay patient. Don't forget that because you've been doing most of the work, you are probably way ahead of your partner in evolution of your thinking about your relationship. [But no need to mention this!][7]

Our Research Says . . .

- Relationships can become strained when a spouse struggles with anxiety. For example, one study found that those suffering with Generalized Anxiety Disorder are twice as likely to have a relationship problem and three times as likely to avoid intimacy with their spouse.
- Research indicates that couples who pray and read the Bible together at home enjoy higher

levels of satisfaction in their marriage. Moreover, a strong spiritual bond helps to buffer the stresses of life.

Recap and Reflect
Talking Points for Couples or Group Study

• •

Much of our day is spent trying to make our hectic lives work *without* God in the center. Yet we still expect Him to cooperate with us—relating to us on *our* terms, revolving around *our* plans, solving problems so we can live the way *we* want to live. And, when turmoil hits, what happens? More turmoil.

> *Do I find myself blaming God when stress hits? How will I change this?*

• Share some practical steps you can take to reduce turmoil.

Marjorie Thompson says:

> While the truth that we cannot escape God's all-seeing eye may weigh us down at times, it is finally the only remedy for our uneasiness. If we wish to hide from the penetrating gaze of holy love, it is because we know it falls on what is unholy and unloving within us. Only under God's steady gaze of love are we able to find the healing and restoration we so desperately need.[8]

• Share two changes that you and your spouse will make.

HOW TO HELP AN ANXIOUS CHILD

WHAT PARENTS MUST KNOW—AND DO

*Worry is a cycle of inefficient thoughts
whirling around a center of fear.*[1]
CORRIE TEN BOOM

In chapter 3 we briefly mentioned four-year-old Evan, who feels so anxious that his preschool teachers are out of ideas about how to help him. The moment his mom drops him off at the beginning of the day, heightened fear washes over him.

"Honey, can you tell me what hurts?" his teacher asks, gently placing her hand on his shoulder.

Evan jerks away with a loud *"NO!"* and dashes wildly to the coat cubbies. He squeezes into one, covers his face with anything he can lay his hands on, and begins to sob uncontrollably.

What's going on? A preschooler's world should be filled with awe and wonder—not panic and anguish.

* * * * *

Standing by the kitchen door, Noah goes through his backpack one more time. *Are all the homework sheets in here? My library book? My lunch?*

"Noah, come on. We're going to be late!" his mother calls.

He races out to the car, backpack slung over his shoulder and science study guide clutched in his hand. As he straps in, his heart begins to race. He has only thirty more minutes until his teacher will pass out the next exam.

His stomach churns as he remembers how fun school seemed last year. "Why do we have to have so many tests in third grade?" Noah asks plaintively.

"Your teachers are going to expect more as you grow up," his mom replies.

"But I've done all my homework. She knows I know it. Why do I have to take a test too? I always do bad on tests." Tears come to his eyes as he thinks about how much he's studied, how tired he is, and how much his stomach hurts. "Can't I just stay home today? *Please?*"

* * * * *

Kellie certainly seems well-adjusted and lighthearted. The bubbly thirteen-year-old flashes a nervous grin at the boys walking by her locker, then laughs at her best friend's joke. On the outside, she looks like most other kids at her school.

But the jumbled-up emotions inside are telling another story.

I feel like I'm in a dark, cold cell, she writes in her journal. *It's really scary because I just can't find a way out. I'm worried all the time—about everything. Is Dad going to find another job? Will we get to keep our house? Is Mom okay? She cries all the time. It's like my life is falling apart, and I feel so lonely.*

Kellie scribbles one last line: *Something's got to change. I can't go on like this any more.*

Growing Up Stressed:
To What Extent Are Parents at Fault?

It's a bit unnerving, and it's definitely humbling, yet it's a reality of parenting: Our children are "watching" us, with every sense and with all their intuition. And, during their early years, their brains are like sponges, soaking up our words, our emotions, our signals, our deliberations, our choices, our actions, our habits.

So what are we really teaching them?

They learn how to follow Christ as they pattern their lives after ours. Little boys learn to be husbands and dads by what they see us *do*; little girls learn to be wives and moms in the same way. They observe and often absorb our attitudes and imitate our communication styles. When they launch into adulthood, their core beliefs about faith and relationships often resemble ours.

Note the word *often*. Some children come to reject their parents' values. (More on that in chapter 11.) Either way, though, here's what I (Arnie) have observed: In most households, children learn how to worry *from us*.

And, whether or not we want to admit it, children are becoming increasingly anxious.

"We are getting requests for therapy for younger-age children," says Dr. Trina Young-Greer, clinical psychologist and executive director at Genesis Counseling Center in Hampton, Virginia.[2] "Before, it was the occasional child. Now we have parents calling in with very young children . . . I can't say the problem is causation, but there does seem to be a correlation with media, the culture at large, and the examples set by authorities in their lives."

In other words, examples *we* set.

As with adults, worry stirs in the hearts of children for a wide variety of reasons: some are genetically prone to be anxious; some have an overproduction of adrenaline in their bodies (flip back to chapters 5–6 for much more on this topic); some are battling emotional disorders; others are victims of trauma, from accidents and relational loss to bullying and abuse.

And, as we've seen, diet, health, lifestyle, and sleep affect everyone's emotional state.

Yet for the largest percentage of children—those who are generally healthy, who are being raised in stable homes, and who have the support of loving parents—here's the biggest trigger: Their degree of anxiety is based on the amount of stress in their families and how their parents are handling it. In other words, our kids worry about what we worry about . . . and we're actually teaching them to do it.

Let's look at a couple different ways by which we transmit worry to our kids. The first is through our own handling of worry. Studies by the American Psychological Association reveal that children worry more than their parents know *and* pick up on their parents' worries, even when the adults think they're hiding it well. According to a 2010 APA study, when their parents are stressed or worried, nearly half of tweens and one-third of teens say that they feel sad.[3] Tweens and teens also worry and feel frustrated in response to their parents' stress.

Second, we transmit worry through how we respond to our children's anxious moments. We have a strong instinct to protect them physically, emotionally, and spiritually. *How* we protect them, how we teach them to address (or exit) situations, and how we equip them to deal with challenges, has a tremendous impact. It's a fine balance between stepping in and taking care of things for them and giving them the support, skills, and encouragement they need to handle it themselves. Every child has a unique personality and his/her own path through development and into maturity; nevertheless, our imperfections and errors play a significant role here, and "upsetting the balance" contributes to kids' worrying. Specifically, when we step in to shield or shelter our child when we should be supporting and encouraging, we can send him the message that he's not capable of dealing with it. The more and the longer he thinks he's not able, the more he's likely to worry, especially about situations when Mom and Dad aren't around.

I (Pam) have found myself rescuing my kids when instead I needed to be encouraging and coaching. I remember several years ago taking my four children to an indoor play area at a local restaurant.

My son, then a preschooler, was eager to follow his big sisters everywhere. That day he tailed them to the top of the play structure—and then stopped short when they took the slide back down. He stood up there, gazing down, his brown eyes big with fright. I tried coaxing him, telling him how *FUN* it would be to slide, also having his sisters go back up and show him again how to do it. He refused to move. Then he sat down and cried, saying he was too scared.

So . . . I crawled up the slide to get him. (Did I mention it was one of those curvy tunnel slides? Not my finest moment.) He stopped crying when his feet were back on the ground. Yet after that day my son's fears increased. He didn't want to go on the play structure at all and was now afraid to go down the slide in the *park* by himself—something he'd been doing on his own for months. It took a while to rebuild his confidence again after my ill-timed rescue mission.

I learned from this experience that there will be times when what our kids need most is help facing their fears. In subsequent years I've stood by shouting words of encouragement (sometimes aloud, sometimes just in my head) as they've navigated camp challenge courses, competed in spelling bees, and performed onstage. Each time it's been such a joy to see the confidence and triumph on their faces as they realize they *are* capable, despite their worries.

The Stuff of Kids' Worries

As an adult, it's tempting to view childhood through rose-colored glasses. When you're dealing with the daily pressures of work, budgets, and health scares, we can be enticed to think that a kid's world is worry-free. This is not the case. Similar to adults, kids fret about the things none of us can control—economic downturns, random violence, terrorism, the death of a pet, car crashes. They also worry about plenty of things moms and dads *can* do something about: how to succeed in school, how to make and keep friends, how to handle seasonal (or everyday) trials.

Put yourself in your child's shoes. Each day she must navigate hundreds of conflicting messages from the media, friends, leaders, and family. The internet and the TV are lightning rods, pumping waves of anxiety into young, impressionable minds.[4] And classrooms buzz with pop culture temptations, like cool-crowd fads, or the latest games and gadgets that for some kids are just out of reach, yet many are being taught to believe that "none of us can live without." Add to the mix a generation that reveres *all things instant*, and voilà: a ticking time bomb of stress.

Observes Dr. Young-Greer,

Today, very young children are concerned about how they look. If a child feels as if she looks different, she may ask herself, *Can I look like those people I see on TV and online? Will I fit in?* To a degree, as we consider what we know through developmental psychology, these things can be normal. There are points throughout our lives when we all feel more self-conscious. But what I'm starting to observe in young children are the self-conscious frustrations that, in past years, were more common among middle-school kids.[5]

Our children's world is much more media-focused and inter-wired than it was just a generation ago. It's more time-pressured as well. For example, between 1981 and 1997 free time and play time for American children declined by an average of fifteen hours per week—more than two hours a day.[6] Time in unstructured outdoor activities, family mealtimes, and family conversations also decreased. At the same time, hours devoted to structured sports and passive spectator sports (e.g., watching a sibling play) have increased dramatically. Evidence suggests that a lack of free time and being overscheduled in structured activities leads to more anxiety.[7]

* * * * *

What can we do to unplug the fear-worry-stress cycle in our homes and help our kids reclaim the healthy childhood they deserve?

The answers form the remainder of this chapter.

The following paragraphs emphasize stress-management techniques that are focused on specific developmental stages. Let's move in for a closer look at the world our children must navigate and gain some insights into what every parent must know—and *do*.

Preschoolers

During the first two to three years of life, a kid learns to relate to others, express herself with words, and comprehend language. It's a time to walk, to fall down and stand up again; a time to sing, laugh, feed and dress themselves, and distinguish pictures and colors.

Preschoolers want desperately to please and emulate their parents. We find them running their toy lawnmower behind Dad or Mom in the yard; sliding their plastic vacuum cleaner around the house, going over each inch of carpet already covered by the Hoover; revel in singing their first version of the ABCs. Over and over they'll practice their new proficiency of language; they add more than two hundred new words to their vocabulary between ages two and four, and most likely they'll learn to write their name.

This is the age of "Why is the sky blue? Can I eat from the dog's bowl? [. . . But why? *He* likes it. . . .] How does [this, and that, and everything else] work?" Preschoolers are curious to the max, exploring their world with abandon and very resistant to rules. As every parent knows, working with them can feel like herding cats.

What They Worry About

Preschoolers will worry about very simple things that are part of their everyday world: not pleasing their parents, having to share a toy they love, or being left out. They may experience frustrations over communication difficulties, particularly if they're somewhat behind in their development. In his own words, a preschooler might express his reason for stress as "Mommy is yelling," or "Mean people are hurting me."

Between the ages of two and four, kids develop a strong sense of fairness and equality. They're learning to share but worry that something might be taken away from them. They're gaining a sense of right and wrong and appreciation for respect, authority, and consequences. And they're beginning to clue in to concepts like "possession" and "loss."

This is also when they start to learn about and understand who God is and to think about His love for them. They recite simple prayers and express their love for God. Reminding them that God will take care of them helps these precious little ones deal with stressful situations.

One spring day my (Pam's) daughters were playing on the back deck. They were three and four at that time and generally got along very well. This day, though, they just couldn't agree. Finally, Charis ran inside saying she was going to play by herself. When Gloria shouted from the deck, "Well, Jesus is still with me!" Charis indignantly replied, "He's with me too!"

When my (Michael's) son, Christopher, was about four, he was in our back yard watching me struggle with decorative torches I was placing around the patio. These weren't the simple bamboo style you stick into the ground and light. (They were annoyingly complicated and required assembly.) As I grappled to put one together, none of the parts seemed to fit.

After watching thoughtfully for a few minutes, Christopher tugged on my shirt and said, "God says to turn it the other way."

I looked down and smiled. "Really—God told you that?!"

He nodded his head, with a very serious look on his face. So, following his instructions, I turned the torch the opposite way. Amazingly, it fell right into place. Christopher nodded once and began playing with some toy trucks.

Simple prayers lead to simple faith—a basic building block to relationship with God.

What You Can Do

- Reassure your preschooler frequently that he's safe and that all will be okay in your home. This is particularly important at times when he may be anxious, such as when there's a storm or he hears of something bad happening in the world.
- Make sure preschoolers understand the routines and rules. Correction should be consistent and fair. Preschoolers thrive when their world is predictable.
- Use simple time-out discipline techniques and be consistent to reinforce the solidity and security of your parental love and authority. This helps preschoolers feel more secure and to worry less.
- Be sensitive to verbal and nonverbal signals that your child is worried or anxious.
- Spend time snuggling and talking about what's bugging him or her. Give your complete attention, and give lots of hugs in the process.
- Model healthy conflict resolution in your home, working through differences with family members and avoiding grudges. Seeing parents argue can be very stressful for children. However, hiding all conflicts from them is nearly impossible and can be ineffective as kids pick up on the tension in the air. Handling minor, everyday disagreements calmly in their presence can teach them the value of compromise, how to use words carefully, and other skills they will need.

Explains Tess Cox (see chapter 6), who for more than three decades has treated the physical and emotional wounds of kids and their families from all over the world:

> I always tell preschoolers, "Use your words," and I say the same thing to moms and dads. Work out differences and problems with one another. This kind of respectful interaction between parents will set the example and will be absorbed by a preschooler.

It builds a strong foundation for respectful interactions between parents and children.[8]

Kindergarteners to Third Graders

Children in this age group are learning to sit still in group settings and practice even greater self-control. They're beginning to understand the concepts of mercy, justice, forgiveness, and loyalty, in their relationships with peers, with their parents, and with God.

During this time they—especially girls—begin to value friendship and love to give little gifts to their closest friends. Just as they had to learn to share their toys, they also must learn to share their pals. They need to realize that it's okay if their BFF is playing with someone else too.

Their energy level is to be envied. For fear of being singled out, they can be shy and not so self-expressive one moment . . . and then with whiplash-inducing inertia become boisterous and squirrely the next. As they practice the art of friendship, many can easily get their feelings hurt. What's more, they commonly have acute awareness of felt embarrassment and humiliation if they perceive themselves to be different from or singled out by their peers.

What They Worry About

- Not pleasing their parents; losing their parents
- Doing well in school; handling assignments
- Rejection by their peers
- Sports performance—especially if they feel they stand out in a negative way
- Personal safety and bullying

As the psychiatrist Mona Spiegel writes,

> Our expectations of ourselves and our children have risen at the speed of new versions of Windows. Babies are taken to

"enrichment" classes, toddlers are expected to have "play dates," and preschoolers are required to know their numbers and letters by the time they enter kindergarten.[9] And it only gets worse. Five-year-olds must have computer skills and fifteen-year-olds top AP and PSAT scores. The pressure is on all of us to produce outstanding results, both in our personal and professional lives. A feeling of urgency prevails, while our sense of safety declines.[10]

What You Can Do

I (Arnie) have repeatedly seen that parents who are absent or too busy to show an interest in the endeavors, successes, failures, and fears of their child can exponentially increase their worry quotient. Adding to the "anxiety mix," husbands and wives who disrespect each other and argue harshly can contribute to a child's behavior problems, especially with this age group. Also, keeping children so busy that they don't have time to rest or play and be creative—that is, too much activity, just like too little—can cause anxiety that leads to sleep and behavior disturbances and even increased blood pressure.

If you find your family running from event to event, it's time to slow down and rethink priorities. Consider ways of decreasing the stress in your home by scheduling plenty of downtime. Other worry-free strategies for grade-schoolers:

- Practice relaxation techniques together. Work with her to figure out what helps her relax most. If she often finds herself stressed or worried, develop a "What to Do When I'm Worried" action plan she can use to neutralize worry.
- Talk through what's bugging him, especially issues or situations dealing with self-esteem, identity, and friendships. Be his advocate without embarrassing him.

- Talk proactively about how to deal with mistakes and failures as well as victories and team-playing. If the issue is bullying, always take immediate action.

Fourth Graders to Seventh Graders: The Tween Years

Children in this age group often struggle with self-esteem and peer acceptance. Cliques are a way of life, which means that rejection can feel like a fate worse than death. Kids create "tribes" where they are accepted and feel protected.

As tweens are beginning to feel more a part of the larger world around them, they're often aware of and concerned about world events: war, pollution, global warming, endangered animals, natural disasters. Cognitively they're able to imagine many more what-if scenarios.

They're also acutely aware of social norms, music, pop culture, and latest trends. They're apt to have a closer relationship with their phone than with their parents. Tweeting, texting, and online video games against other players hold a huge slice of their attention. In addition, they're starting to exercise greater independence and want to begin making their own decisions.

What They Worry About

In our studies, tweens most often worried about school. This includes both how they're doing academically and their relationships with teachers and friends: *I worry about . . .*

> . . . *not doing well in math.*
> . . . *my grades.*
> . . . *having to answer a question in class.*
> . . . *friends in class, and classmates and teachers.*
> . . . *being liked at school.*

*. . . starting middle school, and wondering if I'll attend
     my school of choice.*

Family also is frequently high on the tween worry list. Many of
their concerns are not merely general—for example, about safety
and about remaining together—but also reflect growing awareness
of the larger world and of life's trials: *I worry about . . .*

. . . my dad, with the military in Afghanistan.
. . . my parents dying.
. . . not seeing my dad.
. . . my family getting sick.
. . . my other mommy doing drugs and dying.
. . . Mom and Dad fighting.

Compared with younger children, tweens are much more likely to be
strongly influenced by looks and by the appearance of both friends
and celebrities. They worry about how they look, about fitting in,
and about losing their tribe.

What You Can Do
Any parental effort to single out a child and "make her different"
from her peers usually will be met with fierce opposition. Frequently,
the increasing independence of children this age is a testing ground
for parents, who are learning to trust what they've taught their child
while at the same time stressing over risks and dangers she may face.

Again, parents' stress will affect the child's stress level as well.
It is a delicate balance of children trying to build up their "trust
bank" with parents, and the parents' challenge of allowing them to
make "withdrawals" when opportunities arise for decision-making
and independence.

It's essential that you connect daily with your tween—answering questions, addressing fears, discussing spiritual principles, and

nurturing self-confidence. If he seems to be worried about something, ask about it. Encourage him to put what's bugging him into words; listen attentively as he shares. If he's generally quiet, you may want to gently ask how he's doing when you know he's encountered something stressful. You may find that talking during a shared activity (shooting hoops, or painting a room) is more comfortable and productive for him.

Seek out your tween privately to reassure him that you want to be his resource when he hears things from others that confuse or challenge him. Encourage him that while there's a lot to learn, his friends are living out the same adventure. Remind him that part of your job during this time is to "have his back" and to help him learn the truth so he can make good decisions with good results.

Sharing stories about your own childhood and adolescence can help your tween realize you've been through this and can be a great resource. Speak to her like an adult. If her behavior is a problem, write up a contract and treat the situation as though you are business partners.

Sometimes just talking and opening the door to release what's inside is enough to lighten the load. But make sure you teach her to deal constructively with difficult circumstances. Having a family culture that affirms and accepts her provides a much-needed safe haven, and respect goes a long way at this age; at the same time it's important to have established ground rules that allow you access to her life, in order to help ensure that she stays out of certain dangers.

Mom and Dad to the Rescue:
Three Ways to Boost a Tween's Confidence

Tweens need positive messages in order to build resilience and maintain an accurate portrait of who they are. In this stage they're between the periods of being entirely a child and being entirely a teen. They're starting to want that sense of their own identity.

So, here are some steps a parent would be wise to take:

Emphasize his innate worth. Communicate to him in as many ways as you can that "you are exactly who God created you to be, and very, very valuable—*just as you are.*"

Help her build an accurate and healthy identity. The proficient kids—athletically, academically, artistically, and so on—tend to be the ones who get (seemingly) all the attention; the ones held up by others as the standard for us all. God doesn't value gold medalists more or give special love to A+ students. Build into your child a sense of self that's biblically on target.

Establish together-time. Developmentally, children this age want to feel they're good at something, knowing that they can accomplish a task. It doesn't have to be every day, but strive to spend devoted time with your children. Special moments provide kids with (1) a place of safety, and (2) an opportunity for Dad and Mom to speak encouraging words into their child's life.

"'Together times' can also reinforce in children the sense that, 'Yeah, I can do this. I'm proficient at something; I can be a good soccer player. I'm a good friend," explains Dr. Young-Greer.[11] She points out that such moments and times can be very simple:

- A hug in the morning
- Speaking words of blessing as he/she heads out the door
- A bedtime story
- Kicking the soccer ball in the backyard

- Laughing about crazy commercials
- Making and sharing a snack together[12]

Shared experiences over a period of time have a cumulative effect of building up our kids, helping them to become men and women of God. Children end up with more accurate identities, and they begin to feel safer around their parents. The family unit represents a safe harbor. So as the storms will come, they'll know exactly where to retreat—the arms of a loving parent.[13]

Moms and dads would be wise to build strong foundations right now. Ongoing shared experiences and together-times are vital. Consider this: the tween years represent one of our last seasons to connect before they become much more independent and eventually launch out on their own. See this as a phenomenal opportunity.

Teenagers

As we all know, adolescence is a tumultuous time of hormones, identity crises, relationships with the opposite sex, limits-testing, titanic tantrums, lengthy silences, and parental panic. Wait, doesn't some of this sound like we're back at the two-year-old phase again? Emotionally, this isn't too different.

The current culture of high school students is part of what's known as the Millennial Generation. They typically live at home longer, attend college closer to home, rely heavily on their parents' opinions, and seek their approval consistently before making big decisions. These teens get most of their info through technological means, they watch less TV, and they live in "real time" through social networking sites and Twitter.

Grades begin to take on more value as they grow toward their junior year and begin to think about applying to college or technical school. School workload increases, and the pressure to succeed and fulfill expectations can be tremendous. Teens often become even more time-crunched with part-time jobs, sports, clubs, and social activities. Sleep often gets sacrificed along the way, even though teens need more sleep to stay healthy than do younger children and adults.

What They Worry About

The question might be better asked, "What *don't* they worry about?"

Body image and physical changes occur at wild rates. Coupled with opposite-sex attraction and an overwhelming felt need to avoid rejection, thought processes and perception of reality can become quite skewed and may send teens into tailspins. Inevitable conflict with parents can leave them feeling alone in their decision-making, especially if theirs and their parents' desires are in direct opposition.

Worries can range from the mundane ("do I have enough gas to get to practice?" or "do I have pizza money to hang with my friends?") to the life-changing ("should I have sex?"/"should I use contraception?" or "should I try cigarettes/marijuana?"). Making decisions with desirable outcomes is extremely difficult when you can only see life in the moment and have little concept of future consequences.

Teens may find it difficult to imagine the future except in the framework of fantasy. They fear being alone, are deathly scared of rejection from peers (especially the other gender), and worry about abandonment by their tribe. Their perspective is constantly colored by opinion, peer pressure, and situational ethics, yet without the wisdom of experience to handle any of it. This pile of concern can stack up the worry and anxiety, sometimes on a daily basis.

Those who come from broken homes often find themselves searching for security, love, and acceptance, even if that comes from insecure and dangerous individuals or groups. Even though they're struggling for independence, more than ever they need solid relationships with adults they respect to help them find balance . . . adults who will stay connected to them and struggle with them and tell them the truth.

What You Can Do

Respect where they are, and stay connected. Educate yourself about current problems, social pressures, and issues affecting children today in his/her age bracket. These issues and factors are constantly shifting, but by educating yourself through research and reading and conversing consistently with others (including other parents and those in school authority), you can gather enough information to understand what's happening in your child's larger world and to pray for him/her, especially prior to broaching certain subjects with them.

Once "in the know," you can offer big-picture perspectives. Maybe your son is worried about whether he'll make the team. Let him know that regardless of the outcome, you're proud of him. He tried out and gave it his best shot. If it's not to be, he'll have time and energy to dedicate to something else that inspires and challenges him.

Perhaps she's feeling left out that her friends are partying and want her to join them, or her friends are talking about having sex with their boyfriends. Helping her to acknowledge her struggle, and listening intently to her, to gain understanding—as much as if not more so than to give advice—gives you the opportunity to speak with her like the adult she is becoming and to strengthen your relationship together.

Be willing to let *her* teach *you*. Always approach the subject without heightened emotion and with genuine curiosity. Give her your attention, and ask informed questions so that she perceives you already know something about the pressures she's facing.

Teens believe that the bad things they worry about come true much more than adults do (in part, this may be a result of teens having less life experience). Teens and young adults also feel less comfortable with uncertainty. Once engaged, and without minimizing her feelings, explain that many problems are temporary and solvable, and that there will be better days and other opportunities to try again. Providing a long-term perspective is crucial.

Speak frankly and openly about pressures, drugs, the law, and long-term consequences. Don't preach at him; search God's Word with him and give him opportunities to interpret the words himself. This can give you chances to share your perspective also.

The point here is to treat your child with respect and gravity and take advantage of the opportunity to teach him to keep problems in perspective. This can lessen his worry and help build strength, resilience, and the optimism to try again. At this stage he's very quickly launching into the world, so make the most of the time you have left. Pray with him and over him daily.

Finally, pray for yourself. You will need all the peace, patience, kindness, wisdom, gentleness, and self-control God promises to give you if you ask.

A Checklist of Anxious Behavior

Suspect your child is struggling with worry? Look for these signs:

- Frequent crying
- Frequent headaches and/or upset stomach
- Lack of interest in once-loved activities
- Inability to look an adult in the eye
- Inability to stay focused or to concentrate
- Withdrawal from social interactions
- Sudden drop in grades
- Refusal to go to school
- Constant restlessness

- Problems going to bed and staying asleep
- Feeling tired and worn out nearly all day every day
- *For Teens:* Battling heavy guilt or shame on a daily basis
- *For Teens:* Feelings of worthlessness—to the point of not being able to function with a positive demeanor
- *For Teens:* Weight loss (without trying to lose) or weight gain (more than 5% of body weight in one month), loss of appetite or increased appetite
- *For Teens:* Self-medication with alcohol or other substances

Reading the Worry Signs

In Baton Rouge, Louisiana, Jennifer is confused. Her nine-year-old, Olivia, has retreated to her bedroom after barely touching supper.

What's happened to my little chatterbox? Jennifer asks herself. *She barely takes a breath between stories about her favorite bands and books . . . and girl gossip. And, she can never get enough of my cooking. Something isn't right with her.*

Several hundred miles away, in Portland, Maine, John is trying to figure out why his eleven-year-old won't shoot hoops or do anything else with him. Lately, Ethan just hasn't been the same happy kid, usually eager to hang out with the family.

"It's like we're raising Dr. Jekyll and Mr. Hyde," he tells his wife. "He's withdrawn and sad—like he's seriously stressing over something. The question is, *what?*"

* * * * *

Both parents have reason to be alarmed. While an abrupt change in behavior feels like an hourly occurrence in the lives of teenagers, in young children and tweens it's often the first clue that they may be worried about something.

"A talkative kid who clams up for days, or is on a pendulum swing from happy to sad, should be taken seriously by parents," says Cox. "Children cope with worry and anxiety in very different ways from adults."[14] So, for one thing, we shouldn't merely interpret their apparent feelings through the lens of our own emotions. Here are some other signs to look for.

For Young Kids

Soiling. This is a classic red flag for children who've been potty trained. If there isn't a medical problem—such as a urinary tract infection—probably there is an issue with worry, or possibly he/she has gone through something distressing or traumatic.

For All Kids

Sudden changes in appetite. Some children are picky eaters. But we should be concerned if they suddenly refuse to eat something they used to enjoy. Emotional eating (particularly snacks and junk food) also can be pointing to a problem.

Sudden changes in sleep patterns, especially if they aren't sleeping through the night. Sleep disturbance can be a big clue that something's wrong. At times, most children will fight sleep. But parents should take note if it's recurring, or if children have nightmares and bad dreams more often than occasionally.

Expressions of sadness. Some young children are able to verbalize well how they feel. "Maybe this is a result of our digital age," says Dr. Young-Greer, "but I'm often amazed at how a four-year-old is sometimes able to tell me, 'I'm sad. I'm upset.'"[15] It's plain that if your child expresses sadness in this way, you need to listen and tune in to what's going on. The goal is to get to the root of why he/she is worried.

For Teenagers

Major depressive disorder. Here are some symptoms teens commonly experience when they have a major depressive disorder. Someone with this condition will experience at least five of these symptoms for more than two weeks in such a way that it interferes with daily life.

- Irritable or sad most of the day or all day long
- No longer interested in once-loved activities
- Weight loss (without trying to lose) or weight gain (more than 5% of body weight in one month), loss of appetite or increased appetite.
- Difficulty sleeping, or sleeping too much nearly every day
- Feeling tired and worn out nearly all day every day
- Restlessness
- Battling with heavy guilt on a daily basis
- Feelings of worthlessness—to the point of not being able to function with a positive demeanor
- Lack of ability to concentrate or make decisions

Preparing a Plan of Peace for Stressful Times

While we all want childhood to be a carefree time for our kids, the world has become a more dangerous and stressful place. Gone are the days when it was safe for a kid to ride his bike endlessly up and down the street or disappear all day at a friend's house. I (Michael) cringe when I think about my eleven-year-old son walking home from school alone. While he's a big, tough kid, some bigger threats lurk in our neighborhood.

"Dad, what's a gangster?" he nonchalantly asked me when he was seven.

"Where'd you hear that word?" I asked, my heart skipping a beat.

"At school."

"Was it in a book you're reading—or a story your teacher shared?"

"Nope," Christopher said. "This boy told me his brother is a gangster—and that he's going to be one too."

I groaned. Here I thought moving from a city to a small town would protect my family from stuff exactly like this.

Remember the days when making the basketball team or the cheerleading squad were among a kid's greatest challenges? (For me, it was figuring out how to get a girl to talk to me!) But the world in which my son is growing up is filled with more insidious and unpredictable threats: kidnappers, shooters, terrorists, bullies (physical and virtual) . . . and, yes, Midwest gangs. Every day he's bombarded with repulsive messages in cyberspace.

For some of his friends, life isn't any better or safer on the home front. Financial uncertainty and joblessness have torn families apart. And there's more, so much more: addictions, eroding values, gender confusion, political correctness, lukewarm faith . . . the list goes on and on. All this stuff chips away at the foundation of civilized society: *the family unit.*

Here's how sociologist Daniel Yankelovich explains our plight:

> Americans suspect that the nation's economic difficulties are rooted not in technical economic forces (for example, exchange rates or capital formation) but in fundamental moral causes.
>
> There exists a deeply intuitive sense that the success of a market-based economy depends on a highly developed

social morality—trustworthiness, honesty, concern for future generations, an ethic of service to others, a humane society that takes care of those in need, frugality instead of greed, high standards of quality and concern for community.

These economically desirable social values, in turn, are seen as rooted in family values. Thus the link in public thinking between a healthy family and a robust economy, though indirect, is clear and firm.[16]

Your kids want a deeper connection with you. They need to hear, "I love you," "I'm proud of you," and "I won't give up on you."

They need you to be there for them.

Many children are stressed. Many are anxious. Far too many feel constant pressure; now, more than ever, they need change. They long to be accepted by their peers, but most important, whether or not they're in a place to admit it, they hunger for family support and connection.[17]

They're counting on you to teach them, protect them, and look after their well-being in this often frightening world. They need you to equip them to navigate life as Christ-followers, secure in their true identity and trusting in the promises of the one true God.

Worry-Wise . . . and Live Well:
Action Steps for Helping Kids Manage Worry

Having looked at what makes most kids tick at different stages of development, and having further considered what they fret about and how parents can help, let's get moving with practical ways you can help apply all of this to your family.

STEP 1: Review Your Child's "My Worry Profile" (chapter 4). Did you fill out one for each child in your care? If not, flip back and do so now. With your completed worry profile(s) in mind, and pondering what we've discussed in this chapter, it's time for the next step.

STEP 2: Apply the Worry-Wise Plan (chapter 8) to Your Children. Remember: Our goal is *homeostasis*—moving our kids from an adrenaline-filled worry cycle to a balanced mindset that's hopefully much more peaceful. We accomplish this in three interrelated facets: mind, body, and spirit. With your profiles in hand, and armed with skills you've learned here, fill in the blanks that follow.

MIND: Identify worries plaguing your kids' thoughts and plot a course of action.

"My child / teen, _____, often frets about _____
_____."

Here's what I will communicate as often as needed:

_____
_____
_____

This is a message your child may need to hear repeatedly:

- An encouraging phrase that will help him/her dispute a false thought or irrational fear: e.g., "Your weight is just right" or "You are gifted and talented"

or "You have everything you need to become exactly who God created you to be."
- A verse: e.g., "The LORD is good, a refuge in times of trouble. He cares for those who trust in him."[18]
- A reminder about how much he/she is loved and valued by God. "You are a priceless, one-of-a-kind masterpiece."

Here are some negative behaviors my family will work toward changing and some positive ones we will start doing:

Change: _____.
Do: _____.
Change: _____.
Do: _____.
Change: _____.
Do: _____.

BODY: List key ways in which you'll strive to improve your family's health.

Diet: _____.
Exercise: _____.
Healthcare Visits: _____.
Ways to Relax: _____.
Family Connections: _____.
Sleep: _____.

SPIRIT: Consider how you can encourage your children to turn to God when troubles hit and so avoid spiraling into the fear-worry-stress cycle.

Begin by taking to heart this passage:

> Don't worry about anything; instead, pray about everything; tell God your needs, and don't forget to thank him for his answers. If you do this, you will experience God's peace, which is far more wonderful than the human mind can understand. His peace will keep your thoughts and your hearts quiet and at rest as you trust in Christ Jesus.[19]

As a parent, here's how I'll endeavor to model these words:

_____

_____

These are some biblical lessons I will teach my kids:

_____

_____

Here are some practical steps my family can take that will help build our trust in God and decrease stress in our home:

_____

_____

STEP 3: Set your household's emotional climate. Again, a child's emotions often mirror what his/her parents are experiencing. (They feel worried when we worry.) They're watching us and learning how we react to stress. On both a conscious and an unconscious level, they process and absorb the climate we set. So, one of the best things we can do is *live* Matthew 11:28–30:

Come to me [Jesus], all you who are weary and burdened, and I will give you rest. Take my yoke upon
you and learn from me, for I am gentle and humble
in heart, and you will find rest for your souls. For my
yoke is easy and my burden is light.

• Turn to prayer, not fear, when we're burdened.
• Take time to rest daily.
• Trust the Lord and His plan for our lives.

STEP 4: Don't be emotionally plastic. Yes, our kids are
watching us—that doesn't mean we hide our feelings or
portray inauthenticity about what's going on in our lives.
The emotional distancing between parents and children that
was the social norm in the early part of the twentieth century
resulted in many emotionally stilted children who eventually rebelled and allowed their emotional pendulum to swing
widely in the opposite direction. This in turn ended up defin-
ing the general societal climate of the sixties and seventies.

When you feel stressed, tell your kids (as one example):
"Jesus says that 'In this world you will have trouble. But take
heart! I have overcome the world.'[20] We believe Him. We know
that we can trust God, and because He's in control, everything ultimately is going to be okay."

After you say something like this, make sure you *live* it
in front of them.

STEP 5: Be (or become) aware of your child's emotional temperament. A child's basic personality type can
contribute to his level of anxiety and his "default" stress. Kids
who tend to be a "burden bearer" will often internalize stress,

fear, sadness, joy, and happiness and thus tend to rarely reveal true emotions. Their hearts must be pursued and mined to find the treasures within. This type does lend itself to greater anxiety and, if unaddressed, to possible depression.

Our Research Says . . .

- Tweens state that what helps most is having their parents talk with them about their worries, assist them with studies, and reassure them.
- Two out of five kids sometimes worry that their family will run out of money; one in six worries about this a lot.
- When something bad happens, tweens and teens are more likely to question whether God loves them and are less likely to meditate on Scripture.

Recap and Reflect
Talking Points for Couples or Group Study

Often our kids are worried because we're worried. As parents, we set the tone in our households.

What kinds of things do my kids worry about? Have they learned this from me? If so, what steps can I start taking to help foster a Worry-Wise family?

We're all burdened by information overload. The world is suffering; violence and mayhem seem to be at our doorstep; we battle constant fear for our kids' well-being. The fact is, our lives are hectic. Parents and children are experiencing more stress now than ever, and the fear-worry-stress cycle has been robbing our kids and tearing apart our homes.

- Make a list of what you'd like to change in your household, and jot down some ideas on how you'll be part of implementing those changes.

As we explored various stages of childhood—specifically, how a kid's world looks and feels and what he/she worries about—we discovered that they cope with worry and anxiety in very different ways from us. Naturally, much of their reaction to stress is related to where they are in their development.

- Consider your family:

  What stage of childhood has my son/daughter entered?
  What stresses are unique to his/her age, and how will I guide him/her through?

An anxious child often grows into an anxious adult. Many stressed-out kids are being raised by equally stressed-out parents. Although worry may decrease with age, it often resurfaces in times of transition or stress.

  What are some foundational biblical lessons I can instill now that will help my child in the future?

MEETING A MILLENNIAL AT THEIR POINT OF NEED

NURTURING THE PLANET'S MOST STRESSED-OUT GENERATION

With the cruelty of youth I allowed myself to be irritated by traits in my father which, in other elderly men, I have since regarded as lovable foibles.[1]

C. S. LEWIS

Snapshot of the "In-Betweeners" (born 1989–1995)

Shane, age twenty, glanced out his bedroom window and cringed. He'd spotted a group of boys playing football down the street. *That was me,* he thought to himself. *But I blew it.*

A wave of anxiety roiled up inside.

Shane was a college football player with a promising future. Now he's in a wheelchair. On a dare, he'd tried to smash open a steel door—helmet first. Smoking marijuana beforehand hadn't helped.

"I can't quite figure out why I did it," he says. "I know doing drugs was a factor. But whenever I get with the guys, it's like something else takes over. I feel invincible. I feel charged. And if I don't step up and prove myself, I don't feel like much of a man."

Snapshot of the "Career-Mindeds" (born 1984–1988)

"*Yes*, there are legitimate online jobs!" Becky shouts into her cell phone, then rolls her eyes. The exhausted twenty-seven-year-old is on another "annoying" call with her mom.

"Look, why do you always have to be so practical?" Becky continues. "Just let me be a 'big dreamer,' as you call it. If I work at the deli, I'm afraid I'll be stuck at a dead end forever. Let me give this a try . . . and *PLEASE* stop asking all your friends if they'll hire me!"

When she finally hangs up, she scrunches into a tiny ball on her couch and shuts her eyes. *Oh, Lord,* she prays, *please let my new job come through for me. I can barely make ends meet. And please, somehow help my mom to back off. Her stress is stressing me. Amen.*

Snapshot of the "Young-Marrieds" (born 1979–1983)

"We have no idea what to expect," Janna confesses to her best friend, Nadia, while sipping herb tea. "We *are* excited. But I think I'll scream if one more person says, 'Mothers always know best.' Obviously not. I'm about to be a mom and I have no idea what I'm doing. Can someone please just be real with me?"

The early-thirty-something pauses, then continues: "Am I supposed to be this scared?"

The Young and the Restless

The diverse generation known as the Millennials (broadly, born 1979–1995) share one thing in common: *youth*. Those in their early twenties are torn between the exhilarating freedom and accompanying responsibility of initial adulthood. Often they attend college or are new to the workforce. Overall, they make their own decisions yet are rarely secure enough financially to be on their own. Some live at home and face being "independent" under their parents' roof.

Those in their late-twenties and early thirties have launched their careers and their families—or at least that's what they're striving to do. In the working world, many are dealing with fierce competition, unemployment, and the fallout of a sluggish economy. *Six years of college can only land me a spot in retail?!*

So many in this generational segment mistakenly believe they can be an overnight success. Reality television and opportunities permeating the Internet offer fortune and fame to every average Joe. A college education is sold as a way to more options and a higher paycheck. These expectations frequently are not shared by their parents, who have paid their dues. *"Just get a job—any job."*

Millennials desire the security and the support of a loving family. Too much support, however, can communicate a lack of trust and serve to push them away. Parents and ministry workers must tread carefully as they reach out. For this crowd, brutal honesty mixed with an open mind and plenty of empathy are foundational to connecting. While adult kids will always want their parents to be proud of them, they also want older generations to understand that their world is different.

Young couples tend to be more open to finding creative ways of living. Maybe they move to Germany for the right job, or choose to rent instead of buy, go into debt for grad school, join up for a yearlong missions trip, or opt not have kids right away. But no matter how different their life checklist may look from that of their parents, they still seek support and respect.

Listen to the heart of twenty-eight-year-old Topher Wallace, a Michigan native, married, with kids. While he's hopeful for his family's future, getting his career on solid financial ground has been an uphill climb. He's learning, yet who to turn to during stressful times? . . .

Topher's Story: Wrestling with Worry

I worry a lot. Or, rather, I try not to worry a lot. But that doesn't really work.

Worry comes in from all angles. I worry whether or not my kids are normal. I worry about whether or not I'll have a heart attack at forty-six like my dad did, or if even sooner, since I'm not nearly as physically active as he is. I worry every month when our bills come due and we have to decide which ones we can pay a little late and which ones must be paid right away.

I worry about how I look, that my car will break down, that I'll be out of a job with little to no warning. And I worry that I worry too much, or not enough. I worry that I'm not a good enough husband to my wife, that I don't provide enough. I worry that I'm too tired to spend time with my kids. I worry that they don't have Mr. Rogers on TV anymore so they're stuck with pseudo-educational animated babble. All these things I worry about make my shoulders tense and sore. Yet that's okay, I've got a foolproof plan for getting rid of worry: distraction.

Ah, lovely *distraction*. The internet, my favorite books read over and over again, binge-watching the latest British TV series that's caught my fancy . . . I get distracted from my distractions with more distractions. Am I worried? No, because I can distract myself from worry. What's the point in worry when I can watch TV? Or browse online. Or anything, really. As long as I don't have to embrace those things that truly concern me.

And our culture is built around distraction. The bulk of our media covers celebrities and scandals that help us forget our worries. Electric bill past due? Grab the latest issue of *People*: "Promising young starlet continues downward spiral." Worried about raising your kids? Dive into the latest outrage or firestorm ripping through football, baseball, foosball . . . you name it. Concerned you might be fired? Play some video games. Kill some dragons, kick some goals.

Honestly, the blame is not rightly on video games, or the media. It's mine to own. See, when Jesus talked about worry, He was all about curing the problem, not avoiding it. He essentially said, "Don't worry, because I've got it all under control." Not in the way that we won't have things that concern us or keep us restless at night. Those things will always be here. When the rent's due, God doesn't sneak into my bedroom and hide $500 under my pillow.

What He *does* do is whisper softly and tenderly into my ear. "Hey, these things you're worrying about . . . in the end, they're small potatoes. Remember how big I am. Remember what I'm capable of. I will never leave you or forsake you. I want to take you on a journey—the one for which I created you. And this is just another lesson. Trust in Me. Don't worry. I have you."

And, in those moments, if I'm not too obtuse and obstinate to listen, I understand. He's not asking me not to worry because we *do* have enough money to cover our medical bills. He's not telling me not to worry because our children *won't* ever get sick or I'll *never* lose a job.

He's telling me not to worry because, regardless of what happens, He truly is in control. That doesn't absolve me of responsibility. I still need to work hard to pay my bills. I need to spend that quality time with the kids when I'm exhausted. I need to do my part. Yet I also need to remember that God will do His. And it's up to me not to be weak or drift back toward the distractions that call out to me, but to face those fears and worries head on with the knowledge that, no matter what, *God is in control*.

How Loved Ones Can Ascertain If There's a Problem

Look for signs we've mentioned before, such as . . .

- Being irritable or sad most of the day
- No longer being interested in once-loved activities
- Withdrawal from social interactions
- Weight loss (without trying to lose) or weight gain (more than 5% of body weight in one month), loss of appetite or increased appetite
- Restlessness
- Not being able to sleep or sleeping too much, nearly every day
- Feeling tired and worn out nearly all day, every day

- Battling with heavy guilt or shame on a daily basis
- Feelings of worthlessness—to the point of not being able to function with a positive demeanor
- Lack of ability to concentrate or make decisions
- Self-medication with alcohol or other substances

What should a parent do? Apply the stress-management techniques presented in this book, focusing on a Millennial's specific needs. Here's a relatively brief look at what's bugging this generation and how you might help.

Achieving Financial Peace

Says Mike Hais, a market researcher and co-author of two books on Millennials:

> They are growing up at a tough time. They were sheltered in many ways, with a lot of high expectations for what they should achieve. Individual failure is difficult to accept when confronted with a sense [that] you're an important person and expected to achieve. Even though in most instances, it's not their fault that the economy collapsed just as many of them were getting out of college and coming of age—that does lead to a greater sense of stress.[2]

What should a parent do? Be supportive. Be available. And, if you choose to lend money, do so with no strings attached.

Battling Depression

Depression happens to any of us because of a variety of things—*not* because we're crazy. Sometimes the chemicals in our brains get a little off balance and we simply need to see a doctor who can prescribe medication to help them realign.

Sometimes depression is due to events in our past, and we need to see a counselor who can help us to extract the buried hurt and show us how to deal with it. A common mistake is to think that Christians should never get depressed or ever worry about anything because we have Jesus. With the Millennial in your life, reach out and offer a listening ear, not a lecture on how it was in your day. You want to help her out of cyclical fear and worry and stress.

Navigating Relationships

Yep . . . that once wide-eyed kid is all grown up. And whether he's dating or is newly married, the whole realm of relationships may be a source of much tension for him—and for his parents. Adult kids worry about finding a mate. And, once they're married, they worry about the sure-to-come storms of married life. Likewise, many parents worry that their now-adult child will make a mistake from which he cannot recover.

God wants a lifetime of marital fulfillment for your adult child; one that He designed. (That is, if He leads them into marriage.) The best thing you can do is be a steady example and pray—privately *and* with your child. Pray that . . .

. . . *God will begin molding him/her now into the godly person his/her spouse will need.*

. . . *God will protect his/her future spouse.*

. . . *God will draw the hearts of married children intimately to Himself.*

. . . *God will help married children connect and communicate more deeply.*

Figuring Out What They Believe

We all learn by experimenting and feeling the sting of consequences. It's the same with our faith as in the other realms of life. That's why "religion" is one of the biggest hot buttons within a family—and, often a stressful topic between adult children and their parents. After years and years of telling kids the right thing to do, it's a challenge to learn the art of pulling back and having a simple discussion, even letting go at times. However, if parents can't make that leap, they will find themselves removed from their kids' decision-making process altogether.

*****

The Millennial in your life needs you. What happens if he or she doesn't act on your advice? Do you withdraw support? Will there be an I-told-you-so attitude beneath or behind every conversation? Here's a better approach: Stay close, but let them breathe. Strive to love, respect, and listen as he/she navigates life's many adventures. Above all, don't be a source of stress in their lives; instead, help them find relief from the cycle of fear and worry and stress!

Let's wrap up our conversation with some creative ideas, talking points, and devotional helps that families can use to communicate Christ's love. Take to heart these tips on how to stay positive when troubles strike, be optimistic about the future, and speak encouragement to the ones we love.

Worry-Wise . . . and Live Well:
Action Steps for Helping Millennials Manage Worry

STEP 1: Review Your Adult Child's "My Worry Profile" (see chapter 4). Flip back and fill it out if you haven't yet done so. With your completed worry profile in mind, and considering what we've discussed in this chapter, it's time for the next step.

STEP 2: Apply the Worry-Wise Plan to Your Adult Child (see chapter 8). Remember: Our goal is *homeostasis*—moving our kids from an adrenaline-fueled cycle of fear and worry and stress to a balanced mindset that's hopefully much more peaceful. We accomplish this in three interrelated facets: our mind, our body, and our spirit. With your profiles in hand, and armed with skills you've learned in this chapter, fill in the blanks that follow.

MIND: Identify worries plaguing your kids' thoughts and plot a course of action.

"The Millennial in my life, _____, often frets about _____
_____."

Here's what I'll communicate as often as needed:

_____

_____

_____

_____

_____

_____

This is a message your adult child may need to hear repeatedly. For instance:

"I'm here for you if you need me, but I respect your privacy."

"I'm proud of you, and I'm amazed at how God is using you."

A reminder about how much you value and want to support him/her.

With regard to our adult child, here are some negative relational behaviors my spouse and I will work toward changing and some positive ones we'll start doing:

Change: _____ .
Do: _____ .
Change: _____ .
Do: _____ .
Change: _____ .
Do: _____ .

BODY: List key ways in which you can support your Millennial. (Tread carefully. Never force unwanted help or advice.)

Diet: _____ .
Exercise: _____ .
Healthcare Visits: _____ .
Ways to Relax: _____ .
Family Connections: _____ .
Sleep: _____ .

SPIRIT: Consider how you can encourage your children to turn to God when troubles hit and so avoid spiraling into the fear-worry-stress cycle.

Begin by taking to heart this passage:

> Be anxious for nothing, but in everything by prayer and supplication, with thanksgiving, let your requests be made known to God; and the peace of

God, which surpasses all understanding, will guard your hearts and minds through Christ Jesus.[3]

As a parent, here's how I will endeavor to model these words:

_____

Here are some practical steps my spouse and I can take that will help build our trust in God and decrease stress in our relationship with our adult child:

_____

_____

STEP 3: Clue in to their needs, but be willing to back off. Topher has a few ideas about how stressed-out moms and dads can reach out to equally stressed-out Millennials—without launching World War III. Take a look at his do-this/never-do-that suggestions and then at his heartfelt advice below. Consider how you could apply his advice to the loved ones in your life.

How to Help a Worried Millennial—Topher's List

- Show you care, in authentic ways . . . never just give a bunch of verses to ponder.
- Tune in to what they're thinking and feeling.
- Seek to understand their "anger triggers" and what pushes them away.
- "Please, just let me figure it out on my own."
- "If you offer me money, I'll accept it. If you don't, I'll survive."
- "Every time you criticize my lifestyle, you add more distance between us. Can't you just be proud of me?"

Giving advice to adult children can be tricky—at least that's what my dad tells me. When do you give it? When do you hold back? When do you let them figure it out for themselves, and when do you point out places where you struggled, hoping they won't make the same mistakes?

Your kids struggle with a lot of the same stuff you do: about money, about the future, about our ten-year-old cars breaking down, all of it. We worry that when our kids get the sniffles we may be next on the sick list (and, if so, is SARS making a comeback? Okay, so maybe you don't worry about that one as much).

If we're in college, we worry about term papers and time management and money. If we're young-married, then, as you know, marriage has its own slew of worries too. And then, adding children on top of that—well, you've been there. You understand. So, just a couple suggestions from a former kid, pseudo-adult with two children of his own.

Advice is great . . . but if we haven't asked for it, it feels like you're telling us what to do. And, since we're trying to establish our independence, that rubs us the wrong way. It makes us feel like kids again. And we aren't. We want a relationship with you where there's mutual respect. We might not be peers in life experience yet, but we're getting there. Let us.

Also, hopefully you've helped us grow up in an environment where we know what God thinks about most things. Still, don't just quote Scripture to us. That feels like you're trying to use God to make a point. Let God make His own points. We're His responsibility now.

We do need to know you understand what we're going through. That you've been there, and that it *does* get better. Not that you can fix it, but you know that, right now, life is hard.

Make it known you're there to help if needed, but you won't force it. We need to learn how to stand on our own two feet, and part of that is learning when to ask for help.

I think the most important thing is that we're much like you, twenty to thirty years younger. We're all working through the same stuff... we just have different playbooks.

Our Research Says . . .

- Millennials say the bad things they worry about come true more often than do those of older generations.
- Compared with other generations, Millennials gravitate more toward sedentary forms of stress relief (listening to music, surfing online, video games . . .).

Recap and Reflect
Talking Points for Couples or Group Study
• • • • • • • • • • • • • • • • • • • •

Madeleine L'Engle says, about the importance of restored family relationships:

If the Lord's table is the prototype of the family table, then, if I think in terms of the family table, I know that I cannot sit down to bread and wine until I've said "I'm sorry," until reparations have been made, relations restored. When one of our children had done something particularly unworthy, if it had come out into the open before dinner, if there had been an "I'm sorry," and there had been acceptance, and love, then would follow the happiest dinner possible, full of laughter and fun. If there was something still hidden; if one child, or as sometimes happens, one parent, was out of joint with the family and the world, that would destroy the atmosphere of the whole meal.[4]

> *What are some stress-points between me and the Millennial(s) in my life? What are some steps I can take to open the lines of communication?*

• Consider John 15:9–11:

> *"As the Father has loved me [Jesus], so have I loved you. Now remain in my love. If you keep my commands, you will remain in my love, just as I have kept my Father's commands and remain in his love. I have told you this so that my joy may be in you and that your joy may be complete."*

How should a parent's love be expressed to an adult child? To protect and grow our relationship, what are some boundaries my adult child and I can set?

BIBLE STUDY

30 DAYS TO A PEACEFUL HOME

Day 1: Hope Redefined

Receive

Taste God's Word—Savor These Verses: Revelation 21:1–4

> I heard a loud voice from the throne saying, "Look! God's dwelling place is now among the people, and he will dwell with them. They will be his people, and God himself will be with them and be their God. He will wipe every tear from their eyes. There will be no more death or mourning or crying or pain, for the old order of things has passed away" (vv. 3–4).

Reflect

Family:
- *What causes us to feel hopeless at times?*
- *How can we truly experience God dwelling with us, right here and now, amidst the gritty and difficult struggles?*

Individual:
- *In what ways can these words give me hope, especially in the face of fear and worry?*

Sometimes when we read these promises from God, we recognize them in an intellectual sense but miss experiencing the truth of them in our hearts. We will live an incomprehensibly rich eternal life with Him, but this can feel so far away, so "someday," and we wonder about today—about our present challenges and hardships. *Is God actually with me in the here and now?* Yes, He is, and he offers us hope today, for the very moment we're living out.

DR. ARNIE COLE & MICHAEL ROSS

As Jesus told the disciples: "I am with you always, to the very end of the age."[1]

Not just someday. Already. Right now.

Respond

Ask for Change: "Lord, help us to remember that your hope is with us always. Amen."

Consider What's Real: Think about the bigness of God, how He goes before you and follows you from behind, protecting you on all sides, laying His hands upon you and guiding you toward a deeper, more fulfilling life with Him.

Other Verses to Eat Up: Matthew 28:16–20

Day 2: God's Friendship

Receive

Taste God's Word—Savor These Verses: John 15:12–17

> I no longer call you servants, because a servant does not know his master's business. Instead, I have called you friends, for everything that I learned from my Father I have made known to you. (v. 15)

Reflect

Family:
- *What steps can we take to begin letting go of fear and to start experiencing more peace through our friendship with Jesus?*
- *In our own words, how would each of us describe our relationship with God?*

Individual:
> • *God considers me His friend; how will this truth affect my view of our relationship?*

Think about what Jesus is telling us: All that's His is ours also. This sounds like the kind of connection you might share with your closest friend—and that's exactly what He wants. Yes, the Lord requires us to follow in His steps and live as his Spirit directs. But He doesn't want to be held at arm's length; He knows we'll miss out by merely going through lifeless "religious motions." More than anything, He wants our hearts; our love. Jesus wants a vital, dynamic relationship with us. With *you*.

Respond

Ask for Change: "Lord, I want each member of my family to experience the fulfillment of a real relationship with you. Help us grow closer to you each day."

Consider What's Real: If you're more inclined to practice a formal method of prayer, try a more relaxed interaction with God today. Seek to converse with Him not just at specific, set times but continually, as you go about everyday life (as in, a life of worship, a life of service, a life of prayer—"living out" your faith). Ask for guidance before you make decisions at work. Ask for advice as you parent your children or navigate other relationships. Give thanks for the small blessings He bestows on you throughout the day. Integrate Jesus into your moment-by-moment life.

Other Verses to Eat Up: 1 Thessalonians 5:16–18; Jeremiah 29:12–14

Day 3: This Is Love

Receive

Taste God's Word—Savor These Verses: Mark 12:28-34

> "The most important one [commandment]," answered Jesus, "is this: 'Hear, O Israel: The Lord our God, the Lord is one. Love the Lord your God with all your heart and with all your soul and with all your mind and with all your strength'" (vv. 29-30).

Reflect

Family:
- *What does it mean to love God with all our heart, mind, soul, and strength?*
- *What would our lives look like if each of us lived out this commandment every day? In what ways would our lives change? Who else would notice this change, and how?*

Individual:
- *What's one small step I can take to move closer to loving God in this way?*

Jesus summarizes the Ten Commandments into two steps: love God, love your neighbor. How hard can that be—does this sound easy, at first glance? Whether it is or isn't, though, is not the point. He's speaking not merely of affection, or of not doing harm, but of a love that permeates every facet, every aspect, every "cell" of our lives. Jesus calls for us to love Him with every fiber of our beings, every bit of our essence: not only in our hearts but with our thoughts too, and with all our choices and actions, and in laying before Him all of our passions and wants and needs.

What does this game-changing, all-encompassing love really look like? And is it even possible—can we ever be opened up to that depth and breadth and height?

Jesus says *yes*, absolutely. In fact, anything—*anything* He could ever ask of us, *anything* that would fulfill God's will and be for our greatest good—is possible through Him.

Respond

Ask for Change: "Lord, we want to love you this way, with every bit of our heart, mind, soul, and strength. Show us the way. Take our hands and guide each member of this family into a deeper love for you."

Consider What's Real: Loving others is a real and tangible way not only to demonstrate your love for God but to grow that love too. Today, ask yourself periodically if you are loving others as God desires. Before considering a course of action, ask yourself if that action will demonstrate love for God and love for others.

Other Verses to Eat Up: John 3:16–17

Day 4: God Is Ever with Us

Receive

Taste God's Word—Savor These Verses: Isaiah 43:1–2

> This is what the LORD says—he who created you, Jacob, he who formed you, Israel; "Do not fear, for I have redeemed you; I have summoned you by name; you are mine. When you pass through the waters, I will be with you; and when you pass through the rivers, they will not sweep over you. When you walk through the fire, you will not be burned; the flames will not set you ablaze."

Reflect

Family:

- *God has summoned each of us by name, and He will be with us when we feel spiritually lost. How does this make me feel? How will this help me during life's stressful moments?*

- *God has a specific purpose for each one of us. What do I think this is, for me? If I don't yet know, how will I discover it?*

Individual:

- *Why does God guarantee that He will be with me during life's trials—why doesn't He necessarily prevent those trials from taking place?*

Sometimes we assume that, because we believe in God and have faith in Him, He'll rescue us from or take us out of grief and hardship. This isn't necessarily true. We live in a broken world, which means none of us will walk through life unscathed. God walks *with* us—He doesn't guarantee, for instance, that we'll never experience the wilderness, and yet He will never send us off alone to forge through it. He accompanies us every step of the way—as also through all deep waters and through all blazing fires. He knows us by name, intimately and thoroughly—our fears, our flaws, our deepest desires, and, unequivocally, everything else. He guides each of us on our own path, going before us *and* coming behind us as we navigate life's hills and valleys.

Respond

Ask for Change: "Lord, help each member of this family to know you're right here, now and always. Help us trust with utter confidence that you'll never leave any of us alone."

Consider What's Real: It's easy to trust God in good times, when life rolls along smoothly and our worries are few. The key is to know that He's with us even when we feel alone, even when we might feel abandoned in the midst of a spiritual wilderness. The next time you're in a desolate place, take a moment to reflect on other difficult times you survived with God at your side. And *know* that He's got your back today.

Other Verses to Eat Up: Psalm 139:5–12; Jeremiah 29:11

Day 5: Transforming Words

Receive

Taste God's Word—Savor These Verses: Isaiah 55:8–13

> As the rain and the snow come down from heaven, and do not return to it without watering the earth and making it bud and flourish, so that it yields seed for the sower and bread for the eater, so is my word that goes out from my mouth: It will not return to me empty, but will accomplish what I desire and achieve the purpose for which I sent it. (vv. 10–11)

Reflect

Family:

- *Why is it important for us to prioritize God's thoughts and ways—and plans?*
- *Does each of us truly believe His direction can make a concrete difference in our lives?* (Explain.) *How can we discern His direction?* (Hint: Refer to the verses above.)

Individual:

- *Am I willing to read God's Word with an open heart and mind, with the help of His Spirit, in order to discern what He wants from me?* Commit now to doing this. Go to the Lord in prayer, asking Him for strength, guidance, and wisdom.

God is clear about how He sees Scripture working in our lives. As precipitation nourishes the soil, feeding plants and crops that will grow to sustain those who harvest them, God's Word nourishes our souls, feeding us so that we will grow and flourish and be sustained through periods of drought and difficulty. What's more, Scripture illuminates the purpose He has for us on earth—His Word contains specific direction for each of us. To be led by it, we must seek it.

Respond

Ask for Change: "Lord, I know your thoughts and ways are far beyond our limited ability to comprehend. Yet I also know you gave us your Word as a means to grow closer to you and realize your purpose for us. Help your Word mold our lives into what you intend."

Consider What's Real: Sometimes we try to "get through the Bible" instead of letting the Bible get through to us. Today, slow down as you read; perhaps even meditate a bit on the verses. As Henri Nouwen said, "Meditation means chewing on the word and incorporating it into our lives. It is the discipline by which we let the written word of God become a personal word for us, anchored in the center of our being."[2]

Other Verses to Eat Up: Isaiah 55:1–7

Day 6: The Supreme Giver

Receive

Taste God's Word—Savor These Verses: Ephesians 1:17–19

I keep asking that the God of our Lord Jesus Christ, the glorious Father, may give you the Spirit of wisdom and revelation, so that you may know him better. I pray also that the eyes of your heart may be enlightened in order that you may know the hope to which he has called you, the riches of his glorious inheritance in his holy people, and his incomparably great power for us who believe.

Reflect

Family:

- *Does each of us view God as the Supreme Giver? (Please explain.) What is one thing He has given our family that makes me thankful?*
- *Why does God care so much about His creation?*

Individual:

- *Do I trust Him? What are two ways I can deepen my trust in God?*

God's nature has been described in countless ways—holy, compassionate, merciful, gracious, loving, faithful, forgiving . . . to name a few. In addition, as Charles Stanley points out, there's one essential trait that all of humanity can celebrate—*giving:* "We have life only because God has created us by an exercise of His will. We can receive salvation only because He wills to grant it."[3] God's ever-giving heart welcomes us to approach Him. "Your voice matters in heaven," writes Max Lucado. "He takes you very seriously. When you enter His presence, He turns to you to hear your voice. No need to fear that you will be ignored."[4]

Respond

Ask for Change: "Lord, help us to trust you fully. Help us to know that you are good and that you always and ever want what's truly best for our family."

Consider What's Real: The God in whom you trust is the infinite, holy Creator who has always existed and who made the universe by the power of His Word (Hebrews 11:3). God told Moses, "I AM WHO I AM" (that is, eternally present; Exodus 3:14). There is only one true God (Isaiah 45:5): the sovereign Lord, who acts in His creation and who involves himself intimately in the lives of those He made. God, the Shepherd who guides (Genesis 48:15), is the One who provides (Genesis 22:8), the Lord of peace in all trials (Judges 6:24), the Physician who heals the sick (Exodus 15:26), the Banner that guides (Exodus 17:8–16). God is "the Alpha and the Omega, the First and the Last, the Beginning and the End" (Revelation 22:13). He is Immanuel, "God with us"! (Isaiah 7:14; Matthew 1:23). God is our Father (Isaiah 9:6); He is holy (1 Samuel 2:2); He is love (1 John 4:8).

Other Verses to Eat Up: Romans 8:38–39

Day 7: The Lord's Unconditional Love

Receive

Taste God's Word—Savor These Verses: Matthew 15:21–28

A Canaanite woman...came to him [Jesus], crying out, "Lord, Son of David, have mercy on me! My daughter is demon-possessed and suffering terribly."

Jesus did not answer a word. So his disciples came to him and urged him, "Send her away, for she keeps crying out after us."

He answered, "I was sent only to the lost sheep of Israel."

The woman came and knelt before him, "Lord, help me!" she said.

He replied, "It is not right to take the children's bread and toss it to the dogs."

"Yes it is, Lord," she said. "Even the dogs eat the crumbs that fall from their master's table."

Then Jesus said to her, "Woman, you have great faith! Your request is granted." And her daughter was healed at that moment. (vv. 22–28)

Reflect

Family:
- *Jesus loves us fully, no matter our imperfections and hang-ups. How should this truth affect the way we live?*
- *If we can come to Jesus boldly, despite our flaws and insecurities, why do we sometimes hold back? What steps can we take as a family to be more open with God—and with each other?*

Individual:
- *Am I afraid to approach Jesus for what I really need? If so, why? How can I change this?* (Spend some time in prayer and reflection.)

Sometimes we feel we need to wait until the perfect moment to approach God. We want to hold off until we've gotten a handle on

our troubles or overcome our shortcomings (or, at least, haven't
fallen prey to certain temptations for a certain period of time).
We feel ashamed to be in His presence, with all our flaws and
failures in the light. *If I just work on this problem awhile,* then *I'll be
ready to pursue my faith.* But in waiting, in keeping our problems
to ourselves, we miss the whole point. Jesus wants us to come
to Him when we're *most* vulnerable, when we're *most* in need
of Him. In the above verses, a Canaanite woman persistently
asked Jesus for His help, even though at the time the disciples
plainly saw her as an outsider. She was bold and unafraid, press-
ing on in faith, determined to pursue Jesus no matter what.
And He answered.

Respond

Ask for Change: "Lord, help us to approach you boldly and persistently, without shame. Help us lay ourselves and our sins before you in faith, so that you may heal us."

Consider What's Real: Today, instead of trying to work out your
problems alone, try putting them before God and asking Him
for help. As Jesus says, "Be direct. Ask for what you need."[5]

Other Verses to Eat Up: Matthew 7:7–11; 1 John 5:14–15

Day 8: Jesus the Savior

Receive

Taste God's Word—Savor These Verses: John 1:29–31

> John [the Baptist] saw Jesus coming toward him and
> said, "Look, the Lamb of God, who takes away the sin of
> the world! This is the one I meant when I said, 'A man

who comes after me has surpassed me because he was before me.' I myself did not know him, but the reason I came baptizing with water was that he might be revealed to Israel."

Reflect

Family:
- *What did Jesus Christ come to do?*
- *Does each of us believe that "I am forgiven"? Why or why not? What must we do to be forgiven?*

Individual:
- *In what ways do fear and worry turn me away from instead of toward God?*

Look at John's description of Jesus. He calls the Holy One *"The Lamb of God!"* He could have said, "Behold, the Roaring Lion!" or "Here's the Soaring Eagle!" or "To your knees, folks; it's Supreme Ruler time!" Why would John compare his cousin to a baby sheep? He knew the truth about Jesus, and he didn't want anyone to miss it.

Respond

Ask for Change: "Lord, help our family to place all hope in you. Show each of us your ways; guide us in truth. Amen."

Consider What's Real: John is saying, "This is the lamb God has supplied, the One who will take our place—our sin, our guilt, our blame—and suffer, and die. He'll take every misstep, every failure, everything you've ever done wrong, and dispose of it forever. He will sacrifice himself, take the punishment that should be yours, so you can be clean, and be free!"

Other Verses to Eat Up: Psalm 25

Day 9: Following Jesus

Receive

Taste God's Word—Savor These Verses: Matthew 4:18–20

> As Jesus was walking beside the Sea of Galilee, he saw two brothers, Simon called Peter and his brother Andrew. They were casting a net into the lake, for they were fishermen. "Come, follow me," Jesus said, "and I will send you out to fish for people." At once they left their nets and followed him.

Reflect

Family:
- *Share what it means to leave behind the things that feel import-ant to us, in order to follow our Lord. (What is Jesus asking us to give up?)*
- *Why must we surrender all to Jesus, including our fear?*

Individual:
- Take a moment to reflect on the worry in your life. *How has it kept me from being all God created me to be? In what ways has it kept me from following Jesus?*

Imagine having a face-to-face encounter with the Messiah—gazing into his eyes, hearing his voice, feeling the touch of His hand on your shoulder. Peter and Andrew's own encounter changed their lives for all eternity. Before meeting Jesus, fishing was their life; not only did it put food on their tables, it also was the family business. Little did they realize, God had in mind a far bigger catch. One day, while they were casting nets into the water as usual, the brothers saw a man walking along the shore, not far away. He was like all other men . . . and yet He was unlike any other man. He evinced a gentleness, a strength, a never-wavering love they'd never before experienced. And His *voice*—"Come, follow me!"

Something deep inside compelled them to do the extraordinary, and at once they left behind the security of their old lives and found something—*Someone*—infinitely greater.

Respond

Ask for Change: "Lord, thank you for choosing us, for healing our hearts and renewing our minds. Please keep transforming us, molding us ever more into your image."

Consider What's Real: The nineteenth-century preacher Charles Spurgeon asked hard-hitting questions of believers: "What have you been doing with your life? Is Christ living in your home and yet you have not spoken to him for months? Do not let me condemn you or judge; only let your conscience speak: Have we not all lived too much without Jesus? Have we not grown content with the world to the neglect of Christ?"[6] Jesus still calls: "Follow Me!" Those who are wise listen and leave their old ways behind. They find in him a new direction, new purpose, new identity—a radically new life. They discover real adventure, true fulfillment, and ultimate love. Not love that originates on earth, but the love that is perfect, unconditional and unlimited; the love that comes only from God.

Other Verses to Eat Up: Romans 8:28

Day 10: The Holy Spirit, Our Guide

Receive

Taste God's Word—Savor These Verses: John 14:15-18

> If you love me, keep my commands. And I will ask the Father, and he will give you another advocate to be with

you forever—the Spirit of truth. The world cannot accept him, because it neither sees him nor knows him. But you know him, for he lives with you and will be in you. I will not leave you as orphans; I will come to you.

Reflect
Family:
- *Each of us needs to become sensitive to the Holy Spirit's gentle nudges. In what way(s) have we, individually, experienced these?*
- *Are we, as a family, obeying God? What kinds of things do we sense that we need to change? How are we willing to work together to hold each other accountable?*

Individual:
- *In what ways can God's Spirit deliver me from fear and anxiety when they grip my mind and heart?*

The Holy Spirit is our Guide, Helper, Strengthener, and Advocate, sent to live in us and to be in charge of every aspect of our lives. As with the Father and the Son, we are to believe and obey God the Spirit. In *The Sovereign God,* James Montgomery Boice explains distinctively divine attributes ascribed to the Spirit, such as everlastingness (Hebrews 9:14), omnipresence (Psalm 139:7–10), omniscience (1 Corinthians 2:10–11), and omnipotence (Luke 1:35).

Respond
Ask for Change: "Lord, help each of us to listen to you—not to the fear that sometimes races through our minds. Grant us peace, and direct us when we feel confused."

Consider What's Real: God's Spirit guides, encourages, and comforts; He's the Counselor who lives in us and with us and around us. We can call out to the Spirit for guidance as we follow the instruction God has given us through His Word. He will replace our fears—of rejection, of change, of failure—with the hope and courage we need to face any challenge life throws our way. In times of trouble, the Spirit carries us toward wholeness and peace. We can, and must, trust Him.

Other Verses to Eat Up: Acts 1:8; 1 Corinthians 2:9–16

Day 11: The Essence of True Faith

Receive
Taste God's Word—Savor These Verses: Hosea 6:1–3

> Let us acknowledge the Lord; let us press on to acknowledge him. As surely as the sun rises, he will appear; he will come to us like the winter rains, like the spring rains that water the earth. (v. 3)

Reflect
Family:
- *In what ways must we return to the Lord and begin to acknowledge Him again?*
- *Is there any particular sin in each of our lives that's inhibiting us from pursuing true communion with God? Be brave; share it now, and then let's pray for each other.*

Individual:
- *What can I do to press on in pursuit of the Lord?*

Sometimes it seems as if God is slow to appear, even when it feels like we're pursuing Him wholeheartedly. *Why isn't He answering my prayers?* we might wonder. *Why don't I feel close to Him right now?* If a sin in our life has opened a chasm between us and God, we will need to be honest, with ourselves and with Him, by confessing it and asking for forgiveness. On the other hand, there are times when we simply don't know what's causing a seeming separation. God *feels* absent, distant. We feel spiritually frustrated, and empty, yet we don't know why. In these times, He urges us to press on in faith, to persevere, continuing to acknowledge Him and trusting that no matter what we feel, He will never leave us, whether or not at a given time or in a given season we feel close to or immersed in His presence.

Respond

Ask for Change: "Lord, thank you for being always present, always with us, even when we may not be able to see you or hear you or even perceive you. We have faith that your plan is supreme, whatever our thoughts and emotions. Fortify our spirit, and strengthen our trust in you during these times, so that we may press on in pursuit of you."

Consider What's Real: The Christian life is a journey of endurance. In Paul's letter to the Philippians, he admits that sometimes this requires "straining" in order to "press on toward the goal." Yet the apostle was assured that God *will* appear, and that in the end the reward will be well worth any effort: "The Lord Jesus Christ . . . will transform our lowly bodies so that they will be like his glorious body" (3:20–21).

Other Verses to Eat Up: Philippians 3:12–15; Hebrews 12:1–3

Day 12: Genuine Relationship

Receive

Taste God's Word—Savor These Verses: Psalm 94:16–19

> When I said, "My foot is slipping," your love, LORD, supported me. When anxiety was great within me, your consolation brought me joy. (vv. 18–19)

　　　DR. ARNIE COLE & MICHAEL ROSS

Reflect

Family:

- *When our feet are slipping—and temptations seem overwhelming— do we return immediately to Jesus?* (Describe, individually, how we do so.)
- *And, when it comes to life's worries and stresses, do we trust that Jesus will help us? How should we pray?*

Individual:

- *When I feel God's hand of correction, I can accept it as a sign of His love. How might God be correcting me? When he does, how should I respond?*

It's easy to beat ourselves up over sin, especially when we tend to repeat the same sins again and again in a seemingly endless loop. We wonder how we can call ourselves "follower of Jesus" when we so relentlessly choose against God and His will. Yet this is exactly why we need to lean hard into Jesus' love. If we continue to view faith as a set of rules to obey, then when we fall—and we *will* fall—we'll crash hard and be weighed down with guilt and shame. When we understand faith as a love-based relationship with God, we'll keep turning to Him, we'll know with great joy that He loves us no matter what, and we'll be motivated to embrace the change that only the power of His Spirit can bring about in us.

Respond

Ask for Change: "Lord, I know obedience is crucial, but I also know that you want us to move far beyond simple rule-following and into real relationship with you. Please guide our family so we may continue to learn how to listen to and share with and love you."

Consider What's Real: Timothy Keller talks about the difference between religion and faith, or rule-following and intimacy:

Religion operates on the principle of "I obey—therefore I am accepted by God." The basic operating principle of the gospel is "I am accepted by God through the work of Jesus Christ—therefore I obey"... Faith in the gospel restructures our motivations, our self-understanding, our identity, and our view of the world. Behavioral compliance to rules without heart-change will be superficial and fleeting.[7]

Other Verses to Eat Up: Romans 3:23–24; Isaiah 29:13

Day 13: His Healing Power

Receive

Taste God's Word—Savor These Verses: Malachi 4:1–3

For you who revere my name, the sun of righteousness will rise with healing in its rays. And you will go out and frolic like well-fed calves. (v. 2)

Reflect

Family:
- *What healing touch(es) do we believe we need from the Lord?*
- *Can each of us envision a time when we'll be entirely free from sin?* (Describe this.) *Can we experience that right now? Why, or why not?*

Individual:
- *How do I imagine such freedom—from sin's power and presence—will feel?*

Though Malachi is referring to a time when we'll be forever free from all sin, God gives us glimpses of such freedom in the here and now. Handing over our hearts, minds and bodies to Him, relinquishing control, surrendering to Him, putting our whole lives into His hands, allows us to taste that peace, joy, and freedom. Like the healing warmth of the sun's rays, God wraps us in His embrace and willingly takes from us our burdens. We only need to allow Him in.

Respond

Ask for Change: "Lord, you know how hard it can be for us to hand you our burdens. Help us to open ourselves to you fully so that you may begin to heal us fully."

Consider What's Real: Choose today, or another day this week, to allow yourself to rest fully in God. That might mean doing absolutely nothing for the day, releasing yourself from normal duties and responsibilities. Or it might mean allowing yourself to indulge in an activity that you enjoy but don't often experience. Let God guide your day; allow it to unfold as he wishes. In this place and/or state of rest, ask him to begin healing your heart and to breathe new life into your weary spirit.

Other Verses to Eat Up: Matthew 11:28

Day 14: Our Awesome God

Receive

Taste God's Word—Savor These Verses: Deuteronomy 4:32–40

> You were shown these things so that you might know that the LORD is God; besides him there is no other . . . Acknowledge and take to heart this day that the LORD is God in heaven above and on the earth below. There is no other. (vv. 35, 39)

Reflect

Family:
- *Does each of us live as though God is truly all-powerful and all-loving? In what realistic, practical ways can we nurture this mindset in our family?*
- *How can we maintain that sense of awe in the day-to-day and moment-to-moment?*

Individual:
- *In what ways does God show me His power and love?*

We might read these verses and say, "It was easier to see God's hand at work in Old Testament times, with all the can't-miss miracles and straightforward indicators of His presence, but what about now? What is it that reveals the almighty God today?" The truth is, God shows us His presence every day, through signs and wonders big and small. But at our pace of living we don't slow down so as to even glimpse His work. We don't tune out the incessant cacophony of voices and devices so we can hear the whispers He intends just for us. Our awesome God *is* with us—we need our hearts softened, our senses sharpened, our spirits quieted, to experience Him.

Respond

Ask for Change: "Lord, our family is always on the go, moving frenetically, with our eyes focused on accomplishing 'what's next.' Help us to slow down so we can see and hear you. We want to experience your awesome presence in our lives. Teach us how."

Consider What's Real: Try keeping a simple gratitude list to help you focus on the daily gifts God lavishes on you. Keep your heart and mind and senses open for His presence, and jot down these occurrences in a notebook. Sometimes it's helpful to go back to review a concrete record of God's blessings in our lives and take note of the big picture.

Other Verses to Eat Up: 1 Samuel 12:16; Psalm 46:10

Day 15: Liberating Truth

Receive

Taste God's Word—Savor These Verses: John 8:31–32

> To the Jews who had believed him, Jesus said, "If you hold to my teaching, you are really my disciples. Then you will know the truth, and the truth will set you free."

Reflect

Family:

- *In what practical ways can we let the truth set us free?*
- *Are we allowing ourselves access to this liberating truth, or have we established barriers that prohibit God from truly entering and living in our hearts? Share how we can remove roadblocks (what are they?) to truth.*

Individual:

- *What might be prohibiting me from truly knowing the truth that brings freedom?*

Jesus says that if we follow His teachings, we will learn the truth and be liberated. Sounds great, right? Yet sometimes it looks on the outside like we're following Him pretty well, while in reality we haven't handed over our whole hearts. Remember the story of the rich man who claimed he'd kept all of God's commandments?[8] When Jesus told him to hand over his possessions to the poor, the man went away sad. Jesus knew that the man's wealth was his own personal hold-back from God; he wanted to prove his virtue by rule-keeping but then keep his motives and resources for himself; thus, not only did he refuse to part with what he valued most, he also wouldn't trust Jesus enough to hand over his heart. His inability to surrender and to trust kept him from the truth that would make him and keep him free.

Respond

Ask for Change: "Lord, help us identify the barriers we've erected that keep us from loving you with our whole heart. Help us trust you so that we will be freed."

Consider What's Real: Consider what Jesus might ask you to hand over, if He were to stand before you today—the one "thing" you'd be most tempted to clutch tightly and refuse to place at his feet.

Would it be worldly possessions? Your career? Ambitions? Authority? Physical strength? Family? Friends? Pondering what you might hesitate to relinquish, for whatever reason(s), might illuminate a spiritual barrier in your path toward the truth.

Other Verses to Eat Up: Matthew 19:16–22; Proverbs 3:5–6

Day 16: Engaging God's Word

Receive

Taste God's Word—Savor These Verses: Hebrews 4:12

The word of God is living and active. Sharper than any double-edged sword, it penetrates even to dividing soul and spirit, joints and marrow; it judges the thoughts and attitudes of the heart.

Reflect

Family:
- *As a family, we need to spend time chewing on God's Word—allowing it to penetrate our hearts and to search out our motivations. What simple steps can we take toward this, in the days and weeks ahead?*
- *Why is it important to set our hearts and minds on Scripture? In what ways can it change us?*

Individual:
- *When it comes to cyclical fear and worry and stress, how can God's Word make a difference in my life?*

We might close the Bible and feel good about ourselves after our early quiet time or just before we turn off the bedside lamp. "Hey," we justify, "I'm reading it, right? That's gotta be enough." Reading the Word is a good start, for sure. But God wants us to take another step: He wants us to *live* His Word: to "chew on it," meditate on it, carry it with us, and *act* on it—live it out. He wants His wisdom, his counsel, to guide our everyday decisions, serving as a light that shines along our daily path and as a sounding board against which we can weigh our choices. God intends his Word to seep into our spirit, into our heart and mind, even into our body. It's up to us: Will we allow God's Word to transform us?

Respond
Ask for Change: "Lord, help our family enjoy the full benefit of your Word by slowing down and truly thinking on what you want to communicate to us. Guide us toward a deeper understanding of how you use the Holy Scriptures to transform our lives."

Consider What's Real: Sometimes we try to bite off a bit too much during our reading. We focus on getting through as much as possible instead of delving deeply into smaller amounts. This week, try reading just a few verses at a time, especially if you typically read more in a sitting. Read them to yourself quietly and then aloud once or twice again, concentrating on words or phrases that seem to leap off the page or resonate with you in some way. If a particular verse or sentence or clause or even word seems to be speaking to you, ask God for direction and guidance, and then listen for an answer in your heart.

Other Verses to Eat Up: Hebrews 3:7–8; Romans 10

Day 17: Meditating on God's Word

Receive
Taste God's Word—Savor These Verses: Psalm 119:89–104

Oh, how I love your law! I meditate on it all day long. Your commands are always with me and make me wiser than my enemies. (vv. 97–98)

Reflect

Family:

- *How can meditating on and memorizing God's Word draw us closer to Jesus?*
- *What holds us back from committing Scripture to memory?*

Individual:

- *What's one step I can take today that will help me keep God's Word in the front of my mind throughout the day?*

It's one thing to read the Bible several times a week; it's another to read slowly and thoughtfully to discern what message God might want to highlight. The psalmist suggests that we "meditate on" Scripture "all day long." Repeating a verse or pondering a phrase throughout the day needn't be daunting; it's a relatively simple exercise that, for instance, can serve to help keep us calm and level-headed as we face crises, navigate problems, or make tough decisions. God's Word makes us wise, and true wisdom goes beyond absorbing facts and storing info; true wisdom means learning and then living out what we read.

Respond

Ask for Change: "Lord, we've been reluctant to carry your Word with us in our hearts and minds throughout the day. We tend to leave behind what we've read as we go about the rest of our day. Please help us keep your Word with us always."

Consider What's Real: If meditating on God's Word all day long sounds a bit monastic, don't despair; it doesn't need to be so difficult. Try choosing one short verse that speaks to you personally, and write it out on a handful of index cards. Place the cards in various spots—on or by the dashboard, computer, bathroom mirror, coffee maker—and as you go about your day, glance at them and repeat the verse to yourself. Before long you'll have it memorized and will be amazed at how relevant that single verse is in your everyday life.

Other Verses to Eat Up: Joshua 1:8; Psalm 1:2-3

Day 18: Living God's Word

Receive
Taste God's Word—Savor These Verses: John 5:36-40

> You [Jewish leaders] study the Scriptures diligently because you think that in them you have eternal life. These are the very Scriptures that testify about me [Jesus], yet you refuse to come to me to have life. (vv. 39-40)

Reflect
Family:
- *We need to respond to God's Word—learning to live it daily—in loving Jesus, laying down our lives for others, and moving into abundant life a step at a time. How can we do this as a family?* (Let's spend some time brainstorming.)
- *When we read the Bible, do we ever feel like that alone is enough?* (Explain in our own words why mere reading is not enough.)

Individual:
- *How often do I read the Bible, close the cover, and then not think about God's Word again for the rest of my day? What steps can I take to savor Scripture and then act on God's messages to me?*

God doesn't want us just to read a few verses each morning, close the Bible, consider ourselves "covered," then proceed without a second thought of what we've read. Reading and even studying won't suffice for us, Jesus tells us here. Yes, the Scriptures are about His life—they "testify" *about* Him—but the real key is to take these teachings and *apply them to our own lives,* to live out the Word instead of only reading about it. "The Bible" doesn't provide eternal life; *Jesus Himself* offers us that.

Respond

Ask for Change: "Lord, help each of us in our family to take your Word—your lessons and teachings—and apply them to our lives in meaningful, concrete, and lasting ways."

Consider What's Real: It's easy to say we're going to carry God's Word into our daily life; it's another thing entirely to figure out how exactly we're going to do this (and then, of course, do so). In *The Power of a Whisper,*[9] Bill Hybels outlines a useful exercise he does each morning. He chooses a few verses and reads through them slowly, at least twice, jotting notes about what they mean to him personally and how he might apply them to his life. Then he writes out a simple prayer of commitment to living based on those verses, and prays those words back to God, often several times throughout the day, as a reminder of how he can reliably and regularly live out Jesus' teachings.

Other Verses to Eat Up: James 3:14–17; James 2:20–24

Day 19: A Light in the Darkness

Receive

Taste God's Word—Savor These Verses: John 1:1–5

> Through him all things were made; without him nothing was made that has been made. In him was life, and that

life was the light of all mankind. The light shines in the darkness, and the darkness has not overcome it. (vv. 3–5)

Reflect

Family:
- *In what ways does God's Word expose darkness?*
- *Do we really live our lives entirely in Jesus?* (What does this mean; how is it done?)

Individual:
- *Do I believe that God always overcomes darkness? Why, or why not?* (Take some time to thoughtfully reflect on this question.)

If you've ever weathered a period of grief, loss, or despair, you probably know what it's like to doubt, to question if God can or will overcome evil. Sometimes we feel such anguish and pain that it's difficult to trust God's goodness and love. We wonder where He is, why He's allowed such circumstances, why He hasn't protected us from such misery. It's normal to feel this way from time to time, especially during seasons of great strife. But throughout those periods we must remember, as John the apostle so eloquently reminds us, that God's light always overcomes darkness—even when it doesn't feel true or even possible.

Respond

Ask for Change: "Lord, be with our family today; guide us on your path and shine on us your light of goodness and love. Help us know in our hearts that you are with us always and that your light keeps us from stumbling in darkness."

Consider What's Real: God's love and light are bigger and brighter than any problems or darkness we may face, yet sometimes amidst hardship we forget this. If you're in such a place, perhaps creating a symbol of His light in your home will help serve to remind of His always-burning light. Try lighting a candle in the evening and saying a simple prayer as it burns brightly and steadily on your counter or table. Or keep a small lamp lit as a symbolic reminder of the Light no darkness can suppress.

Other Verses to Eat Up: Isaiah 9:2; Micah 7:8

Day 20: Quenching Spiritual Thirst

Receive

Taste God's Word—Savor These Verses: Jeremiah 15:1–21

> When your words came, I ate them; they were my joy and my heart's delight, for I bear your name, LORD God Almighty. (v. 16)

Reflect

Family:

- *In what ways can Scripture quench our spiritual thirst?*
- *Why is it important to turn to the Bible even when we're discouraged and frustrated?*

Individual:

- *Do I have faith that God is good, even when circumstances seemingly aren't?* (Be honest with your answer, going to the Lord in prayer, sharing doubts *and* praises.)

Jeremiah definitely had no easy time of it. For fifty-two chapters he gives the same message, over and over, one that continued to fall on deaf ears. He urged his people to repent, to rid themselves of idols and false gods, and turn back to the one true God—yet they never listened. Worse, they mocked and imprisoned him, and still God asked him giving them the same message. No wonder he felt discouraged and frustrated; no wonder he doubted God's intentions and fell into despair. But through all hardship, Jeremiah continued to return to God and his Word for comfort and sustenance. Despite everything, God's words brought him joy and delight.

Respond
Ask for Change: "Lord, help us to hear and receive your guarantees of unwavering love as we read your Word."

Consider What's Real: Like Jeremiah, when we find ourselves in a spiritually dark place we might cry out to God in frustration and despair. That's okay—in fact, it's more than okay. He wants us to come to Him with anything we're experiencing; He values all our communication, even when it's anger or hopelessness. When we find we're mired in despair, it's helpful to return to a favorite passage to remind ourselves of God's goodness and love. Keep such verses in your mind so that you can return to them in a time of need to seek and find His peace and joy. Also, try memorizing a couple verses you can repeat to yourself as a meditation of hope when you need it.

Other Verses to Eat Up: Psalm 23; Romans 15:13

Day 21: Releasing Anxiety

Receive
Taste God's Word—Savor These Verses: Luke 21:29–36

> Truly I tell you, this generation will certainly not pass away until all these things have happened. Heaven and earth will pass away, but my words will never pass away. (vv. 32–33)

Reflect

Family:

- *How can we overcome our anxieties?*
- *Does each of us turn to the Bible as a source of strength and hope, or are we looking for quick fixes to our problems?* (Take some time to share from the heart. Discuss how God offers much more than quick fixes.)

Individual:

- *What does it mean to me when Jesus tells me His words "will never pass away"?*

Many of us feel lonely and isolated when we're in the midst of suffering and pain. We retreat into ourselves as we feel unstable, imbalanced, like the world is tilting off-kilter and the ground is shifting beneath our feet. We must never forget that God remains steady, a rock-solid foundation in times of trouble. Furthermore, His Word is as true and timeless as He is. "My words will never pass away," Jesus reminds us—they're always there, available, an ever-flowing wellspring of hope and promise to meet every fear and all worry.

Respond

Ask for Change: "Lord, fill our hearts with the trust to *know* that you are the stronghold in our lives—ever-present, faithful without fail, always available, no matter what."

Consider What's Real: God is our source of strength and hope, but we need to turn toward Him to receive His love. We need to actively participate in being transformed from desolation and hopelessness to renewal and light. One of the ways we can begin this turn toward God is by returning, again and again, day after day, to His Word, from which He speaks to each of us. If we open the pages and listen with our hearts, we can discover it.

Other Verses to Eat Up: Psalm 34:4; 1 Peter 5:7

Day 22: Living by Faith

Receive

Taste God's Word—Savor These Verses: 2 Corinthians 5:1-10

We live by faith, not by sight. (v. 7)

Reflect

Family:
- *What must we do to "live by faith" rather than by sight?*
- *What practical steps can each member of this family take to relinquish control and hand our life over to God?*

Individual:
- *Why do I believe that God is with me, even when I can't sense His presence?*

We've been heavily influenced by our sight-based culture. So much of what we believe we "know" about reality is based on what we see with our physical eyes. Yet what happens when we see events and situations we can't control and encounter broken things we can't fix? What happens when our loved one is dying and we can't help? Or when we witness homelessness or abuse and are powerless to solve or end it on our own? For one thing, such travesties remind us that we must live by faith, in confident trust that God is gracious, merciful, and loving, and knowing that He can work any facet of any circumstance into good. To make any meaningful difference, we must hand over everything—including situations and circumstances—to Him.

Respond

Ask for Change: "Lord, help us relinquish our tight grip; help us hand over control and to surrender entirely to you. Help us embrace true faith in our hearts, trusting that your love and goodness will prevail."

Consider What's Real: Writes Ann Voskamp, in *One Thousand Gifts:*

> Let go of trying to do, let go of trying to control . . . let go of my own way, let go of my own fears. Bend the knee and be small and let God give what God chooses to give because He only gives love . . . This is the fuel for joy's flame. Fullness of joy is discovered only in the emptying of will.

Today, meditate on these words, trusting that God is all-good, all-loving, and thanking Him for the peace He offers in every circumstance.[10]

Other Verses to Eat Up: Hebrews 11:1–12; John 14:1–4

Day 23: Ordinary Heroes

Receive

Taste God's Word—Savor These Verses: Matthew 25:31–46

> Then the King will say to those on his right, "Come, you who are blessed by my Father; take your inheritance, the kingdom prepared for you since the creation of the world. For I was hungry and you gave me something to eat, I was thirsty and you gave me something to drink, I was a stranger and you invited me in, I needed clothes and you clothed me, I was sick and you looked after me, I was in prison and you came to visit me" (vv. 34–35).

Reflect

Family:
- *What is Jesus saying in these verses?*
- *What do people see and hear when they watch and listen to our family?*

Individual:
- *How can I share God's love with those around me?*

A tender word at the right moment, a smile, a kind act—these are marks of a true hero. No need for dramatic feats of strength. No need to outrun a bullet or hurdle a skyscraper. As Christians, we're already empowered with supernatural wonder: The Holy Spirit is the Spirit of Christ in us, and it's the outpouring of His love through our words, our warmth, and our walk that will rescue humanity from evil. Through us, Jesus, the Hero, can open their eyes to eternity. Says Max Lucado, "God desires to take our faces, this exposed and memorable part of our bodies, and use them to reflect His goodness."[11] Are you sharing God's love with those around you?

Respond
Ask for Change: "Lord, teach us to care about and for others; show us how to be selfless, and let us reflect your face wherever we go."

Consider What's Real: Two main centers of obedience to God are our hearts and our mouths. That's why David prayed, "May the words of my mouth and this meditation of my heart be pleasing in your sight, LORD, my Rock and my Redeemer."[12] He knew that by letting his heavenly Father take control of his heart and his mouth he could live a holy life, one that would be a testimony to God's glory and grace.

Other Verses to Eat Up: 2 Timothy 2:8-13; Hebrews 11:1-12:3

Day 24: Fear Factor

Receive
Taste God's Word—Savor These Verses: John 14:1-4

Do not let your hearts be troubled. You believe in God; believe also in me. (v. 1)

Reflect

Family:

- *Are any great fears threatening to flatten our faith?* (Share them together.)
- *In those moments when we find ourselves shaking in our boots instead of standing strong in the Lord, what can we do?*

Individual:

- *Am I ready to let God uproot the "worldly fear"* (see below) *in my life?* (Reflect on your plan of action.)

Fear. Bone-chilling ice-in-the-veins fear. For some believers, it's a way of life: *Lord, I'm trapped. I feel lost and alone. And scared: of being rejected . . . of losing control . . . of the future . . . of risking my heart . . . of surrendering my life.* A healthy fear of the Lord—the kind rooted in respect and reverence for Him—is wise, and pleasing to Him. But He wants to drive out worldly fear—fear that stems from doubt and condemnation and leaves its victims panicked, paralyzed, and in-effective for service in His kingdom. God is greater than anything and everything else, so nothing else is worth fearing. He wants to build in us the courage needed to walk boldly in Him.

Respond

Ask for Change: "Lord, we invite you to build into this family more courage, more confidence, more joy, and more peace."

Consider What's Real: Charles Spurgeon said, of courage:

> You will need the courage of a lion to pursue a course that could turn your best friend into your fiercest foe. For the sake of Jesus Christ, you must be courageous. Risking your reputation and emotions for the truth requires a degree

of moral principle that only the Spirit of God can work into you. Do not turn back, do not be a coward; be a hero of the faith. Follow in your Master's steps. He walked this rough way before you.[13]

Other Verses to Eat Up: Psalm 27; 1 John 4:18; Ephesians 6:10-18

Day 25: Hearts in Motion

Receive

Taste God's Word—Savor These Verses: John 15:1-17

Love each other in the same way I have loved you. There is no greater than to lay down one's life for one's friends. (v. 13)[14]

Reflect

Family:
- *What does it mean to be willing to "lay down" our lives for each other? In what ways up to now have we done this, and not done this?*
- *Why is our love for others so important to God?*

Individual:
- *In what tangible ways will I choose to show more love to family members?*

In the Bible, the word *love* often refers to action—something we *do*. Jesus said, "God so loved the world that he gave . . ."[15] God has *done* this for us; it's love in motion. Scripture characterizes such love in terms of selfless giving to others, manifesting kindness, patience, humility, and commitment in relationships.

Respond

Ask for Change: "Lord, we come to you desiring to be fully open, to confess and to ask your forgiveness. We praise you for your mercy; please breathe gratitude into our hearts."

Consider What's Real: In John 11 we witness an amazing act of love: Jesus raising Lazarus from death. Focus on verses 33–35 for a vivid photo of the Lord's personality: "When Jesus saw her [Mary] weeping, and the Jews who had come along with her also weeping, he was deeply moved in spirit and troubled. 'Where have you laid him?' He asked. 'Come and see, Lord,' they replied. Jesus wept." Whenever He is filled with sadness, it's because those around Him are overcome with mourning. Could it be any clearer how deeply Jesus loves us, how strongly He feels for us? If we're hurting, so is God. He is constantly at our sides, loving us, encouraging us, and feeling what we're feeling. He aches over our defeats just as He exults over our victories.[16] And while our ability to love is limited, His capacity is endless. Jesus Christ took His infinite love all the way to the cross to "lay down His life for his friends"—to make a once-for-all sacrifice that washes away our sins forever. That's ultimate love, in unsurpassable action, with eternal effect.

Other Verses to Eat Up: Romans 5:16–18; Matthew 22:37–40

Day 26: Chicken Soup for "the Blahs"

Receive

Taste God's Word—Savor These Verses: John 14:18–21

> I will not leave you as orphans; I will come to you. Before long, the world will not see me anymore, but you will see me. Because I live, you also will live. (vv. 18–19)

Reflect

Family:
  • *What brings on "the blahs" in our family?*

- *What is Jesus promising in these verses?*
Individual:
- *What steps can I take to get out from under discouragement?*

Shattered hopes. Crushed dreams. Hearts too heavy to sense the One walking alongside us and living within us. Thoughts ooze disillusion: *Loser. Zero—that's me. How could I be more worthless, more insignificant?* As despair takes hold we begin to sink deeper and deeper into a pit, wondering what we've ever done to deserve any of this and questioning why God has abandoned us. We've all been there to some degree. The fact is, our emotions are highly cyclical and can bounce from extremes. If we've failed at something, we usually feel more frustration than faith. If we've had a fight or have been rejected, we're often more consumed with anger than with the comfort of the Almighty.

Respond
Ask for Change: "Lord, sometimes our hearts are so heavy with fear, worry, and anxiety. Sometimes we feel paralyzed by the 'blahs.' Deliver us, Jesus. Let us feel today your power to set us free."

Consider What's Real: Our faith is based on immutable facts: *God* took on human form, came to earth, died for our sins, rose from the dead, and reigns as Lord over all. Nothing can change this—not indigestion, not a bad hair day or school day or work day, and not anything we feel, no matter how intensely and no matter our situation. When we're down, when everything seems to be going wrong and even life doesn't seem to be worth living, we need to ride it out. Emotions may be unpleasant or excruciating for a time, but if we outlast them we'll discover that our circumstances will change. Our world will seem much better. Joy will return; eventually, the blahs always disappear—as do sorrow and grief and anything else we can endure. And, because of Jesus, we *can.*

Other Verses to Eat Up: Mark 4:14–20; Revelation 21:1–4

Day 27: Wholeness: The Full Power of Forgiveness

Receive

Taste God's Word—Savor These Verses: Luke 7:36–50

> Her sins, which are many, are forgiven—for she loved much. But he who is forgiven little, loves little. (v. 47)[17]

Reflect

Family:
- *Does each member of this family believe he/she has been set free by Christ's love? Why, or why not?*
- *God wants us to experience the liberation that comes with His forgiveness and love. How can each of us know this kind of love? How can we pray for each other?*

Individual:
- *Have I allowed God into my darkest places? What must I bring to Him in prayer?*

To be forgiven, we must grant the forgiver access to us. Asking forgiveness of God requires that we open ourselves entirely, admitting our wrongdoing *and* our vulnerability—our innermost self, including all our faults and failures. Jesus knows how hard this is. Just as He knew the risk this woman took, approaching Him in humility to anoint His feet, He knows that when we genuinely seek forgiveness our exposure feels frightening. Only those who've been humbled enough to see the depth of their sin can appreciate the complete forgiveness God offers.

Respond

Ask for Change: "Lord Jesus, we come to you, asking your forgiveness. We agree that we are sinners, and we know you died on the cross, paying the price for our sins. We thank you, and we ask that you fill us with your Holy Spirit and cleanse us."

Consider What's Real: Sometimes we try to hide our sins from God, reluctant to come clean and reveal to Him our most humiliating flaws. However, in doing this, we miss the very best opportunity to understand and experience true love and gratitude. *The Message* renders the verse this way: "She was forgiven many, many sins, and so she is very, very grateful. If the forgiveness is minimal, the gratitude is minimal." Name the sin you've sought to keep even from God himself, and embrace the first step toward being fully forgiven and fully grateful. The more honest our confession, the more thankful we are for God's overwhelming grace.

Other Verses to Eat Up: Psalm 103:1–5; Psalm 51:15–17

Day 28: The Power of Grace

Receive
Taste God's Word—Savor These Verses: Romans 3:9–20

> Whatever the law says, it says to those who are under the law, so that every mouth may be silenced and the whole world held accountable to God. Therefore no one will be declared righteous in God's sight by the works of the law; rather, through the law we become conscious of our sin. (vv. 19–20)

Reflect
Family:
- *Admitting our sins and committing our lives to Christ forever means we'll spend eternity with Him. In what ways has this truth already transformed each of our lives?*

- *How often do we make excuses for our sins, unwilling to admit them or even denying that there's any responsibility for us to take? If we do confess our sins to Jesus, what does the Bible say He will do?*

Individual:

- *Why is it important for me to get real with God about my sins? What steps should I take, and how should I pray?*

So often when accused of wrongdoing we get defensive, unwilling to look at whether we bear responsibility and sometimes just as eager to blame someone else. God doesn't let us off the hook so easily. He holds us accountable—not because He requires us to pay for our sins but because He knows that acknowledging them and seeking forgiveness is the first step in sharing an authentic relationship with Him. In fact, the whole reason for God's law is to make our sins readily apparent to us, prompting us to approach Him in humility and repentance. Even though we will err again and again, with each return to God our relationship with Him deepens.

Respond

Ask for Change: "Lord, we're ready to let go of the sins each of us struggles with. We know we can't do this on our own. We need your forgiveness and your strength."

Consider What's Real: Ask each family member to come completely open and vulnerable with God and to offer Him this prayer of repentance [fill in the blank with the sin(s) each individual holds most tightly]. "Lord, I confess my sin of _____ and ask you to forgive me. Please give me an undivided heart; transform me from the inside out so that I'll come to know you better day by day. Amen."

Other Verses to Eat Up: Romans 5:20–21; Romans 6:14

DR. ARNIE COLE & MICHAEL ROSS

Day 29: Made Right with God

Receive

Taste God's Word—Savor These Verses: Romans 5:12–21

> Just as one trespass resulted in condemnation for all people,
> so also one righteous act resulted in justification and life for
> all people. For just as through the disobedience of the one
> man [Adam] the many were made sinners, so also through
> the obedience of the one man [Christ] the many will be made
> righteous. (vv. 18–19)

Reflect

Family:

- *Through Christ, each of us has found and will keep finding real
  life, real faith, real answers. Are we ready to stop stressing and
  start celebrating?* (Explain the difference Jesus makes in
  our lives—especially how He can deliver us from worry.)
- *When have we, individually, tried to blame someone else and not
  taken responsibility for our own sin and struggles?*

Individual:

- *Do I choose to live by Adam . . . or by Christ? What does it mean to
  live by Christ? What changes must I make in my walk with Him?*

We may read these verses and feel frustrated and resentful that the
sin of Adam and Eve led to our downfall. "Not fair," we're tempted to
complain. "Why should I have been affected by their choice?" But read
on. Jesus gave His life to redeem us even though not one of us deserves
it. Fair? No, that's grace. The fact is, while one sin brought guilt and
condemnation to humankind, one act of righteousness—Christ's
death on the cross—was done for our salvation, for the gracious forgiveness of every single one of our sins. We ought not to protest on
any grounds, and certainly not on those of fairness.

Respond

Ask for Change: "Lord, help us to understand and appreciate the wondrous gift of grace you have given us through the work of your Son, our Lord Jesus Christ."

Consider What's Real: Meditate on God's amazing gift to us as you read these words:

> Sin didn't, and doesn't, have a chance in competition with the aggressive forgiveness we call *grace*. When it's sin versus grace, grace wins hands down. All sin can do is threaten us with death, and that's the end of it. Grace, because God is putting everything together again through the Messiah, invites us into life—a life that goes on and on and on, world without end.[18]

Other Verses to Eat Up: 2 Corinthians 12:9–10; Ephesians 2:1–10

Day 30: I Am God's Unique Creation

Receive

Taste God's Word—Savor These Verses: Psalm 139

> You created my inmost being; you knit me together in my mother's womb. I praise you because I am fearfully and wonderfully made; your works are wonderful, I know that full well. (vv. 13–14)

Reflect

Family:

- *Each person in this family is a unique creation God placed here by His design. Do we truly believe this—even when life is hard?*

How can we start believing and living it? How can this truth keep us strong during those inevitable stressful moments?

- *In what ways can this reality bring us peace in times of trouble?*

Individual:

- *How can I come to learn—and live—what God's unique purpose is for me?*

We all suffer through periods of feeling lost, unmoored, without direction. We wonder if we're choosing well or whether there's even a path meant specifically for us at all. In times like these it's more important than ever to turn to Scripture so we can experience how involved and in tune God is with each of us. He searches us and knows everything about us, and He's always with us, His hand guiding us, His arm holding us close—even when we can't feel it ourselves.

Respond

Ask for Change: "Lord, guide this household today. Help us know and live out the purpose for which you placed each one of us here. Amen."

Consider What's Real: It's normal to experience frustration and weariness. And it's normal to wonder what God has in store for you and to question what His purpose might be. His ways and plans aren't always clear and obvious, and His timeline doesn't always unfold just as we might like. Even so, believe and know that His plans for you *are* right, perfect and good, and He *will* continue to lead you "in the way everlasting."[19]

Other Verses to Eat Up: Matthew 10:30–31; Jeremiah 29:11

Endnotes

Introduction
1. Matthew 11:28

Part One
1. Author calculations from World Health Organization, "Confirmed H5N1 Cases Worldwide 2003-2011." who.int/influenza/human_animal_interface/EN_GIP_LatestCumulativeNumberH5N1cases.pdf and Spectrum, "Number of New Millionaires in the United States in 2012." spectrem.com/Content/300000-New-Millionaires.aspx
2. The CDC estimates that 6% of bats have rabies. cdc.gov/rabies/bats/education/
3. A. L. Wetterer, M. Rockman, and N. B. Simmons. "Phyllostomid Phylogeny: Data from Diverse Morphological Systems, Sex Chromosomes, and Restriction Sites" (2000). Bulletin of the American Museum of Natural History.
4. David Emery, "Are Vending Machines Deadlier Than Sharks?" (2005). urbanlegends.about.com/b/2005/06/29/are-vending-machines-deadlier-than-sharks-repost.htm
5. R. S. Vetter. "Spider Envenomation in North America" in *Critical Care Nursing* (2013): 205-223.

Chapter One
1. *Keep Calm and Carry On: Good Advice for Hard Times* (Kansas City: Andrews McMeel, 2009).
2. APA, "Stressed in America," apa.org (Jan. 2011). apa.org/monitor/2011/01/stressed-america.aspx
3. Melissa Dahl, "Millennials are the most stressed-out generation, new survey finds," nbcnews.com (accessed 2/8/13). vitals.nbcnews.com/_news/2013/02/07/16889472-millennials-are-the-most-stressed-out-generation-new-survey-finds?lite
4. Dr. Mona Spiegel, "Anxiety on the Rise" (accessed 2/11/13). selfgrowth.com/articles/anxiety_on_the_rise
5. John 10:10
6. Matthew 6:33-34 (on "all these things," see vv. 26-32).
7. Ephesians 3:20-21 NASB
8. T. D. Borkovec, E. Robinson, T. Pruzinsky, and J. A. DePree (1983). "Preliminary Exploration of Worry: Some Characteristics and Processes." *Behavior Research and Therapy* (21:1): 9-16.
9. Hans Selye, "A Syndrome Produced by Diverse Nocuous Agents. *Nature* (1936).
10. T. H. Holmes and R. H. Rahe. "The Social Readjustment Rating Scale" (1967). *Journal of Psychosomatic Research* 11(2): 213-218.

Chapter Two
1. Henry T. Blackaby, *Experiencing God Day-By-Day* (Nashville: Broadman & Holman, 1998), 39.
2. Adapted from Michael Ross, "Faith Through the Flames" in *Breakaway* (May 1997):18-21.
3. 2 Timothy 3:1-5 *The Message*
4. Matthew 11:28-30 *The Message*
5. John 10:10 NLT
6. John 14:27 ESV
7. John 16:33 (regarding "these things," see chapters 13-17 of John's gospel).
8. See a longer sample list at anxietycentre.com/anxiety-famous-people.shtml
9. K. Demyttenaere, R. Bruffaerts, J. Posada-Villa, I. Gasquet, V. Kovess, et al. "Prevalence, Severity, and Unmet Need for Treatment of Mental Disorders in the World Health Organization 'World Mental Health Surveys.'" *Journal of the American Medical Association* 291.21 (2004): 2581-2590.

Chapter Three
1. C. S. Lewis, *The Letters of C.S. Lewis to Arthur Greeves*, 18 August 1930 (New York: Collier, 1986), 378.
2. APA, "Stress in America Findings" (2010). apa.org/news/press/releases/stress/2010/national-report.pdf
3. Joshua 1:6-9 ESV
4. D. H. Rosmarin, S. Pirutinsky, R. P. Auerbach, T. Björgvinsson, J. Bigda-Peyton, G. Andersson, K. I. Pargament, and E. J. Krumrei. "Incorporating Spiritual Beliefs into a Cognitive Model of Worry." *Journal of Clinical Psychology* (2011) 67: 1-10.
5. Adrian Wells, *Metacognitive Therapy for Anxiety and Depression* (New York: Guildford, 2008), 25.

6. Daily Christian Quote, "Christian Quotes: Anxiety and Worry Index." dailychristianquote. com/dcqanxiety.html
7. In *Letters of C. S. Lewis,* ed. W. H. ["Warnie"] Lewis (New York: Harcourt, 1966), 256.
8. APA, "Stressed in America."
9. Again, generally, those born between 1979 and 1995.

Chapter Four
1. Matthew 6:25–27 NLT
2. dictionary.reference.com/browse/pathology
3. National Institute of Mental Health, *What Is Panic Disorder?* nimh.nih.gov/health/topics/panic-disorder/index.shtml

Chapter Five
1. Matthew 5:3 *The Message*
2. Edmund Bourne, PhD, *Coping with Anxiety* (Oakland: New Harbinger, 2003), 44.
3. Ibid., 10.
4. Eric T. Scalise, PhD, LPC, LMFT, interview with Michael Ross (08/01/13). Dr. Scalise is Vice President for Professional Development at the American Association of Christian Counselors (AACC), Executive Director of the International Board of Christian Care, Senior Editor of AACC publications, and Vice President for Academic Affairs, Light University Online.
5. Mental health professionals often refer to this guide as they diagnose psychological problems, including anxiety disorders. *Diagnostic and Statistical Manual of Mental Disorders, Fifth Ed.* (Arlington, VA: APA, 2013).
6. *DSM-5*, 197–198.
7. Martin M. Antony, PhD, and Peter J. Norton, PhD, *The Anti-Anxiety Workbook* (New York: Guilford, 2009), 18.
8. Ibid., 22.
9. Bourne, *Coping with Anxiety,* 6.
10. Ibid.
11. Antony and Norton, *The Anti-Anxiety Workbook,* 19.
12. *DSM-5*, 235.
13. *DSM-5*, 191–192.
14. *DSM-5*, 487.
15. Antony and Norton, *The Anti-Anxiety Workbook,* 23.
16. Anxiety and Depression Association of America; see adaa.org/about-adaa/press-room/facts-statistics

Chapter Six
1. Keri Wyatt Kent, *Deeper Into the Word: Old Testament* (Minneapolis: Bethany House, 2011), 79.
2. From "The Anxiety Cure According to Dr. Archibald Hart," compiled by Audrey Wagner, Student Wellness Center (1/22/07), georgetowncollege.edu/studentwellness/2007/01/the-anxiety-cure-according-to-dr-archibald-hart/ (accessed 10/17/13). [Or, search "Archibald Hart anxiety" at georgetowncollege.edu]
3. Dr. Archibald D. Hart, *The Anxiety Cure* (Nashville: Thomas Nelson, 1999), 15.
4. See Antony and Norton, *The Anti-Anxiety Workbook,* 26.
5. Ibid.
6. For a thorough discussion, read chapter 2, "The GABA-Anxiety Connection," in Hart's *The Anxiety Cure.*
7. Dr. Scalise, interview.
8. Hart, op. cit., 28.
9. Tim Kreider, "The 'Busy' Trap," *New York Times* (06/30/12). opinionator.blogs.nytimes. com/2012/06/30/the-busy-trap/?_r=0
10. Bourne, *Coping with Anxiety,* 8–9.
11. Ibid.
12. Gerald G. May, M.D., *Addiction and Grace* (San Francisco: Harper Collins, 1988), 3–4.
13. Nanette Gingery, M.A., interview with Michael Ross (08/28/13). She is a licensed therapist, a life coach, and president of Summit Care and Wellness Treatment and Counseling in Nebraska.

14. Tess Cox, PAC, interview with Michael Ross (09/25/13). She is a pediatric physician's assistant in Colorado with more than three decades of experience in medicine, holds an M.A. in counseling, and has written several articles for the American Academy of Pediatrics.
15. Don Colbert, MD, *The New Bible Cure for Sleep Disorders* (Lake Mary, FL.: Siloam, 2009), 1.
16. See Barbara Mantel, "A Good Night's Sleep Scrubs Your Brain Clean, Researchers Find," nbcnews.com. nbcnews.com/health/good-nights-sleep-scrubs-your-brain-clean-researchers-find-8C11413186?ocid=msnhp&pos=3
17. See Wagner, "The Anxiety Cure According to Dr. Archibald Hart."
18. Romans 12:1–2 *The Message*
19. Susan Krauss Whitbourne, PhD, "Turn Down Your Brain's Worry Center," Psychology Today online (10/9/12). psychologytoday.com/blog/fulfillment-any-age/201210/turn-down-your-brain-s-worry-center

Chapter Seven
1. From Hannah Hurnard, *Hinds' Feet on High Places* (Carol Stream, IL: Tyndale, 1975), 15.
2. "Barbara" is a real person, but to keep her anonymous I have altered details in this account of her story.
3. John 14:27 CEV
4. Luke 21:34–36 ESV
5. Isaiah 43:1–4 *The Message*
6. Matthew 6:25–27 *The Message*
7. See Hart, *The Anxiety Cure*, 25.
8. C. S. Lewis, "Giving All to Christ," *Devotional Classics* eds. Richard J. Foster and James Bryan Smith (New York: HarperCollins, 1990), 9.

Chapter Eight
1. Dietrich Bonhoeffer, *Life Together: The Classic Exploration of Christian Community* (New York: HarperCollins, 1954), 27.
2. Richard C. Halverson, *No Greater Power* (Colorado Springs: Multnomah, 1986), 186.
3. John 14:6
4. Mehmet Oz, M.D., "Dr. Oz's Worry Cure and Diet Plan" (3/12/2012). doctoroz.com/videos/dr-ozs-worry-cure-diet-plan?
5. Elouise Renich Fraser, *Confessions of a Beginning Theologian* (Downers Grove, IL: InterVarsity, 1998), 31.
6. "Dr. Oz's Worry Cure and Diet Plan," op. cit.
7. Nanette Gingery, M.A., interview with Michael Ross (08/28/13).
8. Daniel G. Amen, *Change Your Brain, Change Your Life* (New York: Three Rivers, 1998), 59–60.
9. Psalm 46:10
10. Bob Anderson, *Stretching: 30th Anniversary Edition* (Bolinas, CA: Shelter, 2010), 9.
11. Sara Reistad-Long, "How to Combat Every Kind of Stress," Women's Day online (accessed 08/05/13). healthyliving.msn.com/health-wellness/stress/how-to-combat-every-kind-of-stress
12. "Stress: The Silent Killer," ICBS Inc., 1998–2007. holisticonline.com/stress/stress_diet.htm
13. "Sodium: How to Tame Your Salt Habit," Mayo Foundation for Medical Education and Research, 1998–2013. mayoclinic.org/healthy-living/nutrition-and-healthy-eating/expert-blog/salt-intake/bgp-20056165
14. Ibid.
15. Joseph McAllister, "What Do Salt & Sugar Do to Your Body?" Livestrong (6/3/11). livestrong.com/article/461835-what-do-salt-sugar-do-to-your-body/
16. Ibid.
17. Reginald B. Cherry, M.D., *Dr. Cherry's Little Instruction Book: Health and Healing* (Minneapolis: Bethany House, 2003), 138.
18. David Zinczenko with Matt Goulding, *Eat This, Not That: All New Supermarket Survival Guide* (New York: Rodale, 2012), 117.
19. Maya W. Paul, Melinda Smith, M.A., and Jeanne Segal Ph.D., "Healthy Eating: Easy Tips for Planning a Healthy Diet and Sticking to It," helpguide.org (Sept. 2013). helpguide.org/life/healthy_eating_diet.htm
20. "The Twenty Most Sugar-Packed Foods in America," menshealth.com (6/20/09). eatthis.menshealth.com/content/20-most-sugar-packed-foods-america
21. R. C. Sproul, *Effective Prayer* (Wheaton, IL: Tyndale, 1984), 32.

22. E.g., see Philippians 4:6; 1 Timothy 2:1–3.
23. E.g., see 2 Chronicles 7:14.
24. Mark 11:22–25 *The Message*
25. Margaret Magdalen, *Jesus, Man of Prayer* (Downers Grove, IL: InterVarsity, 1987), 51.
26. Mary Fairchild, "How Do Christians Deal with Stress?" About.com, (accessed 10/9/12). christianity.about.com/od/faqhelpdesk/f/dealwithstress.htm
27. Psalm 91:3–6 CEV
28. Philippians 4:6–7 TLB
29. Colossians 3:15 *The Message*
30. Fairchild, "How Do Christians Deal with Stress?"
31. James 4:8
32. Henry T. Blackaby and Richard Blackaby, *Experiencing God Day-By-Day Devotional* (Nashville: Broadman & Holman, 1998), 360.
33. John 14:1 NRSV
34. John 14:15–17 NRSV
35. John 16:13 NRSV
36. Dorothy M. Stewart, *The Westminster Collection of Christian Prayers* (Louisville: Westminster John Knox, 2002), 9.
37. Ibid., 10.
38. Ibid., 278.
39. Max Lucado, "30 Days of Thoughts (From *Great Day Every Day*)" (3/22/07). maxlucado.com/read/topical/30-days-of-thoughts-from-every-day-deserves-a-chance/
40. See James 4:8.
41. 1 John 4:18
42. See Psalm 25:3–6.
43. Corrie Ten Boom, Brainy Quote (accessed 10/9/12). brainyquote.com/quotes/quotes/c/corrietenb135203.html
44. See John 15:12–13.
45. Romans 12:2 NLT

Part Three
1. Kaleign Shufeldt, "Sing Your Way to a Healthier, Happier You," MeMD Blog (7/10/13). memd.me/blog/sing-your-way-to-a-healthier-happier-you/
2. Rachel Smith, "10 Strange But True Health Tips," MSN Health & Wellbeing (8/5/13). health.ninemsn.com.au/otrivin/8691505/10-strange-but-true-health-tips
3. Mayo Clinic Staff, "Stress Relief from Laughter? It's No Joke," Mayo Clinic (7/13/13). mayoclinic.com/health/stress-relief/SR00034
4. "Stop and Smell the Jasmine," A Woman's Health (accessed 12/21/13). awomanshealth.com/stop-and-smell-the-jasmine/

Chapter Nine
1. *Keep Calm and Carry On: Good Advice for Hard Times* (Kansas City: Andrews McMeel, 2009).
2. This story is adapted from Arnie Cole and Michael Ross, *Unstuck: Your Life, God's Design, Real Change* (Minneapolis: Bethany House, 2012), 137–138.
3. *Keep Calm and Carry On*, op. cit.
4. John Sachem, citing Chinese proverb, "Inspirational Stress Relief Quotes," Yahoo! Voices (4/29/10). voices.yahoo.com/inspirational-stress-relief-quotes-5933076.html
5. Isaiah 41:10 NIRV
6. John 14:27 NLT
7. Dr. Phil McGraw, "Reconnecting With Your Partner" (accessed 11/4/13). drphil.com/articles/article/80
8. In Ruth Haley Barton, *Sacred Rhythms* (Downers Grove, IL: InterVarsity, 2006), 94.

Chapter Ten
1. "Corrie Ten Boom Quotes," goodreads (2013). goodreads.com/author/quotes/102203.Corrie_ten_Boom

2. Dr. Trina Young-Greer, interview with Michael Ross (07/23/13).
3. APA, "Stressed in America," Jan. 2011 (42:1). apa.org/monitor/2011/01/stressed-america.aspx
4. Ondine Brooks Kuraoka, "What Kids Worry About" (accessed 2/27/13). sandiegofreelance-writer.com/clips/kids-worry.pdf
5. Young-Greer, interview.
6. Sandra L. Hofferth and John F. Sandberg, "Changes in American Children's Time, 1981–1997," Advances in Life Course Research 2001 (6): 193–229.
7. Shari Melman, Steven G. Little, and K. Angeleque Akin-Little. "Adolescent Overscheduling: The Relationship Between Levels of Participation in Scheduled Activities and Self-Reported Clinical Symptomology." The High School Journal 2007 (90:3), 18–30.
8. Tess Cox, PA-C, interview with Michael Ross (09/24/13).
9. Dr. Mona Spiegel, "Anxiety on the Rise" (accessed 2/11/13). selfgrowth.com/articles/anxiety_on_the_rise
10. Ibid.
11. Dr. Young-Greer, interview.
12. Ibid.
13. Cox, interview.
14. Ibid.
15. Dr. Young-Greer, interview.
16. See at leaderu.com/orgs/probe/docs/broken.html
17. Michael Ross and Susie Shellenberger, What Your Son Isn't Telling You (Minneapolis: Bethany House, 2010), 12.
18. Nahum 1:7
19. Philippians 4:6–7 TLB
20. John 16:33

Chapter 11

1. C. S Lewis, Surprised By Joy (Orlando: Harcourt, 1955), 160.
2. Michelle Castillo, "Millennials Are the Most Stressed Out Generation, Survey Finds," CBS News (2/11/13). cbsnews.com/8301-204_162-57568735/millennials-are-the-most-stressed-generation-survey-finds/
3. Philippians 4:6–7 NKJV
4. In Amy Mandelker and Elizabeth Powers, Pilgrim Souls (New York: Simon & Schuster, 1999), 120.

Bible Study

1. Matthew 28:20
2. Henri Nouwen, Spiritual Direction: Wisdom for the Long Walk of Faith (New York: HarperCollins, 2006), 6.
3. Charles Stanley, A Gift of Love (Nashville: Thomas Nelson, 2001), 5.
4. Max Lucado, The Great House of God (Nashville: Word, 1997), 90.
5. Matthew 7:7 The Message
6. Charles H. Spurgeon, Spiritual Revival, The Want of the Church in Devotional Classics: Selected Readings for Individuals and Groups, comp. Richard Foster and James Bryan Smith (San Francisco: HarperSanFrancisco, 1993), 333–334.
7. Timothy Keller, Prodigal God (New York: Riverhead Trade, 2011), 16.
8. See Matthew 19:16–29.
9. Bill Hybels, The Power of a Whisper (Grand Rapids: Zondervan, 2012), 23.
10. Ann Voskamp, One Thousand Gifts (Grand Rapids: Zondervan, 2010), 28.
11. Max Lucado, Just Like Jesus (Nashville: Word, 1998), 200.
12. Psalm 19:14
13. Charles H. Spurgeon, Morning and Evening (Nashville: Thomas Nelson, 1994), Dec. 28, evening.
14. NLT
15. John 3:16
16. Bill Myers and Michael Ross, Faith Encounter (Eugene, OR: Harvest House, 1999), 147.
17. ESV
18. Romans 5:20–21 The Message
19. Psalm 139:24